Power and the Spirit of God

Power and the Spirit of God

Toward an Experience-Based Pneumatology

BERNARD COOKE

OXFORD

UNIVERSITY PRESS

2004

OXFORD
UNIVERSITY PRESS

Oxford   New York
Auckland   Bangkok   Buenos Aires   Cape Town   Chennai
Dar es Salaam   Delhi   Hong Kong   Istanbul   Karachi   Kolkata
Kuala Lumpur   Madrid   Melbourne   Mexico City   Mumbai   Nairobi
São Paulo   Shanghai   Taipei   Tokyo   Toronto

Published by Oxford University Press, Inc.
198 Madison Avenue, New York, New York 10016

www.oup.com

Oxford is a registered trademark of Oxford University Press

Library of Congress Cataloging-in-Publication Data
Cooke, Bernard J.
    Power and the spirit of God : toward an experience-based pneumatology /
Bernard Cooke.
        p. cm.
Includes bibliographical references and index.
    ISBN 978-0-19-538264-8
    1. Holy Spirit.   2. Power (Christian theology)   3. Catholic Church—Doctrines.   I. Title.
    BT123 .C6 2004
    230—dc22   2003025903

Printed in the United States of America
on acid-free paper

Preface

The project of this book is extremely broad and at the same time specifically limited, namely, to the relation between power and God as Spirit, two realities that have intrigued and puzzled me for decades. Study of power has resulted in hundreds of books on the subject. Even a "theology of power" has been sketched, though not fully developed. The Catholic Theology Society of America convention of 1980 was devoted to this topic, and the result was a valuable volume of proceedings. John Coleman's keynote address was particularly illuminating and tantalizing in its implications, but he purposely limited himself to one approach to the topic, though arguably a most important approach. Earlier, in his essay "The Theology of Power" (in the fourth volume of his *Theological Investigations*, 1966), Karl Rahner dealt briefly with the topic. Rahner's essay intentionally dealt with the topic from a very specific point of view, namely, physical force in relation to freedom and human salvation. The broader reality of empowerment was left untouched.

At the same time, there has been a recent flurry of books on pneumatology, so that the long-standing complaint about theological neglect of the Holy Spirit is no longer valid. One can truly ask the question: why another book on the Holy Spirit? My answer, perhaps questionable, is that most studies still focus on the trinitarian role of the Spirit in the immanent Trinity, but much remains to be done in clarifying the Spirit as divine "outreach" to creation. Particularly needed is reflection on the role of the Spirit in the reconsideration of "divine providence." Again, as in 1980 with "power," the CTSA in 1998 devoted its national convention to reflection on "Spirit," and the result was a major step forward in formulation of pneumatology. My indebtedness to the theologizing on these two occasions, to the insights and stimulus they provided, is beyond description.

My indebtedness, however, extends farther. In April of 1998, an important symposium on the Holy Spirit was held at Marquette University, and the papers from this meeting were published in 2001 as *Advents of the Spirit*. I know of no reflection on pneumatology that is more extensive or more insightful. Though I was not able to share in this symposium, Professor Brad Hinze (who along with his colleague Lyle Dabney organized the symposium and edited the volume) kindly sent me a copy of the papers delivered on that occasion. They provided a rich background for my own thinking on the topic. Many other theologians have influenced my thinking about the Spirit, but I should mention in a special way Elizabeth Johnson and the late Piet Schoonenberg and Catherine Mowry LaCugna.

I hope that this present book, by bringing together some current thinking about power and about the Holy Spirit, can make a small addition to understanding the activity of God in the lives of humans today. It attempts neither a complete theology of power nor a novel and fully developed pneumatology but may contribute to both by examining the relationship between the Spirit of God and the various kinds of power that operate in human life.

Though there have been debts to persons and academic institutions, to colleagues and students, too numerous to mention, special gratitude is owed to Tom West at the College of St. Catherine in Minneapolis, to my brother David, and to colleagues at the University of San Diego and Loyola University in New Orleans who were kind enough to read earlier drafts of the book and make valuable suggestions. My thanks, also, to Cynthia Read who as executive editor of Oxford University Press encouraged the publication of the book and shepherded the manuscript to production. To Pauline, my life companion and constant support, my tribute to her enduring patience and enriching conversation. An added note: after the manuscript for this book was already in the process of editing and publication two important books on pneumatology appeared: *The Other Hand of God* by Killian McDonnell, one of the world's leading pneumatologists, and *The Spirit in the Church and in the World* (annual publication of the College Theology Society), edited by Bradford Hinze. My book is impoverished because it was not able to draw from these volumes.

Contents

Power and the Spirit of God

Introduction

Fifteen years ago, a symposium was held in Tübingen, Germany, of
seventy leading Christian theologians, Catholic and Protestant, many
of them members of the Concilium group that has been dedicated
since Vatican II to further the progressive currents of thought that
had surfaced in the council.[1] The declared purpose of the symposium was to reflect on the paradigm shift that had occurred in theology during the latter half of the twentieth century. While not all
their conclusions nor especially the limited Euro-American perspective of the conferees would meet with universal acceptance, the basic
premise of the meeting seems undeniable: a major shift has occurred in Christian theology in the past few decades.

It is not only theologians, of course, who have been discussing
the paradigm shift in recent thought. Almost all disciplines of
knowledge, many of them stimulated by Thomas Kuhn's seminal
publication on the paradigm shift in science,[2] have been endeavor-
ing to clarify the fundamental changes taking place. Given the fact
that the Tübingen theologians were attempting to study the manner
in which they have been doing theology, it is not surprising that
their discussion focused on methodology. This, again, is typical of
the current conversations in scholarly circles that invariably turn on
matters of method.

Reflection on Methodology

This reflection on methodology, sometimes quite esoteric and often "in house" in character, is a logical further step in the postmedieval move of philosophical focus from metaphysics to epistemology—not that examination of human ways of knowing was foreign to earlier centuries. Plato's dialogues attempted to explain the manner and extent of thought's correspondence to "reality." Medieval thinkers probed the function and meaning of symbols—linguistic, biblical, ritual—in conveying truth, especially revealed truth. With the emergence of modern mathematical science and the search for accuracy, consistency and verifiability became the criteria by which "scientific" methods were judged. Kant's *Critique of Pure Reason* set up a structure of methodological reflection whose influence continues to this day, but it in turn received important modification with the Hegelian and Marxist dialectics, Freudian psychology, and analytical philosophy.

Quite logically, this led to the emphasis on hermeneutics that has dominated more recent discussion of critical methodologies.[3] In theological circles, the stress on hermeneutical issues is central to the debates about foundational theology, its distinction from classic fundamental theology, and its relation to other aspects of theology.[4] In some circles, research and reflection about foundational issues has received such attention that it is almost equated with doing theology and tends to subsume such traditional topics as Christology.[5]

However, these shifts in methodology are only part of the paradigm shift today. Early in the twentieth century, there was great interest in the history of ideas, in the way that an internal logic among ideas fueled the development of thinking, in the influence of certain master ideas like "evolution." In religious studies, the attempt to create a synthesis of biblical thought that was grounded in the pervasiveness of an idea such as "covenant" led to Walther Eichrodt's *Theology of the Old Testament*,[6] but this quickly gave way, with the publication of Gerhard von Rad's *Old Testament Theology*,[7] to the realization that the Hebrew Bible contained multiple theologies. Much the same happened in New Testament circles where the "Theologies of the New Testament" of midcentury were modified by the pluralistic approach represented by James Dunn's *Unity and Diversity*.[8] While the understanding persisted that a certain heritage of thinking influenced the emergence of ideas, there was greater awareness that the cultural context, the social location of authors, the audience they addressed, and "accidental" influences such as the ability of authors to publish were also major factors.

Another element in the paradigm shift has to do with the focus on experience.[9] From the Greeks onward, universal and abstract ideas played a controling role in Western philosophical reflection. True, this stress on the universal was challenged by various forms of nominalism,[10] but this challenge remained basically in the realm of logic. It is only in very recent times that focus on the existential, on what *is*, has to considerable extent diminished reflection on the essential.[11] This has coincided with increased awareness of the historical character and inescapable contextualizing of any given human experience. In theology, this has led to a gradual (and in official circles reluctant) acceptance of religious experience as the starting point of theological reflection. The classical sources—Scripture, patristic thought, conciliar creeds and other ecclesiastical documents, magisterial theological texts—still were seen to have a role, but it was the role of casting normative light on the experience of a believing community.

Focus on Power

Still another element has had to do with the influence of dominant themes in the narratives/myths used to describe the human journey in history. Structuralist thought, and correlatively Jungian examination of archetypes, had drawn attention to underlying patterns in these societal stories. Much earlier, at least as far back as the writings of Machievelli and Hobbes and then the nineteenth-century emergence into prominence of the social sciences, the nature and exercise of power had been the central object of social scientific reflection upon public life. However, it was different with the hermeneutic that guided historical and literary reflection on human life. As late as mid–twentieth century, Steinbeck's *East of Eden* could assert that the central theme in all narrative was the struggle between good and evil.[12] The centrality of this moral contest had already been implicitly contested by the master/slave dialectic in the philosophy of Hegel and Marx; but it is only more recently, with the influence of the Frankfurt School, Foucault, and postmodern literary criticism, that the dialectic between power and weakness has come to be seen as central to the overall interpretation of human existence in community.

Not surprisingly, the social sciences as far back as Machievelli and Hobbes and Rousseau have been engaged in an analysis of power. In more recent times, Max Weber set much of the pattern of discussion by his *Wirtschaft und Gesellschaft* in 1922, and Emile Durkheim, though not concentrating on an analysis of political power, drew attention as early as the beginning of the twentieth century to the social power of moral attitudes and especially of education. The sociology of power has become notably complex—one author calls it "chaotic"—as "functionalist" and "structuralist" schools of thought debate one another's positions. What seem to be the principal polarities of the discussion are *agency*, that is, the sources and limitations of the empowerment and activity of individuals or groups, and *control/influence*, that is, power over, especially the power exercised by structures. Beneath the difference of views is the enduring influence of Kantian ethics and Marxist focus on conflict. In succeeding chapters, elements of this conversation about power will be studied in their relation to the power of Spirit.[13] One aspect of recent discussion is specially relevant to the perspective of this book: greater attention has been paid to power's distribution in a network of relationships, and there has been increased analysis of these systems of relationship.[14] Organizational theory has become a prominent clarification of the manner in which such a network (system?) of relationships not only constitutes the operational field of the exercise of power, but is also to a considerable extent the source of the empowerment of individuals within the network.[15]

Finally, as "power" has gained center stage in social analysis, literary criticism, and historical writing, there has been growing awareness of the multiple manifestations of power. In general, there is an accepted distinction between coercion and persuasion, but how each of these is manifested takes many forms. Joseph Nye, for example, in his recent *Paradox of American Power*,[16] adds to his discussion of military and economic power an umbrella classification of "soft power"; Marilyn French's 1985 *Beyond Power*,[17] a detailed accounting of the varieties of power, points to the fact that much of the description and critique of power has taken place in feminist circles as women scholars have struggled to clarify and challenge the ideology and structures of patriarchy.[18]

An intriguing aspect of the broadened reflection on power is the parallel, to which Jane Chance has recently drawn attention, between the response of Foucault and Tolkien to the twentieth century's immense abuses of power and to the 1960s popular reactions to those abuses. Though their responses are not the same—in some ways opposed—both concentrate on power as occurring in the various interchanges and relationships between people and on the role of language in this exercise of power.[19]

Power and the Holy Spirit

It is against the background of these growing insights into the character and influence of power that the present volume hopes to reassess the long-standing description of divine power, that is, what Christian tradition has called "the Holy Spirit." Focus on "power" finds an obvious application in the spheres of economic, political, and social life, but the present study will suggest that the deepest questions about conflicting powers are theological and concern what Christians have traditionally referred to as "the Holy Spirit" and "salvation." It is the contention of this book that the paradigm shift in the theological view of "power," in the context of twentieth-century reappraisal of soteriology, represents what may be the most radical shift in mentality to touch Christianity in eighteen hundred years.[20]

In present-day scholarly discussions of pneumatology (i.e., theology about the Spirit), there is widespread agreement that the traditional reference to the Spirit of God as the "third person of the trinity" is both inadequate and misleading.[21] Much more reflection on the notion of "spirit" as applied to God is needed; and using modern understanding of "person" in reference to God's Spirit must be challenged. Granted that, what would replace it? There is no ready answer, and ultimately one is faced with mystery, but greater insight into personal communication and relationships, increased understanding of the function of symbols and rituals, and greater awareness of the sacramentality of creation and especially of believing Christian communities seem to open up new avenues of reflection. These I hope to follow in suggesting an experience-based pneumatology. Reconsideration of the Holy Spirit is not, of course, an isolated theological endeavor but coincides with the shifts in soteriology that probably constitute the central development of twentieth-century Catholic theology. The present volume is not intended to present a comprehensive pneumatology; instead, its more limited aim is to relate pneumatology to today's understandings and exercise of power.

Deeper Elements of Paradigm Shift

However profound and influential the paradigm shift in human thinking, it is not the deepest aspect of what is changing in Christianity and more broadly in human life. To a considerable extent, the shift in human thinking reflects the massive changes in human experience during the past few decades. "Reality" has shifted. Awareness of the centrality of power has come about because the actual structures and exercise of power have changed. There has been a worldwide, but still little appreciated, cultural shift away from patriarchy and the power alignments it represents.[22] Obviously, this is connected with the increasing education and self-awareness of women and the concomitant global effort to obtain human equality. Along with it has been a new experience of the power of nonviolence as exemplified in the careers of Mahatma Gandhi, Martin Luther King, and Dorothy Day and the awakening of the poor of the earth to their oppression and their latent power. As it began to ground itself in humans' life experience, theology was increasingly influenced by that experience. It would take volumes to describe that changing experience—and volumes have already been written attempting to understand it—but certain aspects seem more critical for Christian theology and Christian faith.

First, the world has become truly one world; through increased travel and major breakthroughs in communication, people have become aware of cultures and peoples other than their own as never before. Events in any part of the world now have implications for the entire globe. At the same time, as the political power alignments that prevailed prior to the two great world wars have broken down, there has been a resurgent nationalism[23] that often is linked to religious fundamentalism. As Christians have discovered the reality of other religions, this has challenged the previously claimed uniqueness of Christianity.[24] Second, as a result, the whole question of salvation has entered a new level of discussion. This has meant that previous theology about "grace," "providence," the action of God's Spirit, and the role of the Church in evangelizing and ritualizing needs to be radically reconsidered—something that has been happening since mid–twentieth-century disputes about "the supernatural." Third, and perhaps most basically, there has been a rather rapid "secularization" of Christian thought and life. In its more authentic expressions, this has not been an abandonment of the "mystery" dimension of Christianity but rather a regained appreciation for the importance and sacrality of created reality, especially human bodiliness, and a breaking through semimagical explanations of divine activity to a deeper grasp of sacramentality. Part of this shift has been that people's experience of "the divine" has become more intertwined with the experience of their own personhood. Whether they reflect on it or not, they have a new view of how divine and human power interact in the process of "salvation."[25] Moreover, they have an altered view of what religion is meant to be and what it means to be religious, a growing awareness that some of the worshiping actions that should have been rituals that involved the activity of a believing community had drifted into being observed performances by an ordained elite.[26] Particularly on the part of those Christians who have had the advantages of deepened education about their faith, there has been an almost imperceptible but basic change in their attitudes and understandings regarding religious belief and practice. The ways in which they relate to Christ, to Mary, to God have changed. Fourth, even though not yet officially recognized, the absoluteness of religious institutions and official formulations of belief has been challenged by the relativizing that is intrinsic to humans' historical existing. Fifth, with great pain and conflict, the economic and social life of people is being forced into new patterns of globalization; this has already deeply affected people's religious thinking and activity.

Needed Shift in Pneumatology

Human life is changing at an accelerating rate, and old patterns of thinking can no longer adequately deal with the question: what is going on? Religiously, this question can be rephrased: What really is God doing, if anything, in human life today?[27] How is the power of God influencing human life today? This is a threatening question, for the answer might be that Christians must hope that Christianity has a future as the instrument of divine saving power, but only if it transforms itself quite radically. For such a transformation to occur, human imagination, honesty, and creative effort will be needed; but its accomplishment will be achieved by divine power, the power of God's eschatological Spirit. Hence the importance of understanding as far as we can the character and activity of this Spirit. This enterprise is only the most recent form of a centuries-long process, a form of "reading the signs of the times" that today focuses on the multifaceted phenomenon of power in human activity. Discernment of the Spirit, the power of God, has been central to the life of the Church from its earliest days but never more so than today.

Inevitably, then, any pneumatological reflection today must build upon and draw from the pneumatology of the past. This goes beyond harvesting the insights planted by theologians of previous generations. If today's theologian is part of the same community of faith and memory as those previous thinkers, his/her faith must at some level coincide with their faith and to some extent interiorize and appropriate their theological insights. What the present study hopes to do is to add to this inheritance by relating current reflection about power to traditional understanding of the Holy Spirit.

One thing that needs to be underlined in such reflection is the central influence of people's basic outlook on themselves and the world in which they live. What in any given culture and at any point in history are the overall *Zeitgeist* and regnant ideologies that constitutes the atmosphere of consciousness in which people think and decide and act? In any culture, the institutional forms distinctive of that culture—its political arrangements, its economic activity, the social locations of its members, even its art and leisure—are shaped by the underlying ideology of that culture, even as people's living experiences of those institutions shapes it. To control the basic ideology of a populace is to control its activity—an awesome power, illustrated tragically in the history of the Third Reich.

Such ideological influence comes through verbal expression, but even more profoundly through nonverbal symbols, symbols that are capable of creating the perception of space and time. Along with those "deep down" symbols are the powerful traditional images of legendary "heroes," who embody values that underlie people's judgments about "the good life." There is a social construction of thought through symbol, sometimes overt, sometimes more subtle, but this is inevitably a social construction of the very reality of human life.[28]

If the reality of power and the instances of the exercise of power are shifting, then we must come to think differently about power. The deep images and symbols by which people and societies live and experience, the implicit images that structure our perception of space and time, the classic images of exemplary personages who embody good or evil are undergoing radical shift. All this is receiving profound challenge as a culture encounters other cultures with very different symbol systems and loses the complacency that came with the assumption that it was the norm of "humanity," that it was "the chosen people." There is a social construction of reality that goes deeper than the social construction of ideas about human life; human life is existentially different as a result of social construction. Thought and imagination do more than discover and reflect the reality of "the human"; they create the reality of being human.

PART I

Fear and Force

Power takes many forms, and so the divine involvement with power is a multi-faceted reality. No aspect or manifestation of power is more evident or more constant in human experience than the power exercised in what we might call generically "public life," in overt relationship of humans to one another. In this realm, power is observable in physical violence, in control of people through fear, in the influence of the public image of people, in propaganda and control of information, in the authority of law and official structures. Though it is an imprecise lumping of these distinguishable kinds of power, the term "political power" is often used in reference to this overall arena.

The first two units will, then, explore the interlocking exercises of power in the public arena and the manner in which the Spirit of God functions to influence such activity. Violence and fear are basic phenomena in humans' public interaction with one another; the first unit will deal with this. The second unit will consider "more subtle" public exercise of power: office, law, fame, wealth. Together these two units will deal with various forms of coercion or persuasion, that is, the ways by which an agent is able to influence another to do what the agent wishes. Theologically, this touches topics such as nonviolence, trust and hope, Spirit and law, mediation between God and humans, and the grounds for societal and religious authority.

As in following units, more space and attention will be given to an initial and basic aspect of power, and briefer treatment of allied elements of power will follow—for example, the lengthier chapter on office followed by those on law, fame, and wealth.

I

The Basic Paradigm

Physical (Violent) Strength

History indicates that the underlying, generally taken-for-granted, model of power has always been that of physical strength, whether that strength was found in nature or among humans. Present-day students of culture, as well as the most ancient strains of literature, point to the key role of "the strong man"—whether it be Gilgamesh or Marduk or the heroic "dragon-slayer" of ancient legend.[1] The social patterns of slavery and established possession of property that marked the emerging patriarchal culture characteristic of both East and West came into being through violent domination, in particular the dominating control of women by men. Gerda Lerner in her two studies *The Creation of Patriarchy* and *The Creation of Feminist Consciousness* has detailed the process by which domination and control of women led to other socioeconomic institutions such as private property. Out of the experience of a stronger individual or group controlling others by physical force there quickly developed the ideological identification of "power" with forceful, often violent, control. This linkage of force and control with "power" became the hallmark of the patriarchal cultures that have characterized most human societies for centuries.[2]

While there have been many other forms of power—the power of established systems, of legal structures, of personal charism, and so on, about which I will speak in later chapters—the historical record is basically the account of shifts and developments in human life that occurred because of the use of physical force. Prescinding from the uncertainty of insight into prehistorical "history," the reign of Sargon (2371–2316 BCE) begins a tale of "successful" physical/military domination that continues, through figures like Cyrus, Caesar, Constantine, Charlemagne, Napoleon, or Hitler, to be the fabric of our inherited historical memory, with force grounding all other exercises of power. Examples abound of military activity setting the stage for succeeding human development that springs from other kinds of power. One of the most striking was the sweeping conquests of Islam that laid the foundation for centuries of Muslim cultural and political domination, domination that gradually gave way only to stronger military force in modern times. The jury is still out with judgment about the results of present use by the United States of unprecedented military violence in Iraq, about the influence it will have in shaping future developments in the Middle East.

Recent centuries have brought greater sophistication in armaments, in instruments of destruction that can extend or replace brute bodily strength. Clubs and stones gave way to spears and arrows, which in turn gave way to armor and gunpowder and in our day to mechanized destruction by tanks and aerial bombing, causing the incredible obliteration of Hiroshima and Dresden and Tokyo. Throughout this bloody history, physical might remained the source and basic model of power, and in the ideological order, might was implicitly assumed to make right, despite public protestations to the opposite. True, there was also the accompanying model of political power, but then as now political dominance depended on military support.[3]

In our own day, the military "solution" is still a dominating strategy in international conflicts. This became clear in the immediate wake of the destruction of the World Trade Center in New York; the first, almost instinctive, official reaction was to declare war, to retaliate and reestablish the "correct balance of power" through superior military strength. It is a source of hope that this initial mood was immediately countered by a widespread questioning of the value of matching violence with violent reprisal. Though a major military campaign was actually launched, Realpolitik supported by considerable public opinion was able to indicate other measures that needed to be taken and so modify to some extent the usual governmental policy of using superior military force to punish.

The power of dictators worldwide lies in the size and trustworthiness of their military and police forces. Immense military expenditures rule out the possibility of confronting starvation, inadequate habitation, lack of educational opportunity, and health care for most of the world's inhabitants. Militarism plays a controling role in the worldview of officialdom in the developing world, as well as in so-called advanced cultures.

The paradigm of physical strength extends well beyond the military, however. For one thing, physical strength and prowess are admired and richly rewarded by modern cultures fascinated by professional sports. Not that athletic activities need to engage only those of superior strength, but there is a disturbing focus on violence in many spectator sports and a consequent adulation of the "gladiator." Jokes may be made about the challenge to such athletic preeminence by "the triumph of the nerds," but it is still the stadiums of the land to which thousands flock to witness competition between the physically strong.

There is no need to stress the prevalence and influence of violence in film, television, and mechanical games of various sorts; it is all too evident. Public debate on this issue has drawn attention to the pervasive power of such portrayals of violence, especially on the young. For the moment, there is no clear response to the recent increase of violence in society, violence in the streets, and, perhaps even more disturbing, the rising violence in domestic circles.

The Ideology of Might

Without further detailing what is fairly obvious, namely, physical strength as the pervading paradigm of power, let us move on to what touches the principal object of this study, that is, the ideology and social attitude accompanying this symbol. I hope that will then allow us to relate the power attached to physical strength to that power which is the Spirit of God.

Starting with humankind's most ancient memories, the phenomenon of dominating physical strength has been accompanied/justified/legitimated by ideological creation of the "hero myth." Drawing on the deep symbolic impact of myth, the story of the hero led to a society's self-understanding but also to shared emotions of fear or security, to accepting power exercised in the status quo as "the will of God" or "fate." Incorporated into the processes of education, these myths have reinforced the culture-shaping glorification of physical power.[4]

Despite Plato's admonition that in their education boys not be exposed to the *Iliad* and the *Odyssey* because of the corrupting effect of Homer's stories about the immoral carrying-on of the Olympian gods,[5] young aristocrats of the Hellenic and Hellenistic periods had their notions of "power" shaped by the heroic figures of Agamemnon or Achilles or Hector. It was because of their physical might exhibited in battle that these heroes stood above their fellows and were accepted as leaders. Even though Ulysses was praised for his wit, the account of his return home and slaughter of his enemies featured his strength—he alone was able once more to string the great battle bow and then, aided only by his son, to destroy the haughty freeloaders who greatly outnumbered him. What happened educationally in ancient Athens has been repeated over the centuries in culture after culture when the young have been shaped and inspired by whatever warriors have been remembered in their culture's history.

It is worth noting that in the ideologies accompanying such physical power, there often lay a hint of "supernatural" power at work—only because they were endowed with a share of such power or at least were accompanied in their exploits by "the gods" were those heroes capable of more than ordinary human feats. Behind the adventures of the Homeric heroes and their successes or failures lay the power and the struggles of the Olympian deities. Constantine would claim support by the God of the Christians before the battle at the Milvian bridge, Saladin saw himself as the emissary of Allah at the same time that Richard the Lionhearted saw himself on a crusade blessed and empowered by Christ—and so it went until today when moviegoers who heard Obee bid farewell to young Luke Skywalker with the blessing "The force be with you" experienced hints of some hidden cosmic power working to overcome evil. Was this perhaps the movie creator's suggestion that what Christians call "the Holy Spirit" was at work in the war of the Jedi?

In more than one culture, as with the Zapotecs, who built North America's first city at Monte Alban (in present-day Mexico), the priests who dominated the culture as "the sacred ones," dwelling in an acropolis geographically even closer to "heaven," were also the military leaders who combined physical might with control of "the magic." The gods, of course, were themselves the ultimate possessors of power, being able to employ the forces of nature in their exercise of power—the power of lightning and storm, the power of sea and sun and wind, the power of fertility and plague and death.

Power in Israelite Perspective

For the most part, ancient Israel shared this widespread attitude toward power. While believers can regard the biblical account of the centuries-long experience of the Israelites as "the history of God's dwelling with the people," focusing on divine rather than human power, the fact remains that from the time of Moses onward—even earlier, from the time of their patriarchal origins—this people's culture reflected the same regard for physical might that could be found in their neighbors. Their god, Yahweh Sabaoth, god of armies, was seen as mightier than the armies of Pharaoh, able to defeat the forces of Sennacherib, able to stop the Babylonian invasion if only the people would cooperate.

The central ritual symbol, the ark of the covenant, was Yahweh's battle throne from which in invisible fashion their god would lead Israel to victory against its enemies. This god would, in the decades following the exodus, give them heroes, endowed as was Samson with physical might able to overcome Israel's enemies.

Arguably the most important "hero" of Israelite tradition, King David came to eminence through the use of physical power; he was the warrior who finally achieved the goal of defeating the Philistines who oppressed his people and then went on to establish the kingdom. Though David was blessed with other gifts—as a shrewd military strategist, a musician and poet, and a genuinely spiritual individual—it was still as a triumphant warrior, triumphant with the aid of Yahweh over enemies foreign and domestic, that he was remembered in history, legend, and religious ritual.[6] That the aura of physical power continued to be attached to him in Israel's memory is evident in the Psalms attributed to him, psalms that praise Yahweh for supporting the king in his conflicts, psalms whose implication is that God's power also is that of physical might, that he is the almighty God.

This implication carried on in popular Israelite expectations of a messiah, a future savior figure modeled on David, who would be Yahweh's instrument for restoring the people to glory. The awaited messiah of the Israelite/Jewish people was one who would save the people through military power. Perhaps the strangest application of this view was the idea that Cyrus, the mighty ruler of Babylon, was such a messianic figure (Isaiah 45).

However, looking to physical power as source of "salvation" was not unchallenged in Israel's religious ideology. Constituting at least part of Israel's distinctiveness among ancient peoples was the outlook that came with the great charismatic prophets, the view that another force more powerful even than armies was able to overcome Israel's enemies, whether Jezebel or Sennacherib or Babylon. This "new" force, gradually clarified in prophetic and then priestly traditions, was the power of Yahweh's word.[7]

The ideology of physical power was not abandoned. Instead, there developed a struggle for the minds of the people, a tension between kingly reliance on military strength and reliance on prophetic assurance of Yahweh's other-than-military power. Jeremiah's tragic failure to avert disastrous military resistance to Babylon bears witness to the primacy granted physical might in the popular understanding of effective power.

Yahweh's word was not yet accepted as the ultimate power. That insight would come in the prophetic theology of the word reflected in passages like Isaiah 55 and in the priestly account of creation achieved through divine command; but it took the shattering experience of exile to begin dislodging popular reliance on physical power. The fact that Cyrus was seen as messianic indicates that the "conversion" was not complete.

Significantly, the shift from seeing Yahweh's power manifested in kingly military power to prophetic insight that Yahweh's power was manifested in word was accompanied by a shift in Israel's understanding of the divine spirit of Yahweh. Relevant texts in the Hebrew Bible indicate that there were two distinct periods of understanding about "the spirit of the Lord," each with its own view of what this spirit was and was meant to accomplish. Both equate "spirit" with "power" but differ in the meaning to be given "power."[8]

In the first period, roughly around the time of the origin of kingship in Israel, the spirit is associated with prophecy, but it is prophecy of the more ecstatic variety. Moreover, there are clear links of endowment by the spirit with the possession of unusual physical power by humans or by certain phenomena in nature such as violent wind. To take one striking example from the career of Saul as king and warrior: after his selection and anointing by Samuel to be Israel's first king, Saul is told to join a group of roaming ecstatics. "The spirit of the Lord will suddenly take possession of you and you too will be rapt like a prophet and become another man." Following Samuel's instructions, Saul encountered "a company of prophets coming to meet him, and the spirit of God suddenly took possession of him, so he too was filled with prophetic rapture" (1 Sam. 10). Not long after this, the text says, when he heard the unbearable conditions for peace being offered by the Ammonites, "the spirit of the Lord seized him" as in rage he summoned the men of Gibeah to join him and Samuel in battle against their enemy (11:6). In the battle that ensued, Saul led his troops in a decisive victory over the Ammonites. In these instances, the spirit seems to be a sudden and transitory influence of God that empowers (seizes) Saul "from outside."

But just as the spirit given him empowered him as victorious warrior, as it had done Samson before him (Judges 15:14), when Saul failed in his kingly responsibility and did not follow the dictates of Yahweh, the spirit of the Lord passed from him to David (16:13). Instead of being moved by the spirit of Yahweh, he was from that point on plagued by an evil spirit sent also from God. Here the spirit granted to kings seems to be not Yahweh's own spirit but a charism of ruling/controling power internal to the king. In Saul's case, this is replaced by an evil spirit also sent from God.

Somewhat inexplicably, the spirit of Yahweh receives practically no mention as the source of kingly power in the tradition from the ninth and tenth centuries. Instead it is prophets like Elijah and Elisha to whom the spirit is given, a spirit that endows them with a power able to withstand the power of

kings opposed to them. This prophetic endowment seems again to be an abiding empowerment that extends to the performance of "wonder deeds," for
Elisha after receiving Elijah's spirit is described parting the waters (much like
Moses' action in the exodus) and as healing. Are we already with Elijah seeing
that battle of the spirit-endowed prophets in conflict with royal power derived
from "false gods"? Despite the continuing cultural context of patriarchy, is
God's spirit no longer associated with the power of dominating force?

When we come to Isaiah and the ensuing period up to the Exile, there is
little mention of a spirit of physical/military strength being given a king. Instead, in one of the rare passages in Isaiah 1–39 that speaks of "the spirit of
God" (Isaiah 11—cf. Psalm 72), the spirit of Yahweh will endow the expected
messiah with the spiritual gifts of wisdom so that he can rule with justice.
However, this passage probably cannot be dated as preexilic. Indeed, in some
passages it seems that the power of control, achievement, or destruction earlier
associated with spirit is now connected with the word of God. In Jeremiah the
absence of "spirit" is even more striking. Speaking of God as creator, Jeremiah
10:12 ff. mentions God's power but not God's spirit.

With the Exile, there is frequent and important reference to the spirit. One
cannot but wonder whether this is due to the influence in Exile of priestly
traditions that continue a characterization of Yahweh as creator that had already
begun in some circles of the preexilic Temple priesthood. In any event, the
book of Ezekiel is replete with mention of the spirit. In the opening chapter,
the lengthy description of Yahweh's throne-chariot begins with a vision of a
storm cloud coming from the north, traditionally the dwelling of divinity—the
biblical linkage of wind and spirit needs no amplification. Several aspects of
this chariot are linked with the spirit present in it: it is the spirit that drives
the chariot in one direction or another. This spirit is the spirit of the four living
creatures, yet it is their spirit that is present in the wheels providing their
mobility (1:21–22).

As his prophetic call comes to him, Ezekiel has the spirit empower him,
a spirit that stands him up on his feet to receive his prophetic commission (2:
2). This spirit continues to be mentioned as Ezekiel is sent forth to proclaim
Yahweh's message. Spirit and word now go together with spirit providing the
dynamic power functioning in Ezekiel as he speaks—though as in other prophets the word itself is power. At times, the summons to proclaim the word is
expressed metaphorically by "the hand (i.e., the spirit) of the Lord came upon
me." This "hand" and spirit picked him up in vision and carried him to Jerusalem, as it did also in bringing him to the valley of the dry bones (37:1). In
one place (11:5), it is explicit: "The spirit of the Lord came suddenly upon me

and he told me to say, 'These are the words of the Lord.' " His vision of Jerusalem was "sent to him by the spirit of God" (11:24). In all these instances, the spirit of Yahweh seems to be a force from outside the prophet, seizing him for his prophetic mission.

A more "internal" reality to the spirit is found in other passages. Like Jeremiah 30–31, Ezekiel 36:26ff. speaks of the new covenant: God says, "I will put a new spirit within you so that you will keep my laws." This internal spirit-law actually represents a transformation of the Law comparable to that which took place in the Deuteronomic revision of the Mosaic law. But an inner aspect of "spirit" applies also to the divine gift of life; in the passage of the dry bones, God says to the prophet, "I will put my spirit into you [the people Israel] and you shall live."

Though the same dual meaning of "spirit," a divine force working from outside upon an individual or the people or a charismatic gift of empowerment and life working within a person, is found in exilic thought as had occurred in earlier strains of Israelite faith, there is no hint in the later stage that "spirit" is directed to obtaining God's goal by force.

With the advent of wisdom reflection, especially in the Wisdom of Solomon, there develops an overlap, at times an identification, between spirit and wisdom. Wisdom/spirit in turn is closely allied to word/law. While wisdom as Yahweh's outreach to the world tended now to modify the prophetic/priestly emphasis on the power of word, there is at the same time with scribal developments increased stress on the Law. In Sirach, there is an absorption of word and wisdom into Law: the word that communicates divine wisdom is the Law. One can see this movement as an ascendancy of Sophia as the dominant notion/power,[9] or it can be read as emphasis on Law as the privileged expression of wisdom, which seems to be the case with the Book of Sirach that ends with the chapters praising the wise men who kept the Law.

In the midst of all this, what is the reality and role of wisdom? Clearly it is a spiritual reality, coming to and illumining the minds of humans. It is the divine power that guides and orders creation and is meant to direct human affairs through filling the mind of rulers like Solomon. It brings about justice and works to keep human lives "pure"—so, it is the "holy" spirit. Analogous to the way spirit empowered the prophet to convey God's word, wisdom empowers the king to rule by justice. Erotic language and imagery are used by "Solomon" as a metaphor to convey his longing for wisdom, but the texts do not speak of wisdom itself in terms of divine loving—the eroticism is one-sided and metaphorical. The important point is that God's power of creation and guidance of history is spirit-power, the power of insight and understanding culminating in wisdom, and that this is the kind of power ideally exercised by a human ruler. Wisdom is the essence of divine power, and it is communicated to and empowers humans who are open to it. It is not just that power/spirit accompanies wisdom; wisdom is power.

Looking back over the history of prophecy and subsequent wisdom reflection, one can perceive a clear alternative in Israelite thought to the primacy of physical might and violence as the paradigm of power. Yet, the latter did not disappear as a prominent, perhaps dominant, popular view of power, as the kind of power that one hoped Yahweh would exercise to liberate captive Israel. Certainly, some of the effectiveness of physical might as the instrument of God's liberating activity was illustrated and celebrated in the Machabbean overthrow of Seleucid overlords—the ritual celebration of Hanukah would indicate as much. With Roman control of their land by military might, to many in Judea and Galilee it was quite natural that the power of armed rebellion appealed as the avenue of salvation. Tragically, this led to the destruction of Jerusalem in 70 CE, which forced Jews, both Christian and non-Christian, to reassess the manner in which the power of their God functioned in history on their behalf.

Jesus and the Power of Spirit

Before that assessment occurred, however, violence as a "solution" had been radically challenged by the career of Jesus of Nazareth. That physical might remained the dominant paradigm of power in the Judaism of Jesus' day is the corollary of the strongly patriarchal character of his culture. Patriarchy was well entrenched, ideologically and institutionally, in Second Temple Judaism, though in a somewhat different form than in the Greco-Roman culture that characterized the Mediterranean basin at that time. The omnipresence of Roman troops and the occasional flare-up of revolt made it clear that military means were still looked to as the way of retaining or gaining power. The cycle of violence remained the basic pattern of life.[10]

Early Christian traditions bear witness to the belief that Jesus of Nazareth was the divine parable addressing this primacy of violence. The "revolution" introduced by Jesus was not entirely new, for his public ministry, essentially that of a charismatic prophet, picked up from the preceding prophetic message and stressed the perspective that God's power, that is, God's Spirit, is manifested in "the gentle breeze" (Elijah), in giving life, in "inspiring." More-

over, there is explicit linkage of Jesus with divine wisdom, certainly as
the prophet of wisdom and perhaps more.[11] New Testament texts of Jesus'
desert temptations indicate that Jesus' own experience was one of being empowered and commissioned in his teaching and healing, not by any earthly
ambitions of wealth or power or fame, but by God's Spirit of compassion and
concern.

Whether the Gospels convey Jesus' own explicitly expressed views or early
Christians' reflection on what they remembered as his outlook, those Gospels
describe a clear rejection by Jesus of the commonly accepted notion of and
attitude toward power. The scene of the temptation in the desert, where Satan
strives to sidetrack Jesus' messianic mission, is cast against the background of
Israel's historic temptations, especially the temptation to seek salvation from
earthly power rather than from Yahweh. Jesus is depicted as repudiating such
in Desert false power, refusing to acknowledge that it is the source of salvation (Matt.
4:8–10).

Again, the words of Jesus to his disciples (Mt 20:28), when they were
debating who would occupy the positions of power in the coming kingdom,
are an undeniable rejection of dominating military/political power as the
means of achieving the reign of God. Instead, Jesus proposes the enigmatic
✱ power of servanthood, carried to the self-sacrifice portrayed in Isaiah 52–53, as
the kind of power that he himself would employ and that they as his disciples
must also exercise. It was this view of Jesus as the Servant of God that enabled
the early Christians to come to grips with the scandal of the "expected one"
dying as a convicted criminal, to embrace a wisdom that was a "stumbling
block to the Jews and foolishness to the Greeks."

Philippians 2 witnesses to the fact that earliest Christian reflection absorbed this insight into servant-power. There is good reason to see this passage
as Paul's incorporation into his letter of a very early Christian hymn, perhaps
coming from the community in Jerusalem. The gist of the passage, despite its
poetic genre, is quite clear: it was because of Jesus' acceptance of his servant
role that he possesses power to save, and Christians are to adopt this sacramentality, be guided by this same Spirit.

When one adds to this view the logos theology of John—that is, that Jesus
in all he is and does functions as revealing Word of God—the theology of
servant-power extends even to the divine activity in human history. God's
Spirit-power, embodied and sacramentalized in Jesus' openness ("obedience")
to that Spirit, is precisely the power of self-giving service. Jesus has come not
to be served but to serve and give his life; and in so doing, he makes present
the self-giving and creatively serving power of God.

Tale of Two Messiahs

For the disciples of Jesus who went out to preach the gospel, the death of Jesus presented a major obstacle. The early kerygma, reflected in Acts 2 when Peter proclaims the good news of Jesus, describes the risen Jesus as "Messiah and Lord." To the Jews who were the first audience of evangelization, the notion that the messiah would have suffered the ignominious execution inflicted on Jesus was inconceivable. Christianity needed to reinterpret radically the notion of "messiah."

At the heart of this transformation of "messiah" (which means that the Christian messiah, Jesus, cannot simply be identified as the Jewish messiah) was the application to Jesus' death of the fourth Servant Song of Isaiah 52–53 and the messianic Psalm 22. Probably Jesus himself in the later stages of his public career already related himself to the Servant figure. Certainly Christian reflection very early looked on Jesus as fulfillment of this prophetic ideal and his execution as instrument of divine salvation rather than divine rejection.

Involved in this new understanding of "messiah" was the abandonment of the expectation that the divine activity of salvation was to be accomplished through or allied with military might. Instead, what was revealed in Jesus was the paradox of nonviolence being ultimate power.[12] In Jesus' dying, the cycle of violence was definitively broken in principle, the creative power of God's Spirit was unleashed in fullness to overcome whatever is destructive of human persons. However, that Spirit-power can be effective in history only in conjunction with human free decisions. Tragically, the application of that seminal action to human history still remains unachieved, very largely because nonviolence has never been commonly seen as a realistic exercise of power.

Still, the theologies of the Christian Scriptures are quite clear: the God revealed in Jesus is not the support of those generally regarded as powerful, not the legitimation of patriarchal domination, but instead the God of the *anawim*, the poor and the powerless.[13] It is not just that God protects and justifies the weak; in Jesus, God identifies with the "poor." In the actual context of his historical existing, Jesus of Nazareth was one of the powerless of the earth. He possessed neither political nor economic nor priestly power. Already in the infancy narratives of Matthew and Luke, the divine option in favor of the poor is highlighted as a major theme in the gospel message. The angelic announcing of the gospel comes first to shepherds who occupy the lowest rung on the social ladder. Mary's "Magnificat" speaks of the powerful being dethroned and the lowly exalted.

Such passages forecast the insistence in Jesus' teaching that his auditors adopt a new mindset; external ethical behavior is unquestionably advocated, but the stress is on people's inner attitudes. To act visibly in socially acceptable ways but at the same time to harbor hidden judgments or decisions that run counter to God's will is denounced as hypocritical and a rejection of God's Spirit. Paul's exhortation to the Philippians was "let that mind be in you which was in Christ Jesus" (Phil. 2:5). To have such a "mind" is to possess power, God's own Spirit. Jesus' own "mind" was in complete congruence with the "mind" of his Abba; they had but one Spirit. If one is to be a disciple, that person must open to and be directed by that same Spirit of God.

The fact that one can theologize from the New Testament in this manner indicates how clearly primitive Christian thought had understood and absorbed the transformation of "messiah" that had occurred in Jesus. This insight into and acceptance of the power of nonviolence continued for generations and was dramatized in the history of persecution that characterized the early centuries. Perhaps the most striking case was that of the martyrs of the Theban Legion, soldiers who upon conversion to Christianity went to death themselves rather than continue a commitment to defend Rome through bloodshed. With an exegesis of Paul's occasional military imagery that was more accurate than that of many later interpreters, the early centuries understood those metaphors as applying to nonviolent fidelity in the face of violent oppression.[14]

Beginning with the Decian persecution, the oppression of Christians became more widespread, and as it touched more people, the desire for martyrdom and the courageous acceptance of death began to wane. Christians looked forward to and prayed for an emperor who would rescue them from their enemies, who would be triumphant in battle against those who would continue the Christian persecutions. Such a savior emerged in Constantine. Not only did Constantine by his decree of 313 break with the pattern of persecution, but he did so as a warrior, favored by God with the vision at the Milvian bridge, himself later baptized into the Church.

Granted all the doubts about the actual historical reality of his vision of the cross and its accompanying divine approval, *In hoc signo vinces*, and questions about the motivation for his conversion, there is no doubt that he considered himself to be the head of the Church (indeed of all humanity) and charged by God to care for it all. With imperial arrogance, he seems to have signaled in the arrangements for his own burial that he was the equal of the original Twelve, ushering in a new era in Christianity's existence. This somewhat mythic picture of a new warrior messiah was enshrined in Eusebius's biography. At the time it was written, this somewhat less than factual glorification of Constantine as a divinely-sent savior was criticized for its inaccuracy by eminent figures like the Cappadocian Fathers,[15] but in the course of time it became the accepted story about Constantine's role as the militant savior of Christianity.

What began with Constantine continued with his successors. Now the Christian people were protected by the power of God's representative, the Roman emperor, even favored by Christianity, becoming under Theodosius the official state religion. It would be only a short step to the declaration of Justinian, enshrined in his codification of Roman law, that the emperor was, as the head of both Church and State, the vicar of Christ. With Constantine, a new phase of Christian history began, a new perspective on what it meant to be "Christian" gradually emerged. Previous stress on nonviolence was replaced by a new ideology about the manner in which the reign of God was to be achieved. While it would be wrong to suggest that terms like "the Church militant" and "soldiers of Christ" were now taken with complete literalness, their use did have its own subtle but powerful effect on the "spirit" of the Church. God was seen to work in human history through civil power and parallel ecclesiastical power; civil and ecclesiastical rulers were seen as the mediators of God's salvation.

Still, trust in nonviolent overcoming of evil did not completely drop out of the picture. As we mentioned, not all looked uncritically on Constantine as a new messiah. Ambrose at the very time that Christianity was being recognized as the official religion of Rome invoked a power other than military or political when he forced Emperor Theodosius to do penance precisely because of his violent abuse of military power. More important, as the so-called "barbaric invasions" wore down the military strength of Rome and the emperors themselves could no longer offer protection, power other than that of armies led to the pacification of these invaders and their incorporation into what became feudal society. The ability of Leo the Great, without any use of violence, to save Rome from pillage by Attila's army, was a striking symbol of divinely given power that was other than and triumphed over physical might. However, from the fourth century, if not earlier, the ideal of servant-power gradually weakened, even as Church officials continued to describe themselves as "servants." Without being cynical, one can notice that ordained Church leaders, explicitly in some cases, considered that their service consisted in ruling and controling their nonordained fellow Christians for their own good. Only in rare cases did any of these churchmen themselves use military force to carry out their intentions; but it was not rare for high-level Church leaders to ally themselves with civil rulers who could use physical force to accomplish "spiritual" goals presumably shared by both.

An indication of the extent to which physical/military prowess continued to be a dominant paradigm in Christian thinking is the prominence in church history of military heroes such as Charlemagne, who in his own day was lauded in messianic terms as "a new David" and who, like Constantine, saw himself in practical terms as in charge of the Church. *Los reyes catolicos*, Ferdinand and Isabella, are venerated to this day because of their military victory over the Muslims. Sobieski, leading the defeat of the Turks in the battle of Vienna, is remembered as one empowered by God to save Christendom in its moment of peril. A less glorious instance was the view of Christians on both sides of the sixteenth-and seventeenth-century religious wars who believed that military power would secure the truth and establish themselves in control of Europe's religious life. Up to and including the present, military victory has been consistently seen as a sign of divine blessing, God's approval of successful use of violence.

In a way, this religious approval of violence should not be surprising. The cultures where Christianity took root and flourished were without exception strongly patriarchal cultures. There were instances when the domination associated with patriarchy was less evident, when the impetus to human equality was aided by Christian beliefs, as happened during much of the feudal period.[16] Still, the very structures of Church life perpetuated the early infiltration of patriarchy into Christianity. The relative egalitarianism of early medieval society could not withstand the reintroduction into Europe around the twelfth century of the classical and starkly patriarchal traditions of Greece and Rome. Intensified hierarchical structuring of the Church at the same time itself supported the ideology and institutionalizing of patriarchy. And for better or worse, the domination and control intrinsic to patriarchy as a systemic reality was often achieved then and since through physical/military power.

One of the most intriguing aspects of the century with which the second millennium ended is that a new phase of the struggle between militarism and the power of the powerless may have begun. This seems a cruel statement in light of the genocidal bloodshed of the Jewish, Armenian, and Rwandan "holocausts" or the widespread execution of "dissidents" by military dictatorships in Latin America or the inhumanity of penal systems worldwide. Yet, phenomena such as women's movements, whose global extension was strikingly manifested in the Beijing gathering of 1996, popular unarmed uprisings prior to and causative of the collapse of the Soviet empire, and Vatican II's recognition that "the Church" meant not just ordained officialdom but rather the entire community of the baptized, suggest that the dynamics of history may well be shifting in favor of the powerless. Indeed, the very violence perpetuated by those still in possession of physical power may betray their fear that another power, other than theirs and greater, has been unleashed. Could it be that the scenario of Jesus' triumphant execution is once more being enacted?

If in fact there is a shift in favor of the powerless, this must be grounded in and witnessed to by a shift in the basic ideology according to which most people understand their lives and the communities in which those lives are experienced A new spirit, a new perspective, must root changed behavior on the part of both rich and poor, women and men, upper strata and lower strata in society—in short, the mentality expressed in Galatians 3:28 must become pervasive. In so far as this occurs, there will be a commonly shared "spirit" involving not only understandings but also values, hopes, and goals. Human life in such a context will be "controled" by the Spirit of God; that Spirit will be the power moving humanity eschatologically toward its fulfillment as "the reign of God." Such a global sharing of the Spirit of God will not be a specifically religious phenomenon but something as broad as human life worldwide. If and when it occurs, it will make clear that Christianity was not meant to be a religion in any narrow sense but rather the catalyst for a whole new way of being human.

What all this implies is that a pneumatology that attempts to limit the functioning of "the Holy Spirit" to any specific religious faith or more generally to "religious" activity as a particular activity in humans' lives is truncating the influence of God in human existence. The ecumenical implications of this are obvious, but it extends far beyond what is ordinarily considered the sphere of ecumenical considerations. God's Spirit embraces and transforms what is often—sometimes pejoratively—referred to as "the secular world." This Spirit is coextensive with "the providence of God" and characterizes that providence as functioning in history through the lives of women and men, most of whom are considered powerless.

2

The Power of Fear .

When the terrorists of Al Queda attacked New York in September of 2001, they obviously saw violence as their chosen symbol of power to harm the United States. However, they were shrewd enough to employ also another source of power that was able, they hoped, to dishearten the American people and disrupt their lives. That was the power of fear. They knew that closely allied with physical might as a paradigm of power is fear.[1] Not only is fear one of the most widespread human experiences, it often substitutes for physical might as a source of control. It is a common experience to discover after fearing some threat that the actual carrying out of that threat made us realize that the evil needed not to be dreaded as much as it was. At the same time, the simple threat of violence is often powerful enough to induce people to conform to those who are working to control them.

Like so much of what people perceive as "reality," fear is often socially constructed. By one means or another, people are led to believe that some evil lurks in their future, whether this is actually the case or not.[2] Even when the supposed evil is discounted or eliminated as a genuine threat, fear remains deep in the psyche of many persons or of an entire society, often grounding what today is classified as "post-traumatic stress syndrome." The observed fear is but the tip of the iceberg.

History bears witness to the constant use of fear as a means of control at every level of society. Over the centuries, much of the human race has lived with the threat of being overrun by oppressing armies. Even when war was not in progress, armies were barracked on conquered territory to discourage the locals from starting a revolt. In many other situations, there were overt measures to strike fear into the hearts of people. One need only recall the Nazi attempt to defeat the English by the bombing of London during World War II. As a result, fear has often been a key element in the social "atmosphere" that colored and to some extent controled the attitudes and activities of people.

During the time of Roman rule of the Western world in what was euphemistically called the "Pax romana," Roman troops were part of the daily scene in conquered countries like Palestine. Part of Jesus' experience was one of seeing the Roman troops very much in evidence in both Galilee and Judea. Not all these legionnaires were seen as an immediate threat; some, like the centurion whose servant was cured by Jesus, were regarded as friendly to the surrounding populace. But the Roman practice of crucifixion for any of those suspected of rebellion was clearly intended to strike fear into any who contemplated revolt.

Things certainly did not improve for the bulk of people as the Roman empire collapsed, invading tribes poured south and quite ruthlessly killed and pillaged, only to be followed by centuries of medieval barons battling one another and then setting out on the catastrophe of the crusades with its slaughter of thousands of innocent people. Clearly, fear of military violence must have colored most people's daily experience of life, a taken-for-granted manifestation of the search for power in which they were helpless pawns.

Nor have things bettered in more recent times. Theories of a "just war," used to justify military conquest of various kinds, have usually included the proviso that innocent civilians are not to be killed or even injured; but the reality is that civilians are today considered part of a country's war effort and millions upon millions of noncombatants were killed in the two great world wars—to say nothing of other conflicts such as the Vietnam war. No wonder that most of the world has lived during the twentieth century with fear of thermonuclear extinction. Governments and military establishments on both sides of the threatened conflict have exploited this fear for their own purposes, to cement their own power and legitimate their self-aggrandizing policies.

Behavior of armies in the wars of the past century makes it clear how fear itself was deliberately used as a potent weapon. Leading up to and then initiating World War II, the Nazi use of dive-bombing to terrorize the population of cities like Guernica in Spain or of cities in Poland that lay in the path of the Blitzkrieg was designed to panic the local population and eliminate resistance to Germany's advancing troops. So, too, was the indiscriminate U-2 bombing of London, which was not calculated to target any military installations. Much of the Allied bombing was aimed at nonmilitary targets with the general intent of destroying the morale of the enemy population through fear. And it is hard to find any motivation other than that for the atomic destruction of Hiroshima and Nagasaki.

However, it is not only fear of foreign armies that has been exploited as a source of power. In many dictatorships, such as in Latin America, oppressive governments have been kept in power by armed forces whose willingness to use force is advertised as a deterrent to those opposed to the government. Governments, often on the occasion of public celebrations, display in parades the extent of their military hardware. This can, of course, be seen as a comfort to the populace—"See how protected you are"—and to justify expanding military expenditure. It can and often has been a basis for military recruiting or popular support for military adventures of one sort or another—there is no question about the stirring in one's nationalistic feeling effected by seeing "the boys" marching by. But in many instances, the military display is intended as a deterrent—the massive parades in Red Square with all the latest bombs and tanks and so forth were clear signs: "Just start something and see what you are up against."

I remember on one occasion being in Oaxaca in Mexico at a time when there was a great deal of unrest in the neighboring region of Chiapas and some unrest in Oaxaca itself. It was the annual celebration of Mexico's independence from Spain, a day not unlike the U.S. Fourth of July. Naturally, there was a parade, and it was my good fortune to be staying in an apartment bordering the parade route. There were the usual marching bands, public officials riding in open autos, fire trucks and ambulances, police and firemen, but most prominently the various branches of army and security forces with all their equipment. It was incongruous to see tanks and personnel carriers and mortar launchers and large artillery pieces rolling down the rather narrow street of that attractive provincial city. The message to the populace was quite clear—no rebellion allowed here!

In the acquisition and retention of political power, fear has always been a potent weapon of the powerbrokers. This has involved, of course, fomenting the fear of threats from without; but it has extended to many other fears as well. In the United States during the period of the Cold War, many politicians played upon and nurtured the nearparanoia of the populace regarding communism. The vast majority of people did not have the vaguest understanding of "communism" but were convinced that it was evil and an ultimate threat. Anything that was seen as opposed to or endangering American interests (read "the interests of corporate wealth") was branded "communist," and that was enough to swing public opinion in the direction desired by the government. This applied to developments such as the attempts by oppressed peoples in Central America to free themselves from cruel dictatorships, as well as the rise of the civil rights movement in the United States itself. It is almost comical now to read about the attempts of the FBI to hang on Martin Luther King the label of "communist," and, of course, it is doubtful whether his enemies in high places had any fear of his being linked to the Communist Party. But those enemies were at pains to appeal to people's fear of communism and so discredit the civil rights leadership.

Distasteful as was that episode, it paled in comparison with the witch hunt that one associates with the "McCarthy years." For crass political advantage, Senator Joseph McCarthy and his cronies brought about near panic among large segments of the population, destroyed the careers and lives of talented and responsible citizens, and achieved all this by creating fear that there was a vast Soviet conspiracy to take over control of the United States. One can gauge the power of fear and wonder at it when one remembers the danger in which even highly placed and prominent public officials were put if they openly challenged the operation of the House Committee on Un-American Affairs, the agent of McCarthy's campaign. While the peak of McCarthyism waned, to some extent at least because he made the tactical blunder of attacking General Marshall, the icon of the military establishment, and thus incurring the wrath of then President Eisenhower, charges of communist affiliation continued to be a threat to anyone with political ambitions in the country.

When George Wallace, in his unsuccessful presidential campaign, managed to garner a sizable following, appeal to people's fear of communism was a prominent and powerful element in his strategy. Most recently, Ronald Reagan won wide public support by his repeated attacks on what was presumed to be the great threat to the United States, the "evil empire." Apart from the question about the accuracy of Reagan's assessment of the Soviet threat, there seems little question but that he and the interests he represented were using fear as an incredibly potent political tool. As we will see later, this illustrates the tremendous power possessed by those who in today's world are in control of communications media.

One aspect of fear's power is that the imagined evil is often worse than the eventuality. Bullies, whether on the school playground or on the international scene, gain control of people by the threat of physical harm; and they are successful to the extent that this supposed strength is never tested. However, in many cases, the presumed strength of the bully is found to be nonexistent when it is tested. On the international scene, this was vividly illustrated when, though threatened by massive Soviet military power, the unarmed peoples of eastern Europe faced down and overcame Soviet domination in the 1980s.

What this points to is the link of fear to the imagination and to people's view of "who is in control." Fear is always concerned with a threat, with something in the future that promises to be evil; and it is precisely imagination that enables humans to think about the future. Those whose purpose it is to instill fear into the populace and thereby gain or cement their own power are well aware of this link and so work to create images that will be fear instilling. Clearly, the emergence of television and the Internet has increased immeasurably the power to shape the imagination of an entire populace and create a climate of fear.

Recent presidential elections in the United States are striking instances of this propagandistic use of certain images as symbolic of the evil that will occur if one or another candidate is elected. During the campaign in which George Bush defeated Michael Dukakis, the picture, repeated again and again in TV ads, of the revolving door in which convicted criminals are being constantly returned to society was meant to convey the message that Dukakis's election would result in expanded threat of criminal activity. Connected with this was the figure of Willi Horton as symbol of Dukakis's weakness in handling criminals and thereby endangering society. No doubt, many who saw these TV ads realized that they were not an accurate representation of Dukakis's policies, but the element of fear grounded in doubt still remained. The old adage "A picture is worth a thousand words" was certainly verified in this case. So, the manipulation of imagery is a significant use of fear to gain power.

Imagined evil can have this potent effect on people's attitudes and decisions precisely because the future is always uncertain and therefore often the object of fear. Even though humans do have a certain capacity to determine the future by their own choices, choice itself is risky. One may choose what will prove to be beneficial; on the other hand, choices may lead to unexpected problems or harm. In the latter case, not only does the future bring evil, but to some extent humans themselves are responsible for it, even when they act in good faith and to the best of their abilities. As a result, change—which, of course, is unavoidable—is viewed by many as dangerous. In their eyes, though the present situation may not be ideal, at least one is surviving and even in some cases prospering, and there is no assurance that a future situation will be better or more secure.

History indicates that movements of "restoration" occur regularly when established patterns in society begin to change. After Cromwell and the ascendancy of Protestantism had upset the post-Reformation establishment of Anglicanism and the reign of the Stuarts, Charles II was recalled in 1660 from

Holland to restore the previous situation. In the nineteenth century, the ferment of the years following the French Revolution and the conquests of Napoleon gave way to the Congress of Vienna in 1815, which attempted to restore the presumed stability of the prerevolutionary Bourbon and Hapsburg rule. In our own day, the worldwide phenomenon of religiopolitical fundamentalism is grounded in the desire to return to a previous "golden age," to the time when traditional values had not been eroded by more recent developments.

Opposition to the "new thing" that is coming into being is based on fear of the imagined evils that will flow from abandoning tried and true ideas and processes. History may show that the imagined evil did not happen, but the accompanying fear continues to be appealed to for decades by those in power as a reason for preserving outmoded institutions. The resistance of Vatican officialdom to the modern world, epitomized in the "Syllabus of Errors," is a classic example. Even since the Second Vatican Council shifted the attitude of the Catholic Church toward modern culture, there have remained many in the curial bureaucracy who work to reverse Vatican II and restore things to their preconciliar state.

History records the disastrous effect that pervasive societal fear can have on human life. Perhaps the most striking example of this was the shared terror that gripped much of Europe at the time of the Black Death. Not understanding exactly the cause of the plague nor knowing ways of avoiding or overcoming it, millions of people lived without hope of survival into tomorrow; whole villages were abandoned and their inhabitants became bands of wandering homeless who rapidly became a menace to towns not yet touched by the tragedy; monasteries, which were often the only institution of care for the poor and sick, declined as the monks themselves were caught in the contagion, and a pall of fear and despair fell on the population.

While this pervasive fear gradually dissipated as the plague ended, there remained an excessive awareness of human sinfulness, seen as the reason for "divine punishment," that was passed on for centuries and characterized religious attitudes well into modern times. Generations of preachers drew, sometimes with great effectiveness, upon people's fear of divine punishment as a motivation for conversion to righteous life. This motivation was, of course, not new. At least as far back as Israel's prophets and continuing throughout the subsequent centuries, the threat of retribution for sin has been used to change people's unjust behavior. Given the assumption that this was an effective means of obtaining conversion when it was truly needed, such instilling of deserved fear can be a good thing. However, this places tremendous power in the hands of those religious leaders who claim to be able to prevent or to call down such divine vengeance. This ability to exploit the power of fear means that such religious leadership has the power to shape people's relationship to the divine.

A very important aspect of the power of fear is that its influence extends over not just the dominated and oppressed elements in society but over both dominators and subjects. In a fascinating and insightful analysis of patriarchy as a system, Allan Johnson in *The Gender Knot* makes the case that patriarchy is a system of control grounded in fear.[3] Those in power fear, and often rightfully, that those whom they dominate and exploit will at some point rise up against them and deprive them of their privileged position. Faced with this threat, they devise, sometimes almost unconsciously, social mechanisms that will keep the dominated elements "in their place." As a consequence, fear leads to the dehumanization of both powerful and powerless in society; neither group lives in genuine peace and freedom.

One of the most striking illustrations of this social manipulation by those in control to maintain their control is the way in which gender distinction translated into cultural patterns and laws has been used to preserve male domination. The key social institution has been, of course, the family, as in various societies it has functioned to control the power latent in women's sexuality. Gerda Lerner, in her *Creation of Patriarchy*, has traced out the early emergence of both family structures and the civil state from the control by dominant men of women's reproductive power.[4] While eventually this was formulated into law (as in ancient Assyria), actual rape and the continuing threat of rape functioned as a control mechanism in what Lerner describes as "the exchange of women." It would be a mistake, however, to think that it was only in the distant past that rape and women's prevailing fear of rape have been used as a control strategy and political tool. There is frightening evidence that systematized rape was used in the recent Kosovo/Serb conflict as part of the conduct of war.[5]

One can see the underlying role of fear in this evolving social pattern if one examines the striking history of Christian virgins in Christianity's earliest centuries. In *Lydia's Impatient Sisters*, the German exegete Luise Schottroff has traced the dynamics that lay behind the Roman authorities' persecution of Christian women who refused to submit to arranged marriages.[6] The torture and execution of these women, who insisted on preserving their virginity as witness to their relation to Christ, was not because of opposition to the religious beliefs of these women, but because they were seen as a threat to the stability of Roman patriarchal society. If these women were allowed to challenge the very basis of societal stability, the patriarchal family, the fabric of society was endangered. Actually, it is almost unbelievable to see the extent to which these few women were seen as such a threat; but the fear was justified. Christianity's approach to human sexuality and to basic human equality was fundamentally incompatible with the male domination intrinsic to Greco-Roman culture's patterning of the family.

This fear that Rome had of the strange and challenging group of Christians is but one instance of the constantly recurring fear of change. That people, especially people of affluence and societal power, should be apprehensive about the future, about the change that it will unavoidably bring, is not all that difficult to appreciate. The future is always the unknown; the changes it will bring may not be for the benefit of those whose lives are now quite comfortable. What the future will become depends to a considerable extent on decisions that humans now make; those decisions may be good or bad, may even be irresponsible.

As we saw, a witness to pervasive worry about the future and reluctance to embrace change is the recurrence of political and cultural movements of "restoration." Time and time again, populations—or at least large sections of them—unhappy or worried about where things are going, long for "the good old days" and attempt the impossible, to turn the clock back to what is remembered or imagined to have been a golden age. In its own way, the story of the garden of Eden expresses such longing for a time, irretrievably lost, when human life was undisturbed by the dangers and problems humans now face.

Study of present-day social development makes clear that the relation between men and women continues to be a key instance of the threat of change. Historically, men have dominated women, used them for their own purposes, sexual as well as social and political. However, there was the constant threat that women would try to change the status quo, demand a society of equal opportunity based not on supposed gender superiority but on personal qualifications. So, a strategy of subtle and implicit threats, as well as customs, laws, and social structures, has been used to keep women "in their place." For a variety of reasons, especially the rising level of women's education and the increased employment of women outside the home, this is changing in much of the world. Many men find this change threatening and actively resist it.

More radically, what is happening is that the underpinnings of patriarchy as a system are being researched and challenged.[7] While fear is not the only power used to control both women and men in a patriarchal context, it has without question been one of the most central and effective means. Efforts to resist and abandon patriarchal ideology and institutions constitute one of the most profound changes in human experience. Understandably, there is widespread worry about this change, even if its character is not always recognized.

One of the most prominent instances of fear being employed as power is the process of formalized education. Beginning with the manner in which many parents raise their children, fear of punishment is used to motivate children to follow a pattern of behavior desired by their parents. Obviously, in the process of leading a child from infancy toward maturity, motivation must be employed; but the question is: what kind of motivation? The view that children can simply be left to follow the path of their own wishes is a naïve abandonment of parental responsibility, but the ideal of gradually bringing a young person through childhood and adolescence to mature self-motivation is difficult to achieve. Often, this difficulty leads parents to resort to threats of one sort or another, hoping that fear will accomplish what persuasion or reasoning cannot.

What begins in all too many homes continues in much of formal schooling. Anyone who has taught, especially in the middle school and high school years, is aware of the need for classroom discipline. It would be unrealistic to rule out a healthy recipe of reward and punishment for effort, cooperation, and achievement; but often enough students are motivated, not by an interest in learning, but by threats—usually nowadays not of physical punishment but of incurring parental disfavor and being denied "privileges" such as use of the family car. Or they are threatened by future inability to enter the "right" high school and then in high school to gain admission to a prestigious college and then in college to obtain the high marks that will lead to success as a money-gaining adult. The educational process becomes for many young people a history of continuing anxiety.

One of the most harmful uses of fear in some early school years is to classify classroom misbehavior as "sin," to call restlessness or mischievous behavior "disobedience." This is an obvious instance of domination by using fear as the power to control. What is appealed to in such situations is an unjustified fear of divine punishment: if a child's misbehavior is seen by that child as "sin," and sin is defined as an offense against God, what enters the picture as ultimate motivation is fear of a punishing God.

If the use of fear as power to control is an abuse in the educational sphere, it is even more so in the religious realm. There is a legitimate, indeed a necessary, role for "the fear of God" if that is correctly understood, but abuse of power enters the picture when religious leaders identify their own rules and regulations with "the will of God" and use God as the ultimate policeman to enforce their own control. Fire and brimstone sermons have long been a stock in the trade of evangelists, but the more subtle appeal of ordinary preaching to divine wrath needs also to be evaluated. Humans all need to be helped in accepting the responsibility for sin, but there is a great difference between genuine guilt and guilt feelings and a vast difference between what may be the actual judgment of God upon the sinner and the description of a divine judge sometimes used by religious leaders to maintain their power.

One of the standard means by which religious officials have incorporated fear of an angry God into their own "required" intervention is the performance of rituals that would turn away divine anger from sinners. This has at times been exploited by greed, demanding of the faithful a payment in kind or in cash for removing sins. At other times, performing or refusing rituals of reconciliation with God has been a means of retaining or increasing dominance over their "subjects." In the medieval struggles between *sacerdotium* and *imperium*, entire populations were deprived of normal recourse to sacramental rituals because their nations were placed under interdict by Popes as a means of countering the power of secular rulers. Much more commonly, rituals of appeasement were performed in good faith, the "ordained" believing that they had been called and consecrated in order to help their fellow believers achieve salvation from sin. Implicitly, however, this assumes necessary mediation on their part, and this necessity is supported by people's fear of divine retribution for sin. So, fear of divine judgment is instilled in the faithful, for if they should cease to fear the presumed punishment from God, the power of the ordained would be in jeopardy.

Theological Reflection

Christian understanding of salvation from fear is, like other Christian beliefs, rooted in the revelation given Israel. Jesus' experience and teaching inherited the traditional faith of his people and especially the message communicated in the prophetic writings. In that tradition, fear played a constant but ambiguous role. As the biblical texts narrate it, the career of Moses himself as leader of his people began in a situation created by justifiable fear. He had in anger killed an official of the Egyptian government, and fearing the vengeance of Pharaoh he fled Egypt, where he had been born and raised, and now found himself caring for the flocks of his father-in-law in Midian. It was there, in the theophany of the burning bush, that he was instructed to return to Egypt, confront Pharaoh, the object of his fear, and free the people from their bondage. Needless to say, this was a mission to strike fear into a sane person's heart. Yet, trusting in the power of this divinity who was revealed to him, Moses overcame his fear and set out to deliver his fellow Hebrews.

This scene already epitomizes the forces that will mark the history of the Israelite people: confrontation with what most people would consider a superior earthly power, in this case Pharaoh, acceptance or rejection of the revelation being given them, the need to run the risk of trusting in the superiority of divine power, frequently trusting some earthly source of power rather than

God and suffering defeat or at times, as now with Moses, making the "foolish" choice for Yahweh and flourishing. It is clear that faith implies acceptance of Yahweh as savior from their fears.

Moses' duel with Pharaoh was itself a question of the Egyptian's being gradually forced to fear the power of the god revealed to Moses. Only when the very existence of Egypt was threatened by the loss of the life-power residing in its first-born did Pharaoh finally, in fear of the greater power of Yahweh, relent and allow the Hebrews to leave. Even with the Pharaoh vanquished, the people faced the risky prospect of the desert trek, the uncertainty of food and water, the attacks of those through whose territories they had to pass. More than once, their faith in Yahweh's power to overcome these threats wavered, and Moses was hard pressed to overcome their fear.

In the promised land, the people's need to trust the power of Yahweh was not lessened. The key passage in Josue 24 reflects this. Exegetes are divided regarding the historicity of the event there described where Josue gathers the migrants from Egypt along with some of their cousin tribes already in Chanaan and initiates or reiterates the covenant with his God, Yahweh. Albrecht Alt a half century ago proposed the view that this biblical scene is grounded in an actual chthonic treaty arrangement that united a group in a loose tribal alliance out of which gradually emerged Israel.[8] Whether or not Alt's theory is true, whatever the provenance of the text, its message for later readers is quite clear. Following up on the traditions of the desert passage and particularly on the revelation of the Law and the making of the covenant at Sinai, Josue 24 describes the reiteration of the Sinaitic covenant and its extension to tribes willing to accept that covenant.

What is interesting from the viewpoint of our present discussion is the manner in which fear is used as a motivation for accepting Josue's proposal. Yahweh is not presented as a threatening divinity; no fear of punishment is mentioned for those who do not accept the covenant. What is mentioned is the promise of blessing and protection associated with observance of Yahweh's laws, but with the implicit notion that such blessings will not accrue unless one accepts the terms of the covenant, namely, observance of the Law. Fear is a motivation, but it is fear of losing the good attached to accepting the covenant with Yahweh.

covenant = fear of losing good

With the advent of the prophetic movement, fear of Yahweh's punishments does enter the picture and in a prominent role. While Israel's God is not essentially a threatening divinity, the sinner has good reason to fear Yahweh's wrath. Passage after passage in prophetic literature proclaims the dire consequences unfaithful Israel can expect. It is important to note, however, to whom and for what offenses these threats apply. Most often the prophetic warning is

prophet = fear of punishment

directed to those in positions of power and leadership and for actions of oppressing the poor, misleading the people, and neglecting official fostering of
authentic worship. All in all, fear of a wrathful God is appealed to as the principal motive for observing the Law.

At the same time, the God of Israel is ultimately a merciful God. Even
when the people, misled by their erring leaders, abandon Yahweh and finally
end in Babylonian exile, they realize that the punishment results from their
sin. Without classifying it that way, they see Yahweh's punishment not as vin-
dictive but as corrective. Moreover, inspired by prophets like Ezekiel and
Deutero-Isaiah, they discover that the God they have offended has not abandoned them and that they still possess Yahweh's favor and their identity as
Yahweh's chosen people. So, more ultimate than fear of their God because
Yahweh is a just God is their trust in Yahweh's covenant fidelity.

In some ways, the basic sin of Israel is the people's capitulation to fear—
fear that we might well see as justified. They fear the power of enemies like
Assyria or Babylon or Egypt, and judging the situation only in "secular" terms,
they are conscious of their relative weakness and so search for earthly allies,
refusing to trust the power of their God to protect them. They fear "other gods"
more than they fear Yahweh, so they turn to worship of these false gods and
discover tragically that their faith in these other divinities leads only to disaster.
Israel's constant temptation is to look to earthly power and wealth as "salvation."

Jesus' Freeing from Fear

If one asks the question, "In precisely what way(s) did Jesus of Nazareth act as
savior?" high on the list must be the response, "He saved humans from fear."
This he did (1) by himself confronting the prospect of ultimate physical evil,
death, and not allowing fear of that evil to deter him from total acceptance of
his mission to overcome the more ultimate evil, sin; (2) by sharing with his
disciples that Spirit which led him and them to overcome fear by trust in the
power and love of his Abba; and (3) by encouraging through his teaching a
trust in God that would free people from a variety of fears.

The pages of the Gospels describe Jesus as a psychologically healthy and
mature man, in no way impervious to the threats that faced him in his public
career—threat of rejection and abandonment by those he taught and healed,
threat of condemnation by religious officials presumed to be orthodox teachers
of the Law, threat of public trial, punishment, and execution. He did not embrace any of these threats with an unhealthy martyr complex or with an arro-
gant estimate of his own strength; instead, he avoided them if that did not

involve denying what he knew to be true, abandoning the mission of opposing religious leaders who for their own purposes were distorting people's understanding of God, or infidelity to the movement of God's Spirit working in him. But when these threats were unavoidable, he did not allow them to turn him away from truth and his <u>Spirit-driven mission</u>.

This is what the scene in the garden of <u>Gethsemane</u> dramatizes. In one of the Gospels' most graphic passages, Jesus is described as being in anguish, his emotions rebeling against the prospect of public humiliation as a criminal, suffering, and death. Jesus at that moment was a man gripped with very justifiable fear; yet, <u>he overcame the fear</u>, did not shrink from the threatening prospect that faced him, and despite all the appearances trusted himself to the mysterious will of his Abba. Fear did not rule him—just the contrary.

break violence, overcome fear

That human decision, to die willingly though certainly not eagerly, was the very heart of Jesus' saving role, for its complete coincidence with God's Spirit working against the forces of evil allowed the Spirit to break through unhindered and undiminished to create that life which is the destiny of humans beyond earthly death.[9]

power of inner spirit-driven mission

An important aspect of that decision as salvific was that it constituted a break in the cycle of violence. As we saw in an earlier chapter, the paradigm instance of power is physical violence. Human history attests to the sad cycle in which violence follows upon violence in the struggle for dominating power. No one truly wins a war; all too often victor and vanquished continue to hate and fear each other, and the "peace" that follows upon the end of a war has proved again and again to be a period used to prepare for the next war. Jesus' dying is interpreted in the gospel narrative as his breaking of this cycle. Though he is hated by his executioners, though he is vanquished physically, he does not die hating in return and praying for vengeance. Instead, his dying is a supreme fulfillment of his teaching: "Love your enemies."

Whether or not he actually did speak the words, "Father, forgive them, for they do not know what they do," Luke's passion narrative reflects early Christianity's understanding that this was Jesus' state of mind as he died. With that cycle of violence broken, humans no longer need to fear the inevitability of violence in their lives—there is an alternative to "the military solution." <u>Though it may involve pain, even death, love can overcome hatred and violence by absorbing them.</u>

However, the triumph over fear that was achieved in Jesus' dying was only half of the story. Out of that human openness to God's Spirit in the midst of dying, the divine Spirit created new life. <u>For those who will accept in faith the reality of Jesus' resurrection, the fear of death has been basically overcome.</u> The very reality of death has been reversed; it is a beginning, not an end, of human life. Though the bodily reality of human experience cannot but be threatened by the cessation of organic life as we now know it, one can actually anticipate death—as Paul did—because it is the entry into fullness of life. The power of violence to destroy life cannot compete with the power of love that is the power to create life; death is swallowed up in new life.

The apparition scenes that end John's Gospel constantly link Christ's gift of the Spirit with the gift of peace and the banishment of fear. It is important, however, to realize that this is more than Spirit accompanying peace and fear-lessness—the share in the Spirit given by the risen one is precisely that quiet trusting awareness of a loving God that banishes fear. One cannot be embraced by God's Spirit, bathed in consciousness of divine love, and fear anything, including death, as ultimate evil. One can repeat with Julian of Norwich, "All shall be well, and all shall be well, and all shall be well," or one can, as reportedly did some of the Jewish martyrs in the gas chamber of Auschwitz, recite the Shema and know that God, and God alone, is the Lord of life and the master of death.

Jesus' Teaching

What he exemplified in his own life and death Jesus conveyed in his prophetic teaching. Throughout his teaching, Jesus was at pains to convey an understanding of his heavenly Abba that would dispel people's anxieties. The distillation of his sermons that is contained in the early chapters of Matthew, the "sermon on the mount," repeats again and again the exhortation to trust in the loving care of God. While this exhortation is meant for all, Jesus singles out those who have most to fear in their daily lives, the poor and oppressed and persecuted, and assures them of their role in the reign of God. True, Jesus did threaten some of his auditors with divine punishment; invariably, however, they were those who wielded religious power over the powerless and used that power position to exploit others. Moreover, Jesus' anger and condemnation were directed at some of the Jewish leaders because they legitimated their abuse of power by teachings that caricatured the God of Israel.

That his auditors come to an accurate understanding of and trust in God was the constant purpose of Jesus' teaching. All his parables were directed to this purpose, all were directed to explaining the activity, the reign, of this God he knew as Abba. No place is this clearer than in the three parables contained in Luke 15. Accused by his enemies of behavior unbecoming one who pretended to be a prophet—"you associate with drunkards" and so on—Jesus replied with the three parables that describe God anxiously seeking what is lost. It is significant that the three metaphoric figures symbolizing God in the three parables ran counter to the social judgments of his day: a shepherd— shepherds were considered the lowest in society; a housewife—since women were not even part of Israel, the comparison of God to a woman is striking; a father—who does not exemplify the appropriate attitude of a Jewish father toward a wayward son.

Clearly, the God described in those parables is not an object of unjustified fear, a God who waits in judgment to punish the wayward. Instead, this is a God who takes the initiative to seek out those who need help, those who are valued by God as a treasure to be recovered. Though in the context of the narrative these parables are directed to the official teachers who are critical of Jesus' ministry to the poor and despised in society, the parables encourage these "poor" to trust in the saving activity of God. What Jesus did in such teaching was to share with others the same Spirit that was his, a mindset of trust in his Abba that dispelled anxiety about the present and the future. Another way of describing this in more technical terms is to point to the fact that the Spirit Jesus had and shared is the eschatological Spirit of prophecy. This is the Spirit that is creative of God's reign of justice and peace, working through those who as Spirit-bearers are "minded" as is Godself and consequently are without anxiety the agents of God's future. The response to fear is trust; it is the freeing power of trust that saves humans from the power of fear.

For those individuals or communities possessing this Spirit, change is not an object of fear. Instead of the future appearing as a threat, it is experienced as the Spirit's invitation to a yet better stage in the reign of God. Even the drastic change that is death is an invitation to life and so not fundamentally the object of fear. Central to this view, of course, is trust in God being the God revealed in Jesus, the God whom Jesus trusted in his own ordeal of dying.

What, then, is the essence of Christian belief in humans' salvation from the power of fear? It is the belief in the greater power of love. Love drives out fear, and divine love does this most powerfully. Theological reflection today has come to realize that the entire process of creation is an act of self-giving on the part of the divine creator; all that exists reveals God as lover.[10] This reaches its zenith when creation extends to self-conscious beings, humans, who can personally "hear" and respond to this love. Christian tradition has always seen a link of the divine Spirit with the divine loving; but it has not highlighted the fact that this Spirit is the divine "outreaching" of love and concern which, when humans discover and believe in it, enables them to trust divine love as a power that will overcome evil and the fear of evil. This clearly replaces violence as paradigm of power with nonviolent love and forgiveness of "enemies" as the ultimate power and replaces the power of domination with the power of self-giving service.

Thinking about the loving self-gift of God in this way brings a number of long-standing theological perspectives into question. Perhaps the most fundamental questioning deals with the centuries-long interpretation of Jesus' saving activity and especially his death as _atonement_.[11] The premises of an atonement theory, like Anselm's famous formulation, are that human sinfulness is an offense against God and that divine justice needs to be satisfied. The conclusion is that Jesus suffered in our place to pay the required penalty. In recent years, a good deal of attention has been drawn to the work of René Girard and his study of violence and the religious mythology of the "scapegoat" in the sacrificial rituals that mark religious history.[12] One can make a case that the death of Jesus both fits into and fractures the mythical narrative of the atoning role of the scapegoat; but it is doubtful whether earliest Christianity would have looked on Jesus' saving action in this light. Instead, they viewed what Jesus did as God's doing, as something Jesus did under the impulse of God's Spirit—this is reflected in John 3: God so loved the world that he sent. . . ." A cursory glance at chapter 10 in Hebrews, paralleling Jesus' sacrificial death with the ritual of Yom Kippur, might suggest that the blood of Jesus on Calvary was atonement for sin. However, a more careful reading of the text makes it clear that Jesus' blood is viewed as effective of the new covenant, sealing the bond of humans with God and intrinsically overcoming the alienating evil of sin. Jesus did not appease his Abba; rather, he was the embodiment of God's creative and redeeming Spirit.

Because of excessive focus on human sin and the need for atonement, much of the religious awareness of Christians over the centuries has been marked by fear. With the interpretation of Jesus' dying as his (and God's) triumph over evil replacing "atonement," faith becomes an exercise of trust rather than one of fear. Beyond that, viewing the divine activity in history as loving concern for humans' fulfillment, and realizing the ultimate power of that love to overcome the barriers threatening humans' realization of their destiny, means that fear of the evils humans inevitably face loses its paralyzing power. Love, both human and divine, leads to freedom. History witnesses that despots do not know how to handle those who are free in this way. They can only do what Jesus' enemies did, kill (in one way or another) those who are free in spirit. This also proves futile, for, as Paul teaches in Romans 8, the Spirit of God cannot be defeated—death of the innocent free produces their unending life.

atonement ⟶ fear

creative Spirit ⟶ love

PART II

Power in the Public Arena

As was mentioned briefly in the introduction, social scientific reflection on power has logically focused on exercise of power in the public arena. Despite a wide divergence of opinions, there is a general convergence on the interaction between the empowerment and freedom of agency (whether individuals or groups) on the one hand and the controling and limiting influence or positive support by social structures on the other hand. Though there is discussion of internal motivations and of basic issues of morality (such as "individual interests" as an inadequate norm of behavior), for the most part "power" is thought of as social power, that is, the power that functions in organized public relationships of people, what most people think of when they use a term like "powerbrokers."

Because my interest is basically pneumatological, this book deals with these approaches to power in somewhat different fashion. In the present unit, whose central topic is power as it occurs in public life, disproportionate attention is paid to "office" as such and more specifically to "office" as it has functioned in religious society. Then, in ancillary chapters, "law" and "fame" are studied as influences on the exercise of office. Because of its importance, economic power is dealt with in a separate chapter; obviously, it deeply influences any exercise of public office.

3

The Power of Office

If the power exerted by violence or fear is quite clear, this is not true
of the power that comes into play in public life, specifically in the
exercise of office. In general, power in this sphere is thought of in
terms of authority, but authority attached to "office" needs to be clarified in distinction from other kinds of authority There is an authority that flows from knowledge, insight, or wisdom. There is moral
authority that comes with the role of parents in a family, or of those
who have demonstrated heroism or exemplary living or have been
notably successful. There are those who exert unofficial leadership
in a community. There is a subtle form of authority that functions
in love and friendship, so that one is able to counsel and even correct a friend. Occupation of an office, while often conditioned by
one or other of these, provides itself a distinctive authority that
comes into play even when the character or behavior of the office-
holder gives him or her little personal authority.

Part of the difficulty in describing official authority comes from
the fact that it is never found in a pure form, unmixed with other
kinds of authority. Such complexity functions to an even greater degree when one is dealing with the authority of officials in a revealed
religion like Christianity or Judaism. Tension about religion's role in
a society and the relation of religious and civic officials to one another is a thread that runs through history. The power of "the religious right" in present-day U.S. politics makes it clear that the issue
remains unresolved.

Central to this complicated history has been the exercise of public power and more specifically the distinctive power attached to "office." That raises questions about the appropriate role of "office" in communities based on religious belief and about the nature of the authority attached to such office.

Because the actual interplay of religious and "secular" elements in any given society is so complex and varied, the topic needs to be narrowed in the present study. What I propose to do, in the hope that examination of one instance may throw light on the broader picture, is to trace in what has emerged today as Roman Catholicism the changing dialectic between the official claims and activity of "secular" rulers and Church officials and the shift in Catholic understanding of official authority/power that has occurred over the centuries.

My approach—among many possible ones—will be theological and will be guided by a faith-based thesis: *according to the biblical witness (the Hebrew Bible and the Christian Scriptures), a unique kind of authority/power to contend with evil was given to Israel and then to Christianity, a power that flows from the truth conveyed in prophecy.*[1] Ideally, this truth should mark office and leadership in both the religious community and the secular society with which it coincides but to which it has often been opposed. In the real world, though, prophecy is for the most part suspect and rejected by those in official positions, religious or secular, and the tension between "the establishment" and prophets has remained unresolved.

Any attempt to narrow the examination of religious office can be only partially successful because the reality involved is inseparable from (1) the divine activity referred to as "providence," (2) the nature of "salvation," (3) the authority of tradition, and (4) the mediatorial role in humans relating to God that has long been attributed to religious officials and quite often also to secular rulers. How one views any or all of these issues will inevitably affect the perspective with which one understands official religious authority/power.

The historical evolution of the notion of authority/power within Christianity provides an intriguing picture of the tension or conflict between differing forms of power and illustrates the difficulty of entirely differentiating them as they impact humans' salvation. At its deepest level, the issue is the interaction of divine and human power; therefore, it lies at the very heart of pneumatology and historically found expression in the dialectic of faith and good works.

Before going farther to study in greater depth the enigmatic power of prophecy and its relation to the power of public office, it may prove helpful to do two things: (1) expand a bit more a working description of official authority/power so we know what we are looking for in the historical sequence, and (2) glance briefly at the overall cultural situations in which the historical line of charismatic prophecy took a decisive turn in Jesus of Nazareth and then continued transformed in Christianity.

1. Power of Office—A Working Description

Central to what one is dealing with in the case of governing authority is the power that attaches to office as such—not that authority belongs only to those occupying positions of recognized office. As I mentioned briefly, other kinds of authority, such as the authority that comes with possessing knowledge, derive from other bases.[2] However, it is the authority connected with public office that is uppermost in people's thinking when they refer to "those in power." There is little problem in differentiating theoretically legitimate exercise of official authority from other kinds of power, but history indicates that those in official positions often employ other kinds of power to carry out actions that are claimed to be authoritative but that go beyond legitimate authority.[3]

What, then, is "office," and what is the authority derived from it? Office is an established and publicly acknowledged and accepted role in a particular society. It is established so that a function required by that society is fulfilled on a regular basis. The power to perform that function effectively attaches to the office. It is characteristic of official power that its effective exercise is basically independent of the qualifications of the office holder. Whether the signature of a president on a measure passed by Congress reflects the president's understanding of the bill is not at issue; what matters is the fact that empowered by the authority of the presidency he signs the bill. Appropriate authority pertains to a person, not by virtue of having personal endowments, but precisely by virtue of occupying the office and only so long as he or she occupies that office. While it is generally assumed that one with proper qualifications will be chosen to occupy some office, and those qualifications or lack of them can affect the official's performance, that person's authority as official does not come from these qualifications but from the office itself.[4] One consequence of this is that officials in a given society are not necessarily the leaders of that society, though hopefully they are in many cases. Actual leadership may in some instances be exercised informally but importantly by persons whose personal talents and character equip them to influence the attitudes and actions of their contemporaries, even though they are in no sense "official."[5]

Both Greek and Latin, the languages that shaped Christian theology and doctrine, differentiate "authority" and "power," though they do not confine authority to office. Authority is denoted by the term *exousia* in Greek, *potestas* in Latin, whereas the Greek *dynamis* and Latin *potentia* deal rather with an individual's possession of the intrinsic power to effect something.[6] In practice, however, this distinction was frequently blurred because some officials, such as ancient kings, were believed by virtue of their office to possess magical/divine power, while others, like charismatic prophets, were seen to possess a special authority (exousia) to teach but also power (dynamis) to heal.[7]

Sources of "Official Power"

What are the sources of official power that have functioned in various situations?

The first source of governing authority, whether civil or ecclesiastical, is *direct grant from God*. For centuries, such an endowment of a ruler by God was symbolized and sacramentally effected in the new ruler's anointing. In some instances, the individual may have been elected or may have succeeded by dynastic lineage, but the actual grant of authority came not from this election but from God as a consequence of election or succession. Such a God-derived authority was, of course, the basis for the long-held "divine right of kings." In religious contexts, this principle was honored in the claim that some offices in the Church had been instituted by Christ and therefore exist *de jure divino*. Connected with this notion is that of succession in office—the authority exercised by a bishop today is said to be grounded in the original grant of authority from Christ to the Twelve, and the present-day bishop possesses such authority by virtue of succession in office from the Twelve.

The second source of Governing Authority, though obviously not always present, is *the consent of the governed*. In more modern times, we have become accustomed to this being the foundation for governmental authority in countries like the United States. In many regions, however, dictatorships still flourish, and in many others, the actual participation of the ruled in the choice of their rulers is frequently quite limited.

The third source of authority is that of *genealogical succession*, especially the right of primogeniture. Drawing from the social acceptance of *patria potestas*, whether in its rigid or lenient application, the eldest son is assumed to be the successor to the authority now possessed by the father and upon the latter's death inherits that authority. Generally, this implies not only the control over others' behavior in the family, but the inheritance and disposal of the family property, which, of course, supports his exercise of authority. In the public sphere, this finds application in dynastic succession, which generally but not necessarily involves the primogeniture. Some of the practices connected in ancient adherence to the rights of primogeniture suggest that people thought that some intrinsic power was present in the first-born—in effect, that the first-born carried the life principle of the family.

Still another source of authority is *admission into a ruling group*, which then shares its authority with the initiate. In this case, authority appears to be a collegial reality that an individual possesses precisely as a member of the group. This, of course, raises the question as to the source of the group's authority—at least in some cases, it seems to have simply come into being by natural evolution to provide for the needs of a society, or to have been initially assumed or claimed and then later legitimated by assertions of something like divine establishment or "tradition." A typical case of this sort is the episcopacy in the Catholic Church, where a new bishop through ordination shares in the authority that, it is claimed, comes from Christ's own grant to his disciples This notion of collegial authority was obscured historically by the notion of a monarchical episcopate and only regained with Vatican II.[8]

Finally, there is authority that is *delegated* from a higher official. The power of office that is being exercised in this case remains the power and authority of the higher official and is governed by the extent or limitation of that person's authority and also by whatever limits were placed on the surrogate's representative activity by the delegating official.[9]

2. Cultural Context of Early Christian Exercise of Authoritative Power

It is really anachronistic to pose our questions of religious and secular power when one looks at the dawn of history. In Egypt, a divine pharaoh controled both realms; in Mesopotamia the king's authority was scarcely distinguishable from that of Anu, the great sky god.[10] The doings of Homeric heroes, even as portrayed centuries later than Homer by the great Greek tragedians, were intertwined with the doings of the gods themselves. There were not two realms, one religious and the other secular; there was but one "universe," and it was controlled ultimately by magic. By the time of philosophy's flowering in ancient Greece, much of the attribution of human behavior to the influence of "the gods" was replaced by insight into human psychology, political activity, and secular motivations. Yet, even later in imperial Rome where considerable cynicism marked the educated classes' view of traditional religious mythology, religious rituals and civic ceremonials meshed, and the emperor himself functioned as *pontifex maximus* of the state religion.

In Israel the picture was different, though not completely so. Israel had begun with the great prophet Moses, who, in a process that has not yet found satisfactory historical explanation, led a band of refugees away from Pharaoh's domination to become a people under the sovereignty of the God Yahweh. For more than two centuries, this people managed to survive without officials, at times guided by charismatic figures significantly named "judges," unified in dispersal only by traditions and a developing God-given Law.

Then, kingly office, kings like those of other peoples, was proposed and adopted as a move to protect Israel's fragile existence. For a brief time, kings ruled in Israel, complemented by a priesthood in the royal shrine, but civic power often worked to absorb the distinctive God-grounded power that had given birth to the people Israel. Against this development, the great charismatic prophets, not the official prophets whom they often condemned, spoke out in the name of Yahweh, denouncing the power unjustly assumed by kings and their minions. Prophets spoke truth, called to conversion, and believed that the word of God on their lips and the accompanying Spirit of God were a power that would destroy unworthy kingship in Israel—as it did in the north in 722 and in the south in 600. However, prophets like Jeremiah and Ezekiel insisted that the destruction was directed not against the chosen people but against their sin. Defeat and exile were not fundamentally punitive but corrective, helping the people understand the results of believing the lie circulated by their officials that powers other than Yahweh were the ultimate source of life and salvation.

Returned from exile, the remnant of Judah rebuilt Jerusalem and its Temple, without a king but with a high priestly office that gradually acquired much of the function of kingly rule. Within a short time, prophets vanished, to be replaced by interpreters and teachers of the Law that by now was substantially gathered together and acted canonically as a norm for Jewish life. In this Second Temple Judaism, though for practically all its existence political rule was imposed by foreign rulers, the basic power functioning in people's lives was the power of the Law and the power of those who conveyed to the people their interpretation of the Law. But along with the power of these scribes or: scribe-teachers/teachers that crystallized in the power gradually acquired by the Pharisaic movement was the power of the Temple priesthood. While teaching about the Law was part of the priestly role, the basic source of priestly power lay in the belief, expressed in the Temple Psalms, that the Temple ritual over which they officiated had the power of remitting sin, reconciling sinners with God, and maintaining a positive relation with God that would guarantee support and protection.

Jesus' Authoritative Power

Into this context there was "inserted" the public ministry of Jesus that is witnessed to in the Christian Scriptures. Identifying himself as a prophet, acting as a prophet, and being viewed by those who encountered him as a prophet, he laid claim to empowerment by God's Spirit. Most basically, he claimed to have power over evil and sin. In his public attack upon sin, he focused on officials in his society who exploited people, and the evil he most castigated was the hypocrisy of religious leaders, the fundamental lie about God that was conveyed by their teaching and their behavior. Understandably, such criticism aroused the enmity of the Pharisaic teachers and above all of the Temple officials. But it was his claim that he himself had authority over sin, his forgiveness of sin, that most radically drew their opposition and led to his execution. It was a challenge to the very purpose and existence of the Temple and its priesthood.

What Jesus claimed and—as the Gospels narrate—proved by his healing of physical evils was a further dimension of what had occurred in Israel's great prophets. In their case, judgment on sin and the call to conversion were effective because they possessed the power of God's own word on their lips accompanied by the power of God's Spirit. The prophets themselves did not personally have power over sin. Christianity, however, considered Jesus to be personally empowered. The passage in Mark 2:1-12 is explicit: in the scene in which he cured the paralytic and was challenged by "the scribes" because he told the crippled man, "Your sins are forgiven," Jesus replied, "In order that you may know that the Son of Man has power [exousia] on earth to forgive sins. . . ."

That Jesus was in the actual context of his life without official authority is undeniable. Being relatively poor, he had no economic authority or power; politically, he never held any office nor had any influence with those who did have official authority; religiously, he was unable to hold any priestly office because he was from the wrong lineage. This actually provided a block to his being recognized and accepted as Messiah and required early Christianity to completely reinterpret "Messiah" when applying it to Jesus. The authority that Jesus claimed, that many of his hearers recognized and that his disciples accepted, was the authority of a charismatic prophet. Even in the area of wisdom teaching, where by Jesus' day the teachers of wisdom had been institutionalized in the structures of "scribes and Pharisees" that led eventually to Rabbinic Judaism, Jesus was seen not as one of them but as the prophet of wisdom.

What is as remarkable as the situation itself was the immediate theological recognition of its significance. The Gospels and the writings of Paul both attest to the challenge that Jesus presented to established notions of authority and legitimate exercise of power. What is equally remarkable is the rapidity with which this insight was dimmed and exercise of office came to dominate much of the life of the Christian church.[11]

If one reflects on this pneumatologically, the question must be asked: if in the case of Jesus himself the endowment with God's Spirit was the root of his prophetic authority, and if this Spirit did not endow him for office, can officeholders in later years of Christianity's existence lay claim *as officials* to this Spirit? Part at least of the response to this question must come from developments that occurred very early and were then perpetuated over the centuries. One must evaluate these historical developments with great caution, for "new" institutions and viewpoints that emerged may well have come from the abiding presence and guidance of God's Spirit.[12] Primitive Christianity by itself is not sufficient criterion of genuineness, but it is the first and distinctively important "word" of tradition.

It was Jesus' own prophetic power of effective judgment on sin, the ultimate evil, that the risen Christ conferred on the little group of his disciples that eventually grew into the Christian Church. It was sin, above all untruth, that barred persons from sharing in the kingdom of God; it was to his disciples, beginning with Peter, that he promised the keys to open the gates of this kingdom by passing effective judgment on sin. While Matthew 16:18 points in a special way to this power being given Peter, a later passage (18:18) speaks of broader community leadership passing judgment of excommunication or reconciliation. The Johannine Gospel in its narrative of Easter evening describes the risen Christ giving the power to all the assembled disciples: "Receive the Holy Spirit, whose sins you shall forgive they are forgiven" (20:22).

The theological conclusion from these traditions: the risen Christ conferred on the community that followed him a very different kind of power, the power of passing effective judgment upon evil, especially sin, power that came from God's Spirit, healing power that dealt specifically with the relation between humans and God and not only relationships among humans themselves.

Probing theologically a bit farther, one is reminded that Jesus placed lies as the most basic of sins. He called Satan "the father of lies" and constantly railed against hypocrisy. Conversely, the Johannine tradition in its account of the Last Supper has Jesus refer to the promised Spirit as "the Spirit of truth." This Spirit is, of course, the same Spirit that Israelite and Christian faith sees as the Spirit that inspired the prophets to speak truth in condemnation of false teaching about divine providence. It would seem, then, that what one is faced with is that the power entrusted to Christianity is a power of true judgment (what later Christian theology will refer to as the *potestas judiciaria*). This power is effective in overcoming evil at its roots, this power is to be exercised in community discernment and proclamation of the Spirit's truth that is conveyed to the community in prophecy.

At the very beginning, Christians stressed the power of the prophetic message itself, that is, the gospel, which was the word of God, revealing the freedom-causing truth—the power of the Spirit of truth.[13] So, the basic ministerial thrust to evangelize: the role of Christians was to witness to this gospel. But then there was question of what was the true gospel as instrument of the Spirit—here as the canon of Christian Scripture emerged, the judgment of the bishops provided the principal criterion because of their link with the witness of the original disciples. It was the bishops who, in the second and third centuries, led the Christian churches to judge Gnosticism, and especially Marcion's rejection of scriptural witness to the true God, as untrue.

Emphasis on the word communicated in prophecy is not to deny a charism of governing to which Paul in 1 Corinthians 13:28 refers. There was a certain inevitability in the emergence of designated leadership: as communities increased in size and number, order required that some permanent responsibility and accompanying authority provide needed governance. Governing, however, is not the charism of the Spirit in which human salvation from evil is grounded—that belongs to prophecy, which Paul sees as the preeminent charism. It is through prophecy that the revealed truth that overcomes evil, the truth that makes humans free, enters human life.

What happened, however, and happened very early in the growth of Christianity as an organized religious community were four conjoined developments: (1) The leaders of communities were seen to occupy an *office*, the pastoral office into which all the charismatic functions were gradually absorbed.[14] (2) "Office" in Christianity was modeled on the pattern of official authority in the surrounding Greco-Roman culture. This involved control over people even though in Christian circles this was benevolently pastoral and was named "service." (3) Instead of Christian communities working to overcome the sin of the world, the ministry of overcoming sin became owned by officials in the Church who exercised this power of the keys over fellow Christians who were in sin. Thus, the Christian community was divided into "those who judged" and "those who were judged." The *potestas judiciaria* came to be the possession of Church officials, specifically the bishops, and was gradually extended far beyond power over sin. In their official leadership of the Church, they were believed to speak for God, not in the manner of prophets—though some of them, such as Cyprian of Carthage, did claim prophetic gifts—but as vicars of God's ruling of the communities.

There was a fourth and broader development, namely, the move toward Christianity becoming an *ethical* system and official activity moving therefore toward establishing and enforcing rules. True, the enforcement rested finally with God, but the bishops declared that they acted as representatives of God in passing judgment, and people believed this. Teaching/preaching became increasingly if informally *legislating*. Along with this were the synodal gatherings of bishops that left no doubt that the assembled bishops thought of themselves as rulers.

Space does not allow a full description of the historical process in which judgment against evil, increasingly monopolized by the ordained, was preserved as the heart of power and authority in the Church but was more and more overshadowed by the authority of jurisdiction. However, the basic thrust of this evolution may be glimpsed by viewing the situation at four pivotal points in Christian history.

Ecclesiastical Office in the 200s

By the beginning of the third century, the institutions of Christianity had taken identifiable shape: throughout the Mediterranean basin, communities were headed by a leadership of bishops, presbyters, and deacons; for all practical purposes, the canonical collection of Christian Scriptures was commonly accepted; liturgical forms were recognizably similar in major regions. Working together with the presbyterate, bishops were recognized as the leaders of their respective communities, leaders particularly of liturgical worship. Chosen by his community, a choice ratified by bishops of the region, the bishop was given in ordination the care of that community. Throughout, it was assumed and often stated that the basic power at work in Christianity was the power of the Spirit granted to the Church by the risen Christ.

Much of the emergence of episcopal authority may simply have resulted from the human need to organize the growing communities. The *Apostolic Tradition* of Hippolytus indicates that the new bishop was chosen by the community, a choice that was believed to be guided by the Spirit. This needed to be complemented by the ratification of the choice by bishops of the region; this took place in the liturgical reception of the candidate into the episcopal college. From this joint selection, the new bishop was authorized to do what was required to care for the community that he now headed. Personal empowerment of the new bishops to perform the functions attached to the office came directly from the Spirit—this is the stated petition of the ordaining prayer, as in the *Apostolic Tradition* of Hippolytus.

At this point in the Church's history, there did not appear to be a notion of succession to the office of bishop. What was more evident was—as Irenaeus claimed—a succession of teachers whose authority was grounded in the fact that they had inherited the true gospel, the apostolic witness. This may help explain the special official authority attached to bishops' teaching, but it does not explain why being "official" gave to episcopal prayer (in liturgy?) the special efficacy the *Apostolic Tradition* suggests. The answer seems rather to be that episcopal office was already being viewed as mediation between the community and God.

Bishops clearly had recognized authority to direct the Christian communities in their care. It also seems quite clear that as office and structured exercise of power began to emerge in the Church, the fundamental power being claimed, challenged, and given various interpretations when applied to diverse situations was the power of judgment—judgment over sin and then, by mid-second century if not earlier, power to judge authentic textual and ritual traditions. Episcopal leaders as early as Ignatius were engaged in judging with recognized authority the behavior and belief of their fellow Christians. Whether and in which cases this was only "persuasive" judgment or socially effective judgment is not clear. What is clearer is that the fundamental power at the root of the notion of ecclesial power that developed over the centuries was *potestas judiciaria*, the power possessed by Peter still actively present in the Church, possessed by bishops to whom this power was extended as successors of the early disciples, ultimately possessed by the entire Christian community. This grounds the principal function of a priestly Christian people because overcoming sin is the essence of Christ's own priesthood.[15] Differing levels of that priesthood possess greater or lesser degrees of that *potestas*, and as the community became divided into "those saving" and "those being saved," it became divided into those actively possessing this *potestas* and those capable of receiving its effects—in later theology, the sacramental character of ordination and the sacramental character of baptism.

At the beginning of the third century, the focus of official power was still centered on power over sin committed or allegedly committed by members of the community. In fact, the Church in the year 200 was still embroiled in dispute over the extent of episcopal forgiveness of truly grave sin. In Rome, the rigorist party, especially the presbyter Hippolytus, attacked the bishop Callistus, charging him with laxity because he favored forgiveness of those guilty of serious sin. In North Africa, Tertullian denounced the episcopacy for its betrayal of Christian ideals of purity because they were reconciling sinners guilty of adultery. Underlying these divisions was the shared belief that power over sin had been bequeathed by Christ to his disciples and their successors.

That this centered on the episcopate was confirmed when shortly afterward the restriction to the bishop (Cyprian) of reconciling power was challenged by the dispute in northern Africa over the alleged power of "confessors" to forgive the sin of the *lapsi* (those who had apostatized in the Decian persecution).

For the time being, there was no noticeable interest in the relation of power granted the Church and the power exercised in civil society. Civil structures and authority were accepted, especially the hegemonic power of the emperor to whom Christians pledged allegiance, so long as governmental demands did not run counter to their Christian faith.

In its mission to overcome evil, *truth* was central to the concerns of Church leadership, truth above all in the preservation and communication of the gospel. The controversy with Gnosticism was still in the forefront of Christian claims to authoritative teaching, and bishops were prominent in defending official teaching as true because of its link with the apostolic witness. Irenaeus, who had died just before the turn of the century, in his attack on the aberrations of the various Gnostic sects, laid claim in his *Adversus Haereses* to being in a line of teachers that preserved the true gospel because of descent from the original apostolic witnesses. "Polycarp taught me, John taught Polycarp, Jesus taught John."[16]

It was not only the bishops, however, who claimed teaching authority. Clement of Alexandria (perhaps a presbyter), who headed up the catechetical school after Pantaenus, never justified his teaching role as delegation from the local bishops but only on the basis of his own knowledge. Actually, Clement made practically no reference to the official structures of the Alexandrian church, though by the year 200 that city no doubt had the common pattern of bishop-presbyterate-diaconate. Like Irenaeus before him, he was a vigorous polemicist against Gnosticism, asserting that Christianity was the true gnosis.

Ecclesiastical Office in 545

By the time that Gregory I assumed leadership of the Roman church, the sociopolitical picture had changed drastically. So had the condition of the Church and the role played by bishops. Imperial institutions in the West were a shambles, Rome itself had been three times invaded by Teutonic tribes, and bishops had become enmeshed in civic affairs out of sheer necessity. Not only did bishops continue to exercise the office of civil judges that Constantine had legislated, but they often found themselves as secular caretakers, trying to provide materially as well as spiritually for the people of their communities. In the Byzantine East, the situation was quite different. Caesaropapism and imperial bureaucracy had just been codified by Justinian, and the Church was relegated to being an element in the divinely established state. Bishops were officials, but officials of the civil government, delegates of the basileus to provide the spiritual aspects of his all-embracing responsibility as "vicar of Christ."

The pontificate of Gregory I provides a privileged situation for viewing developments in mid–sixth century.[17] In charge of the Roman see at a time when by default he had to assume many of the tasks of civil government, he was well acquainted with the ecclesiastical situation in both East and West. He had spent years as a diplomat in Constantinople very shortly after Justinian was framing the classic structures of caesaro-papism. He was well acquainted with the Church of Spain and northern Africa because of his friendship with Leander of Seville. His involvement in liturgical unity clearly reflects his self-identity as *sacerdos*. Still, it is his *De cura pastorali* that most tellingly reveals his views on the power and responsibility of bishops.[18] This manual of episcopal behavior, next to the Bible the most influential book during the Middle Ages, explicitly refers to the ruling power of bishops—throughout the book the bishop is referred to as "ruler" (*rector*). In a more gentle and subtle way, he continues the position of Gelasius in defense of the spiritual jurisdiction and autonomy of the Pope and by implication of bishops. Still, the key exercise of episcopal rule is admonition of sinners. It is still by teaching morality and threatening divine punishment for sin that Gregory sees the bishops using "the keys" given to Peter and his successors. The importance of the *potestas judiciaria* did not decrease; indeed, the growing stress on human sinfulness that marked so much of the medieval centuries and continued into modern times made it all the more important that Church officials had power over sin.

The Highpoint of Ecclesiastical Power, Lateran IV

Beginning with Gelasius's controversy with the Byzantine authorities, the metaphor of "the keys" used to justify episcopal power was complemented by the metaphor of "the two swords."[19] In Gelasius's usage, the sword of spiritual jurisdiction belonged to the papacy and by extension the episcopate (the *sacerdotium*), whereas the temporal sword belonged to temporal rulers, especially the emperor. However, by the beginning of the thirteenth century and the ascendancy of the papacy with Innocent III, both "swords" were claimed for the *sacerdotium*, though the sword of secular jurisdiction was delegated to civil rulers so that they could carry out the teaching of the papacy.[20]

This distinction of power rested to some extent on the shift in understanding of "power of orders" accompanied by legal clarification of "power of jurisdiction." During the first Christian millennium, the "power of orders" dealt with a person's "level" on the ladder of social location; those belonging to a higher order were presumed to have power over those of a lower class. This layered ordering of society, borrowed from the pattern of Greco-Roman society and law, was applied to the church and crystallized in the influential writings of Pseudo-Dionysius. By itself, "location" in a higher order did not constitute office, and for the acquisition of episcopal office it needed to be joined to selection to care for a specific community. Episcopal "ordination" meant the raising of a person to the episcopal order/level, which would enable that individual to care for the assigned community. The spiritual empowerment to carry out the tasks that care of a community required was seen to come directly from the Spirit invoked in the prayer of ordination.

A radical shift in the understanding of "power of orders" occurred with the twelfth century reintroduction into the West of Aristotelian anthropology. Ordination came to be seen as causing in the ordinand the internal power of confecting the Eucharist and absolving sins. At the same time, with the rapid emergence of legal study, the training of professional legists, and their involvement in disputes between ecclesiastical and secular rulers, the notion of "power of jurisdiction" was formally distinguished from "power of orders." Jurisdiction was recognized as the authority to direct, even control, the social existence of the Christian community, whereas "power of orders" dealt with the power exercised in the ritual contexts of Eucharist and reconciliation.

As the thirteenth century began with Innocent III, the supreme ruler in the West, and the Fourth Lateran Council legislating the possession by the episcopacy and papacy of both "swords," the triumph of the sacerdotium was complete. Not only had Church officials resisted (in the eleventh-century investiture controversy) the attempts of secular rulers to absorb ecclesiastical structures and power, but Church officials had turned the tables and acquired power over the entirety of the Christian people: the *societas christiana*. Without relinquishing the traditional claim of official power over sin, Church rulers now claimed complete power over the people.

The medieval supremacy of Church official was short lived—but the idea of Church office with its own distinctive jurisdiction was firmly established. In fact, the thirteenth century witnessed a sweeping bureaucratizing of Church administration.[21] Jurisdiction in the spiritual realm, above all in the forgiveness of sin and the condemnation of heresy, continued to be the foundation of ecclesiastical power, but added to this was a widespread exercise of nonreligious jurisdiction that was to continue for centuries in structures like prince-bishoprics and the Papal States. In Church life, the official mediatorial role of the ordained in spiritual matters became so firmly entrenched and unquestioningly accepted that up to the present time special authority has been attached to whatever is considered "official."

By the high point in Church power in the thirteenth century, Church leadership had drifted far from the original Christian grant of power over sin, the *potestas judiciaria* flowing from the Spirit of truth. The theocratic situation brought about by papal claim to the fullness of authority, the *plenitudo potestatis* claimed as far back as Gregory VII, began to be challenged before the end of the thirteenth century. Boniface VIII's overreaching insistence that he possessed all power ran head on into the growing prominence of national rulers, specifically Philip IV of France. The power of secular rulers, overshadowed and challenged by talented popes and bishops for the previous two centuries, began once more to assert itself. Aided by internecine warfare and incompetence within Church leadership itself, kings and princes increasingly broke free and reasserted their autonomy. Royalty and aristocracy still allied themselves to an ecclesiastical leadership drawn from its own class; but a new powerbroker entered the picture and soon played a major role. This new player was the wealthy bourgeoisie, whose power derived from neither lineage nor presumed divine grant but from their commercial success and business acumen. The bourgeoisie's growing prominence and power was not derived from office; in fact, officials, both ecclesiastical and civil, were more and more dependent upon the wealth of the commercial class.

Modern Times and Official Authority/Power

The emergence of modern European society involved a massive and painful realignment of authority and power. At the core of this shift was a basic and progressive secularization.[22] Officials who previously had claimed a certain "sacrality" because their authority was God-given were confronted by those relying on other grounds for authority. This touched not only political activity but authoritative teaching as well. The Galileo case was a prime example: Galileo appealed to his (secular) scientific observation, as opposed to Church officials who still laid claim to possession of truth by virtue of office.

Though their hegemonic power gradually faded in an increasingly secular world, ecclesiastical officials still continued to wield power, much of it secular power grounded in the extensive wealth of bishops/Pope and monastic institutions. Eventually this wealth undermined their religious authority because of the evil of a benefice system that was not dealt with until Trent.

Church officialdom still retained spiritual power through monopoly of sacramental rituals, upon which people's "salvation" was presumably dependent, and through teaching, which, because it was "official," was considered true and to which people's faith and worldview therefore were to conform. With the increasing prestige of scientific knowing, the impact of critical methodologies being applied to traditional religious formulations, doctrinal differences among the various Christian denominations, and the rising level of general education, official teaching was not as immune from questioning as it once had been.

With the Enlightenment challenge to all religious claims of accurate knowledge, the Catholic Church confronted the issue of the relation of revelation and science at Vatican I. Reflecting the modern philosophical shift from metaphysics to epistemology, rather than using the classic medieval categories of "nature" and "grace" the council's decree "De Fide" reasserted the basic compatibility of revealed knowledge accepted in faith with secular knowledge. It then defended office as ground for authoritative teaching: its decree on papal authority claimed infallibility for the highest Church teaching office, the papacy.[23]

However, the authoritative statement of Vatican I did not solve the issue, even within the Catholic Church itself. As more and more Catholic scholars assessed critically the official teaching in the areas of biblical and historical study and moved away from a fundamentalist approach, Vatican authorities adopted a defensive strategy. During the so-called "modernist" controversies of the early twentieth century and the post–World War II attack on theologians epitomized in "Humani generis," Roman Catholic scholars worked under a cloud of official suspicion and condemnation.[24] Throughout those decades, the Vatican based its position on the authority attached to office rather than on the authority of careful research. To a considerable extent, that remains the situation despite the vindication of Catholic scholars that took place in conjunction with the Second Vatican Council.[25] This history has raised in unavoidable fashion the question of teaching authority in the realm of religious faith—a question posed by fundamentalist movements in all the great religions worldwide.

Vatican II did not explicitly deal with the character of the jurisdictional power exercised by Church officials; it accepted the standard description and distinction of "power of jurisdiction" and "power of orders" it inherited from earlier centuries. It may, however, have done something more fundamental by changing the climate of official control of Church life. By its recognition, in the "Constitution on the Church," that the Church is the entire people of God, with rights and responsibilities for the life and mission of the Church, the council removed the assumption of episcopal/papal control over the faithful. Along with this, by reasserting in its decree on religious freedom the individual person's formation of conscience, it shifted official authority from dominating to persuasive power. Exactly how this movement will be translated in future understandings and behavior is not yet clear, but the council has opened up a new perspective on ecclesial authority and power.

Pneumatological Reflection

How, then, from a pneumatological point of view does one judge this centuries-long phenomenon of power attached to office, both religious and secular? More specifically, to what extent and in what way has the *potestas judiciaria* (the power of effective judgment against evil) been understood, implemented, or altered by Christians? A response to this question must keep in mind the uniqueness of this outreach power of God, God's Spirit, and the universality of its influence on all aspects of human life and activity. This means that divine "inspiration" touches civic authority as well as religious authority, with the corollary that some "secular" developments may more accurately be attributable to this Spirit than are some of the attitudes and judgments of religious officials. Some events that were thought to come from the forces of evil attacking the Church, such as loss of the Papal States, have proved to be a blessing, a providential freeing of the Church to pursue its prophetic role in society.

Important to theological reflection is the development in recent centuries of the gradually increasing prevalence of "democratic" civil structures. While the world today is far from a complete awareness and acceptance of the right of peoples to control their own lives and destinies, there has unquestionably been a movement away from an assumed and unchallenged pattern of monarchical rule. The sequence of revolutions of the late eighteenth and early nineteenth centuries marked a turning point that appears irreversible, despite the totalitarian dictatorships that have still persisted into the twenty-first century. This slow movement to "democracy" is one of the "signs of the times" to which Pope John XXIII pointed as manifestation of the Spirit's influence in history, a continuing revelation that theologians must ponder.

At the heart of the power to combat and overcome evil lies the power of truth. Possession of true understanding, commitment to cherishing and defending the truth, courage in communicating truthful judgment upon accepted cultural institutions and processes enables persons to escape the bondage and personal diminution that comes with deceit. The ultimate source of such evil-destroying and person-creating truth is God's communication in Word and Spirit. It is this truth, shared by God with humans through the charism of prophecy, that forms and nurtures authentic human community and underpins the right relations among people that constitute justice and lead to peace. It is in communicating truth that God reigns.

In a dispute between secular and religious authorities, who can lay claim to the guidance by the "Spirit of truth"? Perhaps only the course of history itself can respond to specific instances of such conflict, and perhaps an awareness of what history has been can provide a trustworthy guide for judgments in the present. However, the nagging question remains: what is there about some activity of religious officials—or for that matter, secular officials—that makes it more authentic, more acceptable as true, *because* it is official?

In what way and with what legitimacy was the Spirit/power granted to Christianity increasingly attached to "office"? Episcopal authority and power have been justified by the contention that bishops inherited the authority of the Twelve, who possessed it by Jesus' grant, that is, *de jure divino*.[26] Given the fact that careful historical scholarship has indicated Jesus never commissioned the Twelve as bishops, never gave them power to rule, is there a different and perhaps more valid understanding of the link of bishops to the early disciples, an understanding that grounds "office" as a source of authentic authority?

As never before, the question has been posed: when clear dissonance marks religious doctrinal teaching and the careful research of "science," to what extent can any teaching claim to be true because it is "official"? Certainly, part of the religious response can be an appeal to "tradition," but this only leads to further questions: what precisely is "tradition"?[27] To what extent does it consist of impulse from God's Spirit and to what extent and in what ways has it been the result of human culture and decisions? Even if one accepts in faith that Christianity has been given potestas judiciaria, power to pass effective judgment upon evil, how is such judgment to be exercised?

Unquestionably, a key element in this discussion is the phenomenon of prophecy that in both religious and civic society has always existed in some tension with official judgments. Further study of prophecy as it has occurred in history and as it exists today is needed to identify and evaluate the precise authority of "office." The Spirit of truth promised the Church is the prophetic Spirit, linked with the "inspiration" of Sacred Scripture, animating the human community as it moves toward eschatological fulfillment, transforming communities of faith in the enactment of ritual. If this Spirit has guided the process of bringing order into community life, order in which some leadership in Christian communities acquired authority because "official," office itself should be regarded as part of the Spirit's guidance. This need not, however, imply that the exercise of official jurisdiction is itself a cause of sanctification.

Even though it runs contrary to centuries in which officials, especially ecclesiastical officials, have taught that they are required mediators for the transmission of grace and salvation, as vicars of God acting *in persona Christi*, careful reflection may lead us in the direction of saying that the role of officials *exercising jurisdiction as officials* lies not in such direct effecting of "grace" but in keeping communities orderly and unified so that they (i.e., communities) can become the more immediate agency of salvation. This would preserve the need for jurisdiction and office not as a source of power to heal and sanctify but as a source of effective unifying leadership.

This still leaves the neuralgic issue of authoritative religious teaching, crystallized in Catholicism in use of the term magisterium. If, as I will develop later, magisterium should not be restricted to the episcopacy but seen as a broader function to which various voices in the community make distinctive contributions, what is the authoritative role of the episcopacy in this activity?

A brief response: since Christian faith and life are rooted in an historical event—the life, dying, and rising of Jesus, the Christ—all teaching is grounded in the actuality of that event. It follows, then, that at the center of Christian teaching stands *witness* to the gospel, to the risen Christ who is the Truth that passes judgment on history. Giving such witness throughout history is the basic role and responsibility of bishops as a "college." This is the indispensable heart of their magisterium.

However, there is then question of the meaning of this event. To give such explanation is always a matter of a teacher drawing from his or her own knowledge, cultural perspective, and social location, which implies that, beyond witness, teaching is always conditioned, inadequate, or authoritative to the extent that the teacher possesses the understanding that legitimates his or her teaching. Obviously, the century-long shared memory of the episcopate gives that college an advantage in grasping the meaning and implications of their fundamental witness, but their explanation stands in need of amplification, clarification, and at times correction—as well as communication. It is here that other agents enter into the magisterial activity of the Christian people.

4

The Power of Fame

Nature has made us enthusiastic to seek after honor, and once we
have caught, as it were, some glimpse of its radiance, there is nothing we are not prepared to bear and go through in order to secure it.
—Cicero, *Tusculan Disputations*

Cicero is not alone in this view of honor; indeed, the acquisition of
fame (glory) was considered by ancients in general as a principal de-
sideratum in human life. By some, it was considered the supreme
good for the sake of which no cost was too great.

For those who did not expect any continuation of life beyond
the grave, it was their fame that would grant them immortality as
they lived on in the memory of future generations. This was, of
course, truer of those who were considered to be or considered
themselves to be "important" persons; it was precisely the extent
and character of their reputation that made them important in people's eyes.

Such concern about one's fame is not confined to ancient times.
It is a commonplace that public figures today, such as U.S. Presidents, are deeply interested in their place in history. Television pun-
dits speculate about the place in history that will be gained by these
public figures and about the legitimacy of their claim to such enduring remembrance. Something similar happens to sports figures who
wonder how long their athletic records will stand to remind people
of their physical skills. Associated with such desire is a subtle but

influential area of the exercise of power, the power to influence a person's reputation. Some instances of such power are not all that subtle; one is immediately reminded of the immense power of Eusebius's *Life of Constantine*, which brought into Western memory a glorified image of Constantine and attributed to him a divine call that would shape subsequent Christian thinking about the way God works in history. As we already saw, this was the substitution of a militant Messiah for the nonviolent Messiah, Jesus of Nazareth.

At the root of the power associated with fame is the strong desire many humans have to possess a positive and acknowledged public image. It is intriguing to watch the way in which politicians worm their way into "photo-ops" where they can be seen on TV along with other politically powerful figures. The vast majority of humans do not, of course, cherish any notion that they will be known and remembered beyond the small group of friends and acquaintances that make up their lives. Nor do they, for that matter, have much concern about their place in history. For them, it is sufficient if their small world views them as decent persons who in some way have blessed the world with their existence.

Still, if one reflects a bit more deeply, it becomes clear how basic to the self-image of all individuals and societies is the way they are viewed by their contemporaries. From infancy onward, the understanding one has of self is shaped by the approval or disapproval of those who make up one's world. To give or withhold positive approval is perhaps the principal reward or punishment that parents can employ in the training of a child. We are well aware—as psychology and novels and films make clear—that the need for such parental approval carries into adulthood. And as one grows, the way in which he or she is viewed and judged by an extended family, by teachers, and above all by one's peer group during adolescence and by one's professional associates in adult life remains a powerful force in supporting or undermining a healthy self-image.

Much the same dynamic works in regard to social groups. Protecting their "good name" is an ongoing effort and activity, even when that good reputation is hardly grounded in reality. Church groups, like the Catholic Church, will go to great lengths to hide information that would damage their public image. People are often sacrificed, maligned, and misrepresented, as denial about unjust activity by Church officials seems the ordinary response to reports or charges of criminal offenses. At times, the victims are described publicly as the offenders and the dominating authority depicted as safeguarding truth and virtue. If nothing else, "stonewalling" is employed in the hope that in time people's memories will dim. All this is legitimated by the claim that officials are attempting to avoid scandalizing the simple faithful.

In public life, particularly in international relations, this touches on an important element in what Joseph Nye calls "soft power," namely, an individual's, group's, or nation's credibility. The delicate conduct of diplomacy is often a matter of asserting one's own credibility and assessing the credibility of a potential foe. Political campaigns prior to elections focus to a considerable extent on a candidate's credibility, even as it is assumed that campaign promises are regularly ignored when the election is over.

If one takes the notion of "fame" to a more general level of experience, it appears to be the common human desire and need to be liked, even loved. Though some may disavow it, humans wish to be loved by at least someone and ideally by a wide circle of friends. In addition, people seek to be esteemed by some others, even if that for which they are esteemed is successful criminal behavior. No one glories in being recognized as a failed or insignificant. Leaders of street gangs expect respect from their underlings and contentiously demand it from other gangs.

To put it in other terms, the power that is operating in this regard is the motivating attraction of "the good." In this instance, a good reputation, especially when this is extended to fame, is seen as a great good. To be regarded by others in the manner in which one wishes to be regarded is a powerful motivation; and those who can influence public opinion in one way or another wield great power to create or destroy. Abuse of such power to influence public perception of one's reputation has been seen as far back as the Mosaic law's proscription of "bearing false witness" as morally unacceptable; calumny and detraction have long been classified as "grave sin."

Even civil law regarding libel recognizes the importance of a person's good reputation. Deliberately to misrepresent a person's words or actions in a way that seriously harms that person's good name is judged to be a violation of a basic human right, an injustice that needs to be publicly repaired. Such laws are, however, notoriously difficult to enforce. Attack ads during an election campaign that are quite obviously intended to question a candidate's character are disguised as "issue-oriented advertising."

The existence of libel laws reflects the fact that the ability to create or destroy a person's "fame" is recognized to be a power that society needs to control. However, it would not take the existence of such laws to make clear the power to affect an individual's public image that is exerted today by various elements of the media. Given a rumor of misbehavior by some notable public figure, there occurs what is aptly termed a "media frenzy," a scramble to discover and disseminate the latest tidbit of titillating information about suspected misconduct. Less scurrilous, though not more honest, is the industry of fabricating the image of a candidate running for public office.

In our day, "public relations" has become big business. Special interests, such as the insurance industry or pharmaceutical firms or tobacco companies, spend huge amounts of money to develop a public perception of themselves as benefactors of society so that this can reinforce the huge sums of money they expend to lobby governmental decision makers. They are not alone—every academic institution of any size has a public relations office with a budget that is the envy of academic departments of the school. Whether the school has the facilities and qualifications that are advertised is not exactly the question; what matters is the image of the school that is projected. One could point to similar endeavors of religious groups, sports franchises, or auto manufacturers—and the list goes on.

One of the important aspects of power exerted by the media is the shaping of public acceptance of people's behaviors as "respectable." Respectability is not identical with moral goodness; the distinction is not a new one. Especially in an ethically pluralistic society like the United States, there is some hesitancy in judging a person's inner moral values and the intrinsic morality of one's behavior; but it is expected that a person, in particular a "public" person, will not go beyond certain bounds of respectability that society has determined informally are socially unacceptable. Some exceptions are made, of course, for "artists" or the very wealthy; their misbehavior is viewed as eccentric or even in some circles admired as "daring."

However, as I mentioned, public media (in the broad sense including the arts) have the power of gradually modifying the limits of respectability. Not too many generations ago, divorce was for the most part looked at askance. While it was known to occur, families were reluctant to admit that one of their members was divorced. Today, on the contrary, divorce is taken for granted, and it no longer detracts from a person's "fame" if he or she has been divorced, perhaps more than once. Hidden in this power to mold people's views of respectability, however, is the power to alter a population's moral standards and the character of a culture.

Some of the most prevalent and distinctive exercises of the power to affect a person's fame occur in societal subsets. For instance, there is a certain code of behavior that is expected of men and women who are considered to be "professionals"—physicians, lawyers, clergy, bankers, and so on; this can at times relate even to the manner in which these persons dress. To say that an individual does not act professionally is an indictment that can affect or even destroy a career. The professional standards in question can change over the years, at times quite drastically and suddenly; and a series of scandals in any group can begin to undermine the public's trust that truly trustworthy activity can be expected from that group. So, there exists the power of some unscrupulous members of a group to deprive others in the group of the public esteem they deserve and the power of those who publicize the unprofessional deeds.

Apart from more obvious cases of public betrayal of the respect and trust usually granted to professionals, there is the less public ostracizing of individuals within a group because they are considered to be, or at least rumored to be, unobservant of the expected attitudes and code of "ethics" of the group. In many cases, this is not really a question of ethical behavior but rather of fitting into certain patterns established by custom or by dominant controling interests within the group. Nothing looms larger in the professional appraisal of such deviants than the charge of being unfaithful to "the club," a charge that gains intensity if the person in question publicly challenges the ethos of the group.

Another interesting phenomenon that appears in the search to gain the power of fame is the claim to superiority by one or another group of professionals. This is achieved in a variety of ways, by referring to greater length of academic training or the academic prestige of the institutions that provide such training, or by signaling the higher scale of the charges for their professional service, or by pointing to the secret ("more scientific"?) character of the knowledge shared within their group, knowledge not possessed by "ordinary lay persons," or by creating the public perception that society is dependent upon them. There are interesting parallels between the arrogance of such groups and the attitude of ancient Gnosticism. Every historical period has had Gnostics who laid claim to "the real secret understanding" of what is "good" and how to achieve it. People's acceptance of these gnostic claims is conditioned by the "fame" of a particular group; hence the power of those who can enhance or diminish this fame.

Nations, of course, also lay claim to superiority; and if the claim is justified, it leads to considerable power—the nature of the power linked to the character of the superiority in question. Certainly, the claim of the United States today to military and economic superiority is unchallenged; but there is also the power exerted by respect for "the American way of life"—not that this respect is total, for there is criticism mixed with admiration. However, the notoriety generated by U.S. films, music, lifestyle, as well as the openness of life in this country, project an image of the United States that continues to draw millions of immigrants and that leads to widespread imitation.

Theological Reflection

At first glance, there does not seem to be much connection between the activity of God's Spirit and the use of power related to a person's or a group's public image. Yet, an important insight arises from Jesus of Nazareth's vehement denunciation of hypocrisy. It is clear that the Jesus of the Gospels finds repellant the public dishonesty of some of his enemies, the dissonance of their inner views and character with the public image they project. Their lack of authenticity is completely out of accord with his genuineness as a charismatic prophet.

However—and this is the connection with God's Spirit—the revulsion Jesus experiences is precisely the expression of the Spirit he shares with his Abba. That Spirit is the Spirit of truth; it is intrinsically inimical to a person's false public persona, to a public image created artificially to gain recognition that that person does not truly deserve. This negative judgment on hypocrisy is the flip side of Jesus' stress on honesty as a basic moral principle.

Further reflection suggests that the power of the Spirit as it opposes false public images of either individuals or groups is a redemptive process. It is not good for either individuals or groups to pretend to be what they are not; nor is it good for those who may be misled and harmed by assuming such false images to be true. True human community is grounded in authentic communication; only in honest interchange can humans share themselves and their experiences and be truly present to one another. Creating false public images, undertaken to gain wealth, political power, or professional prestige, is ultimately incompatible with the influence of God's Spirit manifested in Christ and destructive of the society within which this "sin" is committed. On the other hand, the power of that Spirit works through the sacramentality of the authentic lives of Christians and others to redeem humans and their societies from the corrosive and destructive force of dishonesty.

There is another subtle but pervasive activity of Christ's Spirit in combating the power of calumny and detraction, whether real or imagined. Many people have a lack of self-confidence, a fear that they are judged somewhat negatively by others—or at least ought to be. What can offset and "redeem" this situation is for a person to encounter the esteem that comes with love and friendship. Clearly, God's Spirit, which is the spirit of infinite love, by making a person aware of being the object of divine love, is a powerful antidote to people's diffidence about their own worth and worry abut their public image.

In the course of history, one of the most influential facets of the power of "fame" has been the impact of those who are considered to be "sacred," whether this sacrality came from the person's own holiness or from the office a person occupied. Traditionally, those who have occupied the top levels of society, particularly of religious society, have been looked upon as closer to God and therefore as sharing some of the divine sacredness. As we saw, this was crystallized in Christianity in the notion of "holy orders" and its explication in the works of Pseudo-Dionysius. Even when the behavior of some of those occupying such lofty positions raised doubts about their personal reputation, there was a basic assumption that top officials were "specially good" people and were in a position to powerfully influence those "below" them. It is interesting to note that at Vatican II, where the central issue was the relative power of papacy and episcopacy, the adjective constantly used by the bishops to describe themselves and their activity was "sacred."[1]

Somewhat different, though at times linked to this influential regard for officials, is the power exercised by those who are regarded as "saints." There is a grassroots, homiletical and catechetical, recognition of what has been termed "good example" or its contrary. On a more theological level, one of the leading explanations of the redemptive power of Jesus' life and death has been the moral influence of his example. Within a culture, continuing power is exercised by the fame of those considered to be moral heroes. Probably the unparalleled instance of this is the power exercised during the past two millennia by the memory of Jesus of Nazareth. One of the striking aspects of the influence of Jesus is the fact that he who never sought his own "glory" during life and who was unknown to the "powerbrokers" of his day has become perhaps the most famous and admired person in history.

Finally, one theological topic that bears on the power of "fame" is the allied issue of "the glory of God." Certainly, if the issue of the "majesty" of an earthly king was central to people's attitude toward a ruler in the days of monarchies, the majesty of God was considered something to be respected, an aspect of divine power to be acknowledged. While humans could not add anything to the infinite intrinsic goodness of God, they could, "extrinsically" as it were, acknowledge God's glory. Theologians differed somewhat in what they considered this "glory" to be—for biblical thought, it was God's "manifested salvific intent"; for Irenaeus, it was "the human person fully alive," for others, it was the intrinsic eschatology of creation leading back to the divine creator as its goal.[2] The *Spiritual Exercises* of Loyola and the *Constitutions* of the Jesuit Order reflected the common understanding of Christians when they summarized the goal of dedicated Christian life as "the greater glory of God." History attests to the power of commitment to that goal in the lives of countless believers. In the final chapter of this book, it will be suggested that it is precisely the Spirit of God that manifests God's glory and attracts humans to honor that glory.

5

The Power of Law

No pneumatology can ignore the classic tension between Spirit and law. So, a study of power and Spirit must probe the kinds of power associated with law and how they relate to God's Spirit as ultimate law. Obviously, this topic is closely linked with one we have yet to study, namely, the power connected with the words of command spoken by one in authority. However, there is a distinct question I hope to study here: how is law itself a form of power?[1]

As far back as one can trace the history of humans' reflection on their experience, there has been a focus on the phenomenon of order (or its opposite, chaos) in nature, in society, and in human existing itself.[2] The regularity of dawn and sunset, of the seasons of the year, of the consistent patterns of stellar constellations, all testified to some basic controling force or "divinity" that guaranteed the orderly pattern of nature. Their interest was not just theoretical fascination. Human life depended on this regularity; if at the time of the winter solstice the days did not begin to grow longer and darkness increasingly took over, human existence was at peril. And when the normal pattern of nature was disrupted by earthquakes, floods, or drought, not only questioning but terror could ensue. Instinctively, people discerned that, at least in times of normalcy, nature was governed by inner laws.

More sophisticated reflection attributes to "law" a pervasive governing cosmic role. In Eastern thought, Dharma is one of the most basic notions in explanations of reality. Beyond the laws governing the growth of crops and human well-being lies an overarching cosmic law, which people should discover and observe. Much the same insight is found in Egyptian teaching about *ma'hat* or in the strains of Greek philosophy that lead up to Stoicism's view of cosmic Logos. Israelite/Jewish theology has its own distinctive emphasis on the Law—we will examine this a bit later. In all these cases, the order in the world and in human society is seen to flow from law as a unifying and ordering force. In terms of causality, inner law such as that found in nature is for all practical purposes identical with finality.

Apart from humans, created realities all function according to determined inner law that directs them to fulfill their purpose in the universe. Humans, too, as part of the created universe are subject to law, to their proper finality. Yet, the "natural law" is that they as free persons are meant to decide many of the actions that will appropriately fulfill their purpose. How truly free humans are has, however, been a topic of doubt and debate for most of human history. While responsibility for one's actions has always been recognized, and without such accountability there is no basis for legal action against aggressors, there has also been a consistent belief or concern about some force like Fate, which mocks humans' presumption that they are free. Indeed, the ground for perennial belief in magic is the notion that there exists a fundamental determining pattern to which all human and cosmic realities are subject.

To spell out the demands of life in the world and especially in human society, cultures have developed explicit laws, a development clearly recognized as important because legendary figures like Solon are revered for their role in formulating these laws. Presumably, such humanly formulated bodies of law spell out the more basic law of human nature's demands. Yet, up to the present, competing theories of jurisprudence propose differing bases for interpreting correctly a nation's laws. Heir of the British tradition of common law, which in its own way is an application of "natural law," the legal tradition in the United States has based judgment on precedent, that is, on the accumulated wisdom of previous official decisions. In any case, all legal systems recognize a certain power that law possesses, a power backed up by coercion beyond simple persuasion, a power that regulates humans' external relational behavior and guarantees the orderliness of social existence.

What, then, is the character and source of laws' power? Certainly, we are dealing with a group's need to guarantee order, to eliminate or at least punish violence, to safeguard the basic rights and rhythms of people's lives. This requires, of course, that laws be accompanied by procedures and structures able to implement them—and this introduces the relation between the power to legislate and the power to judge and enforce, something we have already studied under "office." However, there is another power that laws possess, especially if they are just laws. This is the demand they make on the conscience and responsibility of members of a society. In some circumstances, this can be abused, when illegitimate use of authority demands what is improperly called "obedience" to unjust or wrongly interpreted laws. Actually, what is being asked in such cases is not truly obedience but rather unthinking or fear-motivated submission.

To mention conscience is to open the door to the entire enterprise of ethical reflection, to the revolutionary changes in Christian moral theology that have occurred over the past century. To deal with this far-ranging topic is far beyond the purpose and possibilities of this volume, but reference must be made to the discussion of the Spirit's role in exercise of conscience. James Hanigan has drawn attention to the almost complete absence of mention of the Spirit in writings on moral theology, but he has also hinted at the fact that there has existed in the new developments a good deal of implicit reference to the Spirit's role.[3] Heralded by the writings of Fritz Tillman, Bernard Haring, and Gerard Gilleman in the late 1950s, some Catholic moral theologians returned to the relation of Christian morality to the New Testament, to Christ, and by implication to the Spirit that animated Christ's own ethical judgments. In addition, the line between morality and spirituality became increasingly blurred as more attention focused on prayerful discernment of the Spirit as central to Christian moral judgment. It is instructive to see how psychological insights into human maturation, theological examination of conversion, and reflection on the spirituality of Thomas Merton complement one another in Walter Conn's foundational moral theology, *Christian Conversion*.[4] Another increasingly transformative influence on ethical reflection and spirituality has come with women theologians' entry into the field and the impact on them of feminist exegetes' studies of Sophia-Spirit.[5]

Law and Social Context

In the course of history, a number of different sources and grounding of laws have prevailed, depending on the extent to which people have lived in a situation of genuine democracy or in a theocratic or "secular" context. In an absolute monarchy, the will of the ruler roots the laws; the ruler is legislator, judge, and executive. In an oligarchy, this is extended to influential aristocracy, whether that be a political or economic aristocracy. Such situations always invite question about the humanly binding force of the laws, whether they are just or not; but usually, the laws possess a certain "awe" that leads to their being followed without questioning, to providing a pattern for policing, or to their being an effective means of official legitimation.

In a democratic/representative civil context, laws are grounded in the grant from the people of power to legislate and are meant to express the accumulated wisdom of the community. The power of the laws resides in the consent of the governed. This principle may find an unusual application to authority in the Church: It is rather widely assumed that the authority/power of ordained Church officials comes directly from God, as in the case of pope and bishops, or from God through higher officials, as in the case of presbyters and deacons. The Church is not a democratic structure—or should it be, since it is a voluntary society? At the time of the Great Western Schism when the papal authority was in crisis and at the Council of Constance where that crisis was resolved, the canonical basis for the resolution viewed the entire body of the faithful as source of official power. The canonical theory espoused by Francesco Zabarella and Jean Gerson that granted legitimacy to the council's proceedings did not deny the fullness of papal authority but saw that authority as flowing from the entire Church.[6]

A special case provides laws with an unquestioned power, namely, in religious groups where the officials who legislate can claim that the laws come, not from themselves, but from their god. This can overlap, and often in the past has, with the civil sphere. Whether expressly subscribing to "the divine right of kings" or not, many an autocratic political leader has laid claim to divine appointment and support and claimed that his legislating is a surrogate act for that divinity. At times, this takes the form of appealing to "destiny," of the ruler and of the group he or she rules. Obviously, the context in which a claim to divine support is most potent is that of religion itself. In one way or another, religious leadership teaches that it can "save" the faithful, that it has a privileged insight into the will of God, and that it is entrusted with the means of grace. The path to salvation is, of course, the moral and religious behavior that is proposed as "the law of God." In this instance, much of the power of the religious leadership derives from the supposedly God-given laws, which can at times be much more the will of these leaders than the will of God.

Source of Law's Power

What, then, is the source of laws' power? One obvious response is that laws are effective if there is some penalty for their nonobservance that exerts coercive force. Clearly, the authority and/or the power of the law-giver lies behind any given law.[7] More basically, in a civil situation, the "covenant"/constitution on which the society is founded provides the grounds for any specific legislation and legal interpretation by the courts. This norm, however, requires adjustment as decades or centuries witness to a changing mindset on the part of the populace, a change that is represented effectively by the choice of legislators. Still more basic is "human nature," that is, the distinctive character of humans as persons with common potential, rights, and responsibilities.[8] What this involves is legislators and judges deciding whether a certain course of behavior accords with the good of the persons involved or with the common good. Such decision would have to be based on existing laws or on legal precedent that stated the accumulated wisdom of a given culture, whether this had been explicitly stated in a code of law or whether it was "common law." Finally, religionists would see the will of a creator divinity as the ultimate empowerment of all legitimate law.

Ideally, formulated law is intended to safeguard and foster the well-being of all the "citizens" under its umbrella. History indicates, however, that legal structures can be an effective instrument of oppression and domination. Under the guise of "law and order," powerful rulers can maintain control over others, exploiting others' labor, talents, and sexuality for their own benefit while depriving the dominated of even the most basic of human rights. As noted above, in her book *Lydia's Impatient Sisters*,[9] the German exegete Luise Schottroff details the way in which the marriage laws of the Roman Empire supported the supposed rights of men at the expense of women's freedom to choose their marriage partner. Christian women who defied this pattern of patriarchal domination, because they chose a life of dedicated virginity, paid the price of martyrdom. While perhaps more striking than other examples, there is no lack of examples of laws being used to manipulate economic or social patterns to the advantage of the more affluent and powerful.

Pneumatological Reflection

The resources for Christian theological reflection on law—its nature, power, limits, sources, and abuse—are very rich. Christianity's roots lie in the career of Israel, a career in which law played a central role. It is not an exaggeration to say that the Law created Israel, shaping and uniting a disparate group of wandering refugees into an identifiable people, providing a coherent pattern of social behavior, and creating ordered life in and among families and tribes.

As early as the exodus, the leader of the people, Moses, was most importantly a law-giver. However, the law he and others who succeeded him formulated and promulgated was believed to be the Law given by Yahweh, their God. It is a distinctive feature of ancient Israel that this people had no separate body of civil law; the all-encompassing law of their social existence was the divinely given Law. This Mosaic Law was the power behind kings, priests, and even prophets. Kings were judged by it and were not free—though they tried—to substitute their own edicts. Priests in shrine and Temple developed their own codes of behavior, but these were always subsumed under the Mosaic Law and judged by it. In Israel, charismatic prophets were not a challenge to the Law but a challenge to those who would abandon or neglect the Law or those who would distort and misinterpret the Law for their own ends.

Inevitably, the fundamental Law was spelled out by Jewish teachers in the postexilic period in a large number of specific regulations that were meant to guide the life of the people. Essentially a beneficial process, this could and to some extent did during the Second Temple period of Jewish history develop into a legalism that suffocated the religious authenticity of many and led to religion's being a fear-based observance of practices. The Law became to a large extent not a guide for free-spirited relationship to God but an end in itself. Faith gave way to moralism.

Yet, this was balanced by another development within the circles of Jewish wisdom reflection. Among wisdom thinkers and teachers, Judaism's distinctive form of response to the questions, what is the good life? who is the truly wise person? attributed wisdom to God alone but saw divine wisdom shared with humans. This is imaginatively described in terms of the divine figure of Wisdom, a personification and not a distinctive divine person, an epitome of the guidance given the people by Yahweh. Wisdom's teaching goes beyond the Law in so far as it draws from greater depths of human response to life. It is closely linked, though not identified, with the Spirit of God that moves the hearts, as well as the minds, of humans.[10] Yet in the final analysis, wisdom reflection comes back full circle to the Law: in the book of Sirach, the teacher of wisdom sees the Law itself as the privileged statement of divine wisdom—the final portion of the book describes the wise figures of Israel's history as having been the faithful observers of the Law.

Christian Theological Reflection

In Jesus' own life, in the Judaism of his day, and in the Jewish and Christian anguished attempts to come to grips with the destruction of Jerusalem and its Temple, the tension between Law and Spirit was central. For Jesus and his contemporaries, the radical importance of the Law was unquestioned. But the question was: what truly was the Law? What did the traditional formulations of the Law mean? Whose interpretation—and there were many schools under masters like Hillel or Gamaliel, each with its distinctive teaching about the meaning of the Law—was truly Yahweh's law? For Jesus himself, this debate about the interpretation of the Law took on a unique character to which the gospel narratives testify. For him, the "demands" of God flowed from the experience he had of his "heavenly father"; the Spirit of God that empowered and inspired him was a more radical understanding of the Law than any of the current Pharisaic teaching.

A superficial glance at Jesus' teaching might suggest that for him there was an opposition of Law and Spirit. However, this was not the case. Though the Law was an expression of God's will for Israel, an expression of God's Spirit, it could not adequately "translate" that Spirit because it was always formulated in human language. Built into this divine/human interchange was an inevitable tension: if the Law was institutionalized as a final statement of God's will, it cut off openness to the deeper "law" of the Spirit that remained always as a further word of challenge to the finality of the formulated Law. Judaism's own wisdom movement honored (as did later Rabbinic Judaism) this need to probe further the reality of the Law when it brought together God's Wisdom, God's Spirit, and God's Law. It was this coincidence of divine "personifications" that Jesus lived out as Wisdom's prophet empowered by the Spirit.[11]

In his treatment of Jesus' parable of the Good Samaritan, Thomas West draws attention to the power of agapic love to transcend human laws and customs.[12] Though it does not explicitly draw a connection to the Holy Spirit, West's analysis of the Samaritan's action has important implications for pneumatology. Classic explanation of God's Spirit has always related that Spirit to divine love and the Samaritan, motivated by love, exemplifies the manner in which the impetus of the Spirit overrides the restrictions of dehumanizing laws and customs.

Early Christianity and the Law

Inheriting both Jewish respect for and adherence to the Law and Jesus' freedom of Spirit, the earliest Christians wrestled with this tension. Internally, this was manifested in the Judaizing controversy that severely tested the unity of the earliest communities. It was in the context of this struggle that St. Paul stressed the primacy of the Spirit of freedom as guide for Christian faith and life.[13] After the destruction of Jerusalem, the role of the Law took on a new dimension, but the nature of this new role was a matter of debate, sometimes acrimonious debate, between Christian and non-Christian Jews. One view would lead to Rabbinic Judaism, the other to historical Christianity. Though Christians saw Jesus the Christ as embodying the law of the Spirit and providing a final "translation" of the Law, it is important to remember that in keeping with the Hebrew Bible as part of its own sacred scriptures, Christianity did not jettison the God-given Law of Israel. Ultimately, there is no fundamental opposition between Law and Spirit, in the history either of Christianity or of Judaism. For both communities, there remains the tension between honoring freedom and restricting its abuse. For both, there remains the need to interpret Word by Spirit and vice versa.[14] For both, "obedience" remains a question: to what and to whom?

One of the neuralgic issues linked with this Law-Spirit tension is the character of *obedience* to institutionalized authority.[15] There is often the tendency to translate obedience as simply the acceptance of laws formulated and enforced by official authorities. However, obedience is quite different from submission; obedience is the honest response to the demands of "reality" in any given situation. In a particular situation, reality may include some official dictate. A truly obedient response proceeds from basic moral principles but is not an unquestioning acceptance of official decisions; while respecting such decisions, it must always proceed from a person's own conscience. In some instances—and they often are painful instances—a responsible decision of conscience must give preference to Spirit rather than to laws.[16] Such decisions when they dissent from official teaching are often prophetic but for that very reason are criticized and opposed. In his book *Ministry*, Edward Schillebeeck raises this issue when he points out that new developments usually face a period of being "illegal" before receiving acceptance and approval.[17]

In summary, theological reflection sees God's Spirit as the ultimate law, for it is identical with "the will of God." This Spirit is not imposed restriction on human behavior but rather an eschatological invitation to fullness of personal life. It is an invitation to personal relationship with God, a relationship that is its own ultimate law. Gospel texts reflect Jesus' own response to this invitation: "I do always the things that please my heavenly Father" (John 5:19). Because humans are personal creatures, the invitation of the Spirit is none other than the transcendental relationship of creature to creator that Aquinas describes as a human's "obediential potency" and Karl Rahner refers to as "the transcendence of the human person."[18]

6

The Power of Wealth

One of the temporary "victims" of the September 2001 terrorist destruction of the twin towers in New York was the growing campaign against international corporate monopoly. For three years prior to the Al Queda terrorist attack, there had been mounting international demonstration occasioned by meetings of the Big Seven, the WTO, and the IMF/World Bank, demonstrations intended to draw attention to the increasing power of corporate wealth. Unhappily, the news media in reporting these demonstrations in Seattle, Washington, Genoa, and so on focused on the disruption caused by small groups of violent protestors and for the most part missed or ignored the deeper and broad-based protest that was being made. What was happening and is perhaps of lasting import was the international alliance of groups—organized labor, social justice activists, representatives of small nations, environmentalists—gathered to alert the world to the threatened control of human life by huge corporations linked to the power of the world's most affluent nations and to organize an effort to resist this impending monopoly. However one may wish to assess the validity and effectiveness of these protests, it is clear that they were confronting the power of wealth.

While it is true that a small portion of the protestors still sought to combat massive economic power with the power of violence, the basic antimonopolistic appeal was to a much different kind of power— "people power" exerted through citizen activity, organized use of purchasing patterns, and educating people worldwide to the monopolistic practices of large special interests. The problem these protestors, who represented a much larger constituency, were facing was not new, but it has been greatly magnified by the processes of globalization taking place today. These processes are to some extent irresistible; factors such as the communications explosion have made the world into one "global village." Yet, the accurate interpretation of this globalization, its potential for human benefit or for exploitation of the powerless, and its actual implementation remain a task of the present and the future—a task in which competing powers are bound to clash.[1]

The true nature of this fundamental power struggle for the "soul" of the world needs to be clarified. Radical fundamentalists like Al Queda try to frame it as a worldwide war between Islam and the West. While this is a distortion, there has existed just enough ethnic discrimination and social arrogance on the part of the affluent Western world to give credence to this theory. On the other hand, and not too different in its limited perspective, is the "clash of civilizations" view espoused by Sam Huntington in his recent book by that title.[2] The difficulty with such interpretations of the dynamic in present-day world affairs is not only that they are inaccurate and superficial, but that they divert attention from the real issue dividing humanity, the disparity of rich and poor.[3]

Such disparity is at least as old as recorded history. However, the relation of wealth and its power to other power has shifted. From antiquity and up to the end of the Middle Ages, it was the militarily and socially powerful who acquired possessions because of their class location and a superior economic situation because of the accompanying possession of military and political power. True, there were always "merchant" entrepreneurs who acquired wealth by their creative use of property or by clever salesmanship, but it was only with the emergence of a commercial bourgeoisie toward the end of the thirteenth century that wealth began to replace aristocracy as a basic source of power. From that point onward, modern times—at least in the West—have been marked by increasing power coming with material possessions and especially with capital for investment.

While violence and political domination may have remained prime symbols of power, wealth has become a primary source of power.[4] Wealth has bought political office and paid for armies; its acquisition has also been a goal of wars and political struggles. At no time in history has this been more true than it is today. Vast wealth guarded by large-scale military establishments supports any number of dictatorial regimes, regimes that are favored economically and militarily by the world's most powerful nations so that they can in turn feed their natural resources into the rich world's economy. Obviously, there are very wealthy people who benefit from today's economic activity, but wealth is for the most part acquired and increased by huge transnational corporations whose power seems to be beyond the control of any national governments—is actually abetted by governments that are largely controled by these same special interests.[5]

More and more critical attention has recently been paid to this worldwide economic structure. In the United States Congress, for example, there is a struggle taking place to lessen the influence of money in elections and of lobbying by wealthy special interests in legislation. Increasing attention is being drawn to the extent to which government at every level has been engaged in subsidizing big corporations. Free trade arrangements such as NAFTA are still being negotiated and presidents still seek "fast-track" power so that they are freer to act without congressional restraint. However one may wish to judge all such developments, it is clear that the power of wealth is fundamental in today's world and its exercise is a matter of the gravest importance.

Theological Reflection

So, what is the perspective of the world's religions on this growing power of the wealthy to control and impoverish the great majority of humans? Do they have at their disposal more than a next-life appeal to divine punishment for abuse of wealth? Their ethical reflection about the injustice of this economic imbalance may be academically insightful, but is there any power upon which they can draw to oppose the excessive power of wealthy individuals and wealthy nations and wealthy corporations? One must even ask whether religious communities themselves have not succumbed to the power of wealth. It is no secret that it is the wealthy who have access to religious officials, whose ideas and interests are regarded by religious authorities as worth consideration, whose values and economic decisions are seldom challenged in homilies or pastoral letters, and whose oppression of the poor is rarely denounced. To be honest, however, there is increasing and encouraging resistance by religious leaders to worldwide economic domination[6]—but money still speaks powerfully in the life of the "Churches."

Several of the world's great religions have their distinctive approach to the issue; but in the West it is the Jewish and Christian traditions that have been most prominent. Both find their roots in the prophetic movement of ancient Israel that attacked the exploitation of the poor by the wealthy. It is important at the outset to point out that the prophetic voice in Israel does not denounce wealth as such; on the contrary, material prosperity is considered a blessing from God, a reward for fidelity to the Law. What does draw the wrath of a prophet like Amos, who speaks for Yahweh, is wealthy people's lack of concern and care for the indigent, even worse the exploitation of the poor by the rich.

Radically, this evil divided a covenant people into two classes, denying the human equality that was intrinsic to the covenant, thereby caricaturing God, and making the community of shalom impossible. Behind the word of the prophet leveled against abuse of the power inherent in wealth was the prophet-empowering Spirit/power of God. So, in what many would see as naïveté, Jewish and Christian faithful believe that in mysterious ways the divine Spirit works through humans to counter unjust gaining or use of wealth. The finality of the Spirit's operation in history is the creation of the reign of God, a situation of right relations among people, that is, justice, and authentic personal community; abuse of wealth runs directly counter to this by causing social discrimination—and obviously harming the indigent and causing them undeserved suffering.

The Christian response to this question springs from the teaching of Jesus. Recognizing greed as a constant temptation of humans, that teaching advocated a radical shift in people's attitude toward material wealth. Using a certain amount of rhetorical exaggeration to gain attention, Jesus urged that trust in God's watchful providence replaces obsession with gaining possessions as the means of overcoming economic anxiety. What this represented was a basic application of the most central of Christian moral principles: people are more important than things and never to be subordinated to things.

The gospel texts narrating the temptation of Jesus in the desert highlight the centrality of this attitude toward riches. Satan's suggestion that Jesus exercise his messianic role by using economic and political power ("all the kingdoms of the earth") as the source of humanity's salvation is repudiated; and Jesus' use of Deuteronomic texts in response to the tempter recalls the repeated failure of Israel to resist this temptation. Like the Israelite/Jewish traditions, the teaching of Jesus and the witness of earliest Christianity do not repudiate possession of earthly goods within reasonable limits. What they do criticize is reliance upon such goods as the key to "the good life" and gaining of wealth as a person's main objective.

There is no question but that the teaching of the Christian Scriptures advocates poverty as a force working to achieve "the reign of God"; but the precise character and inherent power of this evangelical poverty has been disputed for most of Christianity's history. Nowhere is the split in interpreting evangelical poverty more obvious than in the sometimes acrimonious divisions of opinion within the medieval Franciscan movement, controversies that led to actual split within the Franciscan Order. Put in stark terms, does evangelical poverty require one to live in actual poverty, or is it enough to "hang loose," to remain detached and personally free from the possessions one may have and that are used to benefit the lives of others as well as one's own? The dispute remains unresolved up to the present time and probably is not subject to theoretical solution. Differing spiritual traditions will no doubt continue to stand in tension on the issue.

In our present study, however, the questions are: why attach the notion of "power" to any form of poverty? Is not lack of power inseparable from lack of wealth? Are not innumerable efforts to achieve justice and charity stymied for lack of funds? The response would seem to be fairly obvious, yet today there is broad interest in and discussion of "the power of the poor."[7]

One of the most interesting and instructive cases of such discussion is the debate going on among the Catholic bishops of Latin America. What is well known is the historic decision they made at Medellin, Colombia, in 1968, when they turned away from their long-standing class identification with the rich and politically powerful and advocated a "preferential option" for the poor. What is less known is the gradual extension of this position that occurred at the bishops' 1979 gathering in Puebla, Mexico, and their 1992 meeting in the Dominican Republic. At Puebla, despite some opposition from the Vatican that was expected to be voiced by Pope John Paul himself as a participant in the sessions, the bishops not only reiterated the decision of Medellin but spoke of a Church *for* the poor. Again, prior to the Santo Domingo meeting, there were rumors that Vatican pressure would lead to a repudiation of Medellin and Puebla; instead, the bishops went a step further by speaking of "the Church *of* the poor."

So, what is "evangelical poverty" as practiced for centuries by organized religious groups and advocated as a virtue to be developed by all Christians? One element is common to the diverse responses to this question: a greedy quest for wealth and the "rich" lifestyle wealth provides is to be avoided if it entails the impoverishment of others. Essential to evangelical poverty is freedom from excessive acquisition and obsession with riches, a genuine appreciation for and observance of the principle "people before things." It is in this focus on a person's or a society's *attitude* that the power of wealth can be controled and directed to true human betterment.

At this point, one can see the entry for the influence of the Spirit. Harnessing the power of riches requires a set of priorities, a perspective on what human life is all about, a wisdom that provides insight into the authentic meaning of "the good life." As both the scriptural message and Christian tradition attest, this is precisely what the Spirit/Wisdom provides. The "mind of God" as transmitted through revelation is constantly portrayed as opposed to unjust use of the power of wealth, committed instead to special care for the economically disadvantaged of society (the widow and the orphan). Wealth as such is not seen as evil but its possession brings with it responsibility for "the neighbor." If embraced by humans, this divine wisdom is a power capable of contending with abusive use of wealth.

The divine wisdom communicated by God's Spirit understands the "good life" in terms different from "having things." To be prized above possessions are freedom and friendship and beauty and peace of mind. Riches can contribute to these, but all too often they promise to substitute, a substitution that proves to be illusory. Realizing the true nature of happiness and prioritizing their goals according to the principles of the gospel would empower people to withstand and counter the power of wealth.

It is important to stress that this "solution" to economic injustice, while it may well require a revolutionary shift in economic theory and practice, is most radically a conversion of people's thinking and desires. Presently, the study of economics takes human greed as a given and explains "scientifically" the ways in which greed can become more profitable. In order to maximize profit, humans' need and labor are exploited and subordinated to ever increasing economic gain. Two examples of this illustrate the need for "conversion":

(1) To maintain and hopefully increase a corporation's profit, thousands of people are deprived of employment and benefits such as health care in what is euphemistically referred to as "downsizing"; and top executives of these corporations are sought and richly rewarded for their ability to engage in such person-denying decisions. Obviously, economic enterprises of one sort or another must be profitable or they cease to exist. Ethical and theological reflection on economic behavior must deal with reality and take account of the actual functioning of financial institutions. Having said that, there is need to insist that a set of priorities expressed in human decisions ultimately rules the activities of the wealthy. "Market forces" are real, but they are all too often appealed to in order to mask the underlying power of executive decisions, all of which says that there is need for the decisions controling the functioning of the world's economy to be guided by "the mind of God" that places concern for people before concern for profits.[8]

(2) On the marketing side of economic activity, there is also a fundamental difference between presently dominant theory/behavior and the perspective of the gospel. It is a basic principle of economics that the price of some article should be increased in proportion to people's need. So, if there is a shortage, real or artificial, of gasoline, one can expect the price of gasoline to rise; people need gasoline to get to work, to shop, to get their children to school; despite the hardships that involves, they must pay the higher price. The situation be-

comes even more painful when it is a matter of people's need for heating oil. On the other hand, the message of revelation is that the need of people rather than business profit alone should guide pricing. Businesses are meant to function within the context of the common good; they are meant to have the purpose of providing for people as well as making profit. So, within reasonable bounds, prices should be such that people can meet their basic human needs.

That such reasoning is regarded in many quarters as "pious and naïve" is not surprising. Christianity's worldview has since the days of St. Paul's letter to the Corinthians been seen as a "stumbling block and foolishness." There is an opposition of "powers"—as Walter Wink's writings have insisted, Paul's "fight against principalities and powers" can in our day be seen in terms of the power of wealth confronted with the power of the Spirit.[9]

Is there hope that the power of wealth, particularly corporate wealth, can be matched by Spirit-power, so that the massive impoverishment of most of the human race can be overcome? Theoretically, it would seem that the entire situation of destitute millions would be remedied if people in the affluent parts of the world underwent the conversion just described.

However, there is a second attitude against which the Spirit of God must work, the apathy that Rollo May in his *Love and Will*[10] underlines as the great "sin" of our day. Most people are not engaged in purposely doing evil, working to destroy the lives of others. Rather, it is that "good" people are not concerned enough to be engaged in doing good. Geiko Mueller-Fahrenholz says much the same thing when he describes the phenomenon of "numbing" in which, without much awareness or passion, people become accustomed to a situation that is truly inhuman and feel powerless to remedy it.[11] This is closely allied with what Dorothy Soelle criticizes as the banality of so much middle-class existence today.[12] Opposed to this is the vitality associated with the action of God's Spirit in direct contrast to Stoic stress on *apatheia*. Paddy Chayefsky has caught this in the line from his play "Gideon," which paraphrases the book of Judges, "Passion is the very fact of God in man."[13]

Linked with this action-activating vitality is the power of the poor in today's world, a phenomenon to which Gustavo Gutierrez among others has drawn attention.[14] Clearly, to speak of the power of the powerless, especially the economically poor, can make sense only in the context of faith. But precisely because it is a question of faith, it is something that a pneumatology cannot ignore. Recognizing the apparent "folly" of such a view, Gutierrez argues for the reality of this power in the socio-economic context of the world today. Basically, the power to persevere in their struggle against the oppressive forces that demean their lives comes to the poor because of their faith and hope in the liberating activity of God. At one level, the poor have always, despite appearances, trusted in a protecting God. By and large, this found expression in the hope of reward for the just and suffering poor in a life to come. What is different today is that large segments of the poor, particularly in Latin America, have come to believe that divine assistance is at hand to support them in this present lifetime in their efforts to liberate themselves. That is why the starting point of a theology of liberation is not simply the context of oppression suffered by millions but rather the effort of those oppressed to free themselves from the forces allied against them.

What they rely on is a "preferential option for the poor" that begins with God but is meant to find translation into the responsibilities of Christians worldwide. One of the things that suggests strongly that this power of the poor is very real is the violent opposition of the powerbrokers. Previous Christian generations have had martyrs who gave their lives in witness to their beliefs in the revelation that came in Jesus of Nazareth. Today, there are martyrs, probably many more than at any period in history, but they have been killed because of their role in the struggle for justice, killed because those in control of the guns and the money have seen them as a very real threat to their power. What is animating this phenomenon and in the context of faith gives it irresistible power is precisely the same as in Christianity's infancy, the impulse of God's Spirit.

PART III

Nature

Probably the earliest human experience of power was people's encounter with the force of storms, earthquakes, and floods. This required incipient reflection on this power, not to arrive at theoretical explanations but to find means of dealing with it practically by naming it or portraying it in art or ritual. That will be studied in the next unit. This unit will focus on the *positive* powers that produce and sustain life, particularly human life. Human empowerment, however, extends beyond biological manifestations of life; this unit will contain chapters on *creativity* and on what is the source of creativity, human *imagination*. This will lead logically to the next unit that studies the power of symbol and language.

7

Power in Nature

A theological study of power must take seriously the power that resides in nature. It was the experience of this power—in storms, in floods, in growing things, in the generative power that produced plants, animals, and humans themselves—that led prehistoric humanity to search for the "divine" powers that underlay these blessings or threats of the world in which they lived. Ultimately, the power that controled creation remained a mystery; and even as modern understanding of nature has led to scientific explanations that have demystified many of the previous somewhat magical views, the power operative in the universe remains a vast unknown.

Science, correctly, absolves itself from any religious explanation of the created world. Indeed, some scientists openly oppose or ridicule any religiously oriented cosmology.[1] That "supernatural" explanations of physical phenomena are the object of educated skepticism is at times justified, for "religion's" explanations have often proved superficial, magical, or just plain wrong.

A classic example, of course, was the reaction of many religious groups to Darwin's views on evolution when these groups resorted to a fundamentalist, noncritical appeal to Genesis to counter Darwin's theory. To resolve the conflicts between science and religion, if there truly are such between authentic religion and responsible science, is not the purpose of this chapter. Rather, it attempts (often with the aid of contemporary scientific thought) to observe the various kinds of power that reside in nature and relate them to the ultimate *power of creation* that is the Spirit of God. This will, of course, run afoul of the claim made by some scientists that in the last resort the created universe is self-explanatory (or basically chaotic) and that any appeal to a transcendent creator is a *deus ex machina.* On the other hand, I believe that a carefully crafted pneumatology can prove consonant with any understanding of the world that is arrived at by appropriate scientific methods.

Origin of the Universe

While not universally accepted by astrophysicists, the theory of the universe's origin in a "big bang" has received quite wide credibility. This presupposes the fact that the universe we know did have a beginning—with some implication that the source of its coming into being defies scientific explanations and that the notion of creation deserves a hearing. Christian belief attributes the world's origin and existence to a transcendent creator—and it is not alone in doing so. However, when one takes seriously the extent of this claim in the face of the universe as we now know it, it defies easy acceptance—how could any "God" be responsible for such immensity and complexity? And if there is such a transcendent divinity, what must it be like, what is the nature of its creative power?

"Spirit" is a kind of being quite different from bodily being though not foreign to it;[2] and not only can spirit-being come to know and imaginatively embrace the universe (as we human spirits are progressively doing), but transcendent Spirit is capable of bringing even this awesome created world into being by spiritual power. To put it quite simply in human terms: a transcendent creator is "thinking" and "loving" the universe into existence.

Bracketing for the moment the truth or falsity of this claim, it is indisputable that the natural world exhibits a wide range of power at work—the incredible power that from the "big bang" raced out to shape galaxies of stars and planets, power of gravity and antigravity that apparently feeds a still-expanding universe. But the power within each of the limitless atoms in this cosmos, the incredible energy exerted in the interaction of all these elements—most of this is still hidden and unknown to us, only in the most preliminary fashion harnessed and controled by us. What can either philosophy or religious belief provide as understanding of all this? One thing it seems can be said, something simple but basically important: everything in this universe exists relationally; everything strives for some kind of completion or fulfillment. The universe is moved by "eros." Much of the scientific community rejects the notion that some form of teleology guides this entire development, but it seems difficult to assume that all this complex cosmic activity is accidental and without purpose.

Rejection of teleology in the world's evolution was probably the deepest scientific objection to the vision of Teilhard de Chardin.[3] No doubt one can point to oversimplifications in his magisterial *Human Phenomenon*, but Teilhard's theory of "radial energy" provides an intriguing insight into the fundamental developmental thrust in the universe.[4]

Beginning with creation's origin, with the "big bang" if you will, there has been a constant force, a radial energy, working to bring to realization created beings' interlocking potential, maintaining, despite the incredible diversity of things, a unity we call "the universe." This is not an entirely new vision because for centuries before mechanics took over as the acceptable shape of "science," there had been a competing and at times dominant scientific view of the world as a living reality.[5] Teilhard, of course, does not espouse this ancient "living world" explanation, nor can Christian faith, because it verges on pantheism; but it does reflect the common sense understanding that there is unity and purpose in the universe.

If one accepts the fact of creation and attempts to give it some philosophical explanation, it becomes clear that human understanding is incapable of grasping the divine activity that would be involved in bringing something into existence. The other side of the picture, however, the created character of things, is subject to human reflection. To make a long story short, any created "thing" is a transcendental relation beyond itself; its very be-ing is an appetite for existence beyond what now is. Apart from the human, this relatedness is determined and unable to achieve direct "linkage" to the creator; it is only created spirit that finally is capable of relating beyond mediation to the divine—and at that point the relation is subject to free choice.

Triggered by increased exposure of the world's religions to one another, there has recently been renewed interest in explaining the relation of God to creation in a way that would avoid pantheism and at the same time not make the Transcendent a distant and uninvolved reality. Prominent in this discussion has been the notion of "panentheism": God is not everything, but somehow God is "in" everything. It seems that one can provide some intelligibility to this view by introducing the idea of "presence." Starting the analysis with the human phenomenon of presence and then extending it to the whole of created being, one can distinguish personal presence from proximate spatial location and see that presence to another person is a matter of communicating through appropriate symbol, a communicating that in its fullest form is a self-gift in love of one person to another, a "being-for." Obviously, such self-giving communicating takes place fully only when the "recipient" of the communication is open and accepting. It is in such loving presence that even the Transcendent, ontologically other to an infinite degree, can be "in" a creature without losing its distinctive otherness.

Because divine presence is brought about through love, one can gain some insight into the kenotic dimension of creation: if it is in divine loving that the power to create consists, a creator God can relinquish the dominating control that would seem inseparable from divine activity and allow randomness to creaturely happenings and freedom to created persons.

Clearly, such personal being-in and being-for another that requires consciousness does not take place in the nonpersonal elements of the universe, but there is a divine-to-creature self-communicating at the even deeper level of existing itself. The act of creating is a communicating of being itself, the reception of which is determined and necessary. Even in the case of human persons, the communication of existing is more radical than the communication of divine to human that takes place on the level of consciousness that is intrinsic to human existing.

Giving Teilhard's radial energy a religious interpretation, one could say that within the entire dynamism of the universe, the creative power of God, that is, God's Spirit, is at work, "drawing" all that exists toward its fulfilling union with the creator. God's Spirit is not identified with radial energy; rather, the latter is the "being drawn" caused by the Spirit, infused into the cosmic processes. Divine Spirit is not constitutive of the universe, "immanent" in that sense, but it does not work at a distance—its transcendent character has to do with distinction in being between creator and creature, not with "distance."[6] The creator God of Jewish, Muslim, and Christian belief is not the God of Deism nor the Brahma of Hinduism.

Though recent centuries have witnessed a remarkable advance in scientific understanding of the universe and a revolutionary harnessing of some deep-down powers of the physical world, there no doubt remain aspects of nature's power that we do not yet so much as imagine. What we do know is that the horizons of scientific research appear boundless; each new discovery opens up unexpected "mysteries" to be explored and reveals more clearly the powers that affect human life.

Before turning to study the power of nature manifested in living beings, brief mention must be made of a subtle but important power of nature, the power it has to both humble and exalt humans' spirits by its beauty. The awesome splendor of snow-capped mountain ranges, the crashing surf at oceans' shores, the shifting colors of an autumn sunset, the promising blue of spring's first crocuses—one could go on and on listing instances of beauty that have delighted or comforted or uplifted humans and still do. If nothing else proves the power such beauty has to inspire, it is the fact that artists and poets have found nature's beauty the challenge to their own creative power.

Life

Among the various forms of power at work in the world is the power of life. For obvious reasons, humans have always been interested in the forces at work in life, especially human life. Ancient peoples tended to think about life as "some thing," that life was a fluid carried by the rain to bring forth crops and so pass into humans, that in humans blood and breath were identified with life. For Israelites, blood was so closely linked with the God-force enlivening people that it was considered sacred, belonging specially to God. Recent developments in molecular biology or the retention of bodily organs as "alive" and usable for transplant indicate the extent to which science has probed the structures and energies of living organisms, but the distinctive character of life itself still eludes us. How does a blade of grass manage to break through concrete, or the ability to become a living plant survive for millennia in seeds found in an ancient pyramid? How in a heart transplant does the life force of the recipient take over to enliven the new organ in a way that is different from artificial mechanisms? What is the life force that flows into healing?—medical attention does not heal people; it merely provides the means for the organism to heal. What is the power of genes or hormones to influence the structure and behavior of humans?

Most tantalizing are the questions that surround the distinctiveness of *human* life: When in human generation does human life occur? When can one equate the life of a fetus with human personal life? When does life truly cease for a person with flat brain waves but kept on so-called life support? Must one in such cases draw a line between human organic life and personal life? What is the reality of the "self" in these cases?

To turn again to religious understandings, the traditional belief of Judaism and Christianity has always linked the Spirit of God with life. The valley of dry bones vision of Ezekiel describes the Spirit of God breathing life into the skeleton remains of exiled Israel. Jesus' wonder works, attributed to God's Spirit working in him, often end with the words "Your faith has made you whole," raising the tantalizing question about the power of faith to influence organic life. And the Nicene-Constantinopolitan creed in stating Christian belief in God's Spirit characterizes that Spirit as "life-giving." Most important, Christian understanding of risen life as it occurred paradigmatically in Christ follows Paul in identifying that future life with life in the Spirit.

It would be a mistake in this reflection not to go beyond bodily organic life; for the basic life in humans upon which even organic existence depends is spirit life, the life of thought and love and imagination and freedom, life of conscious experience and intention. This level of human living clearly does not have complete control of the bodily dimensions of life; physical suffering and death make that clear. But the organic development of fetal life is directed toward spirit life; it provides the organic infrastructure for thought and self-aware sensation. Humans are not rational animals but rather incarnated spirits. It would seem, then, that if there is divine influence upon human life, it lies in the effect of God's Spirit upon the human spirit.

Further insight into the manner of Spirit's influence on the human spirit is at present crippled because of our relatively limited understanding of the physical power of human thought, imagination, and emotion. At least as far back as Galen, there has been some recognition of psychosomatic medicine. Traditions of employing psychic power to affect bodily functions have been stronger in the East than in standard Euro-American medical practice, though such approaches to physical healing are receiving more respect and attention today. Consequently, despite the danger of quackery, one cannot dismiss the evidence that there exists a realm of spirit's and Spirit's influence on human bodiliness that opens up reflection on the character of faith healing.

Sexuality

One of the two or three basic operations that exist in all life forms is the process of reproduction, the activity by which life passes from one generation to another and so guarantees the existence of a species. So powerful a force is this drive to reproduce that in some species the life of the generator is sacrificed so that life can be communicated. As it occurs in human reproduction, sexual activity has always been a central interest and an expression of a mysterious and wild force that needs to be brought under societal control by institutions like marriage. Men did not understand and often feared female sexuality, saw it as a threat to social stability. Governments like Greece and Rome legislated "household codes" to safeguard patriarchal control. In Israel's Mosaic Law and in the Mesopotamian law codes from which it drew, the rights of men and the responsibilities of women in sexual matters were carefully delineated. Typically, over the centuries, different cultures have either divinized or demonized sexuality. Human sexual experience opens up a unique way of appreciating the eros of the universe in which it shares.

Perhaps the attraction connected with sexuality is the most powerful in human experience, an attraction that is certainly related to the attraction of the beautiful but involves much more. Superficial "sex appeal" focuses on the physical features of a person, especially on the erogenous areas of the body, but deeper and more mature sexual attraction arises because of the beauty of the beloved *as a person*. No doubt a most important source of sexuality's attraction flows from the drive toward reproduction that humans share with other living beings. The physiological links between hormones, vigorous health, perception of sexually stimulating images, and sexual arousal are deeper than people's conscious decisions or refinement. It is this instinctive linkage that can often cause anxiety and guilt feelings in adolescents who lack open and accurate explanation of their bodily and psychological sexual makeup.

In its human context, sexuality is much more than the drive to reproduce, fundamental and undeniable though that is. Human sexuality is focal in humans' spirit-existing, a central player in persons' move toward mature self-identity. It is a key impulse to establish relationships at the same time that it is a profound revelation of created persons' interdependence. However, it is not the deepest level of human relationships, for friendship is both more extensive and more basic. It is friendship that can function in human experience as the key symbol of relationship to God. But even in friendships, the power of sexuality is never completely absent and works to intensify or threaten. It is in this important aspect of human experience that the religious use of erotic imagery by some of the great mystics points to the largely unexplored power of divine love, that is, God's Spirit, to clarify and transform human sexuality.

Mature and loving sexual intercourse involves neither control nor dependence. It is not the experience of power over but of power with. For this reason, mature sexuality is basic to a positive and healthy self-image. With it comes the realization of one's importance, unique importance to another person who is the object of one's respect and love. This kind of mature sexual attitude and activity is actually a creative process, creative of the personhood of the two lovers and for heterosexual partners creative of the children who are the desired fruit of their love. It is to the creative interaction of men and women that the initial chapter of Genesis alludes when it says that the creator God made humans in the divine image and likeness, "male and female God made them."

Such a positive view of sexuality is well and good; but there is also "a dark side." Despite its tremendous power to refine and enliven human life, sexuality has often been abused to harm, demean, and even destroy people. Sexual attraction seems to have built into it a certain "warp," the attraction of "the forbidden," a tendency to voyeurism, an immature seeking for titillation, that work against an open, balanced appreciation of sexuality's enrichment of human experience. There is a profound beauty to sexuality; but the attraction of that beauty in the context of true love and true art is utterly different from the attraction of pornography, the gratuitous presentation of sexual imagery for the purpose of titillation, often connected with financial gain. What is difficult to explain is that such pornography, even when it is recognized as immature and exploitative, still retains a certain attraction. Part of the answer may lie in the fact that it is related to pleasure without responsibility. Another element of the answer is that within a given culture, the attitude toward sexuality is socially constructed by influences such as use of sexually stimulating imagery in advertising.

Casual sexual intercourse may seem to be a harmless though irresponsible game, but all too often it leads to betrayal and heartbreak; for there is something in the inescapable symbolism of this action that promises a deeper commitment. By far the most harmful abuse of sexuality comes in its employment as a means of domination, of control, of angry revenge—the paradigm abuse being the forcible rape of another, which is essentially an action of violent aggression and control rather than of sexual enjoyment.[7]

However one wishes to characterize it, there is no question but that human sexuality is a powerful force in our psychic existence, though perhaps not quite as basic as Freud would have us believe.[8] Certainly much of its power lies in its deep symbolism, linked with the promise of both life and death, symbolizing even when apparently used only casually a commitment of enduring love and fidelity. In the context of genuine love between two persons, the moment of sexual ecstasy involves an experience of personal union, of possession and self-gift, of personal worth, unlike any other. It is both the satisfaction of what may be the most dominant appetite and physical drive and the greatest sensible pleasure. And the passion with which it is linked is power that rationality can scarcely control.

The most powerful expression of sexuality comes when it is the manifestation of mature and unique love, and the more powerful attraction is that of love. Committed couples who cherish a deepening friendship, who remain lifelong lovers, find their sexuality expressed and fulfilled in the whole ambit of their interactions with one another. On the other hand, in situations where genital sex is the only bond between a couple, where friendship does not grow and personal communication ceases, sexual experience proves incapable of maintaining the relationship and itself grows less attractive.

It is here that we can perceive the transforming influence of God's Spirit on human sexuality and therefore on human maturation. Working particularly through the sacramentality of human friendship, the love-power of the Spirit introduces a meaning and depth that is able to transcend and render ineffective the superficial pleasure-only and titillation attached to immature capitulation to sexual attraction. This is what can give positive meaning to the Christian practice of celibacy that is freely chosen for the reign of God. Exemplified in Jesus himself, abstention from genital activity need not reflect a lack of affection or lack of personal warmth or even of intense passion. Rather, it can be a tribute to an individual's profound love for God. Authentic celibacy is no barrier to sexual maturity since love is the force working in the human psyche to give sexuality its genuine meaning and evaluation.[9]

Human Imagination and Creativity

Creation, if understood in the full sense, pertains only to the Transcendent, but there is something analogous to it in what is called human creativity. We will study it more fully in another chapter, but in the present discussion of creation it is important to notice that the intrinsic evolutionary thrust of created reality finds distinctive expression in humans' ability to better human life by producing something truly new—in poetry, in art, in music, in social arrangements, in technological inventions, in generating a child. While many factors feed into the creative process, its heart lies in imagination, where insight and emotion, thought and affectivity intersect and interact. Study of the power of imagination will prove critical to the present reflection on the Holy Spirit because the traditions of Jewish and Christian belief have linked the Spirit with prophecy, that is, with insight and imagination that are central to human creation of the future.

8

The Power of Creativity

Humans can approach divine endowment and activity most strikingly in what is referred to as "creativity." The very term suggests that women and men are capable of actions similar to the divine creative action. Strictly speaking, of course, humans cannot "create," for they cannot bring something into existence out of nothingness—which is what divine creation is all about. Still, there is something of creation in the composition of a symphony or the painting of a great piece of art or the composition of an inspired poem. Though the "pieces"—of color or word or sound—that the artist uses already exist, in a work of art, an arrangement of these pieces that had not existed before comes into being and has a distinctive existence. Analogously, a breakthrough invention or a truly revolutionary restructuring of economy or society comes from a creative individual or group.

Though it can be recognized when it occurs, creativity remains somewhat mysterious and beyond purely theoretical explanation. An internet listing of studies about creativity reveals a flurry of interest in creativity among psychologists and psychiatrists, but the interest extends to creativity in business, governmental structures, educational techniques, and even sports. Different as are these varieties of creativity, all coincide in examining the human power to imagine, that aspect of human consciousness that lies between the rational and the affective and influences both. Without imagination, there can be no thought; without imagination, there can be no desire; without imagination, humans could not anticipate and plan for the future, could not even think about the future, could have no linear notion of time. To arouse images in others is to "control" their thinking, stir their emotions, and prod their desires. For this reason, the ability to create and convey images is a source of unique power.

Inevitably, imagery is an intrinsic element in all human experiences; and the extent and intensity of one's power to imagine is a measure of the vividness and richness of one's experiencing. The further ability to convey imagery is a measure of the power to share life by bringing about vicarious experience in another. When the playwright presents a sequence of images of seeing and hearing, he or she allows the audience to experience the "history" of the play's characters. With more "static" imagery, the poet uses images to lead the reader to metaphorical insights that draw from the reader's previous experiences, give them new meaning, and lead to "dreams" about future experience. In a more mysterious process, the musical composer taps into the sound imagery of others to affect their emotions. Because true creativity is rather rare and be- cause great artists are "born, not made," the artist has often been seen as inspired. Geniuses speak of their muse, an inspiration that enables the artist to produce when the muse is present; but in the absence of this muse, the creative process is thwarted. In the religious sphere, such inspiration is be- lieved to occur in charismatic prophecy; but in this case, the "muse" is God's own Spirit. The prophetic oracle is inspired; the written canonical text, along with the author of that text, is believed to be inspired and therefore "word of God."[1] The prophecy of Joel (the text quoted by Peter in Acts 2) links the Spirit's inspiration with human imagining when it "predicts" that in the day of the Lord, because of the "Spirit poured out on all flesh," young and old, slave and free, women and men, will "dream dreams." Filled with God's eschatological Spirit, believers will be capable of imagining a future that is truly new and therefore be the agents for creating the future as reign of God. In our own day, Vatican II has spoken of the Christian community as a prophetic people and in "Gaudium et spes" ("The Church in the Modern World") has spelt out the ways in which Christians are meant to be agents for creating a truly human future.

A dream of a new humanity, however, is not always one that proceeds from the Spirit of God. The twentieth century, for example, has witnessed the power of a dream in the struggle of Gandhi to free his people from colonial domi- nation. But it has witnessed also the seductive dream of Nazism, a dream that Germany would become the "new Roman Empire" dominating a world without Jews. And the nurturing of that latter dream by Nazi propagandists is a textbook case of using symbolic imagery to create the ideology and control the behavior of an entire nation.

Not all "social engineering" is as blatant as that in Germany of the 1930s. There is a common and subtle process by which cultures, through their ideological use of imagery, create the definition of what it means to be human. Probably the most basic and most influential instance of such social construction of reality is the differentiation of humans as "masculine" or "feminine." It is instructive to notice the way in which the original Christian egalitarianism of Galatians 3:28 is quickly blunted by Greco-Roman strident sexism, slowly reasserts itself to some extent during feudalism, only to be negated again by the reintroduction of classical culture in the twelfth century and later by the demands of industrial and commercial structures. Today, there still function powerful socially constructed images of a "real man" or a "real woman," though shifting imagery (e.g., of professional women athletes) is causing a changing view of women and men in relation to one another.

Theological Reflection

Creating "reality" by use of imagery has its religious applications as well. Pictures of Jesus or of Christian saints have shaped countless Christians' "understanding" of these individuals. Images of the Vatican or of the Pope, whether immediately observed or seen in the media, are a powerful influence on many people's notion of the Church. An interesting illustration of this occurred a few years ago at a national conference of the Call to Action. One of the principal speakers, whose topic was contemporary views of Mary, the mother of Jesus, distributed just prior to the talk a picture of Mary as a woman of fifty to sixty years in age. The impact of this picture was palpable. Most of those in attendance had had their understanding of Mary shaped by pictures of her as a very young adult, dressed in a blue gown, and so forth; and this picture of her as a real middle-aged woman came as a bit of a shock—a healthy shock, I hasten to add.

However, the power of imagery to create the "reality" of religious faith goes much deeper. The notion of God as trinitarian possessed by most, if not all, Christians has probably been influenced more by portrayals of three "divine persons" in Renaissance paintings or medieval stained glass than by the creedal statements of Chalcedon. Christology has been radically structured by Christian imagination placing the risen Christ "up in heaven," and connected with this the images of a heavenly home to which good people will pass after death.

Such images are not false; their origin in large part is biblical. However, the misleading influence they have comes because they are not recognized as metaphors for what is unimaginable but are, rather, taken as "real." It is easy to forget Paul's statement that "[i]t has not entered into the human mind what things God has prepared for those who love God" (I Cor. 2:9–10).

It is instructive to examine the function of images in the traditions of Israel, to see how they shaped the people's understanding of their God, of that God's activity of revealing self in the course of their history, and of themselves as "the chosen people." The images attached to the narrative of the exodus, of the gradual conquest of "the promised land," of David's founding of Jerusalem as his capital, and the image of the Temple as the dwelling place of Yahweh— these were at the very heart of Israelite understanding of Yahweh. One can construct the entire history of Israelite growth in religious faith, from the primitive beliefs of a wandering group of migrants to the more mature insights of a Deutero-Isaiah during Babylonian exile to wisdom reflection in some of the later Psalms, by tracing the development of key images for God.[2] Biblical thought, though obviously not irrational, transcends the purely rational by the use of images. Israel's great charismatic prophets were Israel's great poets. Still, Israel's justified fear of misleading imagery was enshrined in the second commandment: You shall not make graven images.

A clear witness to the power of images is the challenge presented by prophetic imagery to official employment of imagination as legitimation of authority. Much like other rulers, the kings of Judah and Israel tried to create a view of themselves as powerful leaders and possessors of ultimate authority by displaying wealth and military strength. Such justifying images of themselves as kings were supported by adding to the ancient view of God as Yahweh Sabaoth, Lord of armies, the notion of Yahweh as king. At least to some extent, this represented the kings' exploitation of the divinely given Mosaic Law, using the Law for their royal advantage rather than as an instrument of bettering the life of the people. Countering the dangers of this royal image for God, the eighth-century prophets introduced the husband-wife imagery, the picture of Yahweh as a loving but betrayed God, though still a Law-giving God. But the Law itself now underwent a basic shift as in its Deuteronomic formulation it began with the precept: "You shall love the Lord, your God."

Christian mystical experience reflects the inadequacy and distortion intrinsic to human imagining of the divine. Images cannot possibly portray the reality of God; to mistake and accept them for "reality" is the essence of idolatry. So those whose personal relationship with God deepens through a life of contemplation are forced at some point to abandon imagery about God—in the "dark night of the senses." The divine presence to which they are directly exposed is radically incompatible with the limitations intrinsic to any image. Religious images, even the most accurate, can do no more than point to what they cannot portray. That is not to deny the value, even the need, for the sensible images in which divine revelation is communicated—such denial is the heresy of iconoclasm. But the monastic theologians who defended the images against iconoclastic Byzantine emperors were also theologians who espoused apophatic theology.

Creativity, however, finds multiple expressions outside the realm of either art or religion. Today, as we have seen, there is discussion in almost every area of human life of a paradigm shift that is directing humanity toward a new and only vaguely foreseen future. The question is: what is the source of such a reorientation of human thought? And the response must include the human capacity to imagine possibilities that have not yet been actualized. This implies several things: (1) The imagining of "the new" is to some extent a deep insight into the potential of the present. Here we are reminded that authentic prophecy is not prediction but rather an awareness of what the future could be on condition of certain human conversions. But we are reminded also that paradigm shifts of the kind we face are revolution and not simply reaction.[3] (2) The imagining connected with a true paradigm shift is inseparable from a degree of hope. Unformulated though it may be, allowing oneself to accept the uncertainties involved in a shift from the familiarity of what has been does demand a trust that something better can come to be. (3) As Hans Kung has pointed out, the search for a new paradigm comes often as a response to a crisis, to a situation in which "the old way" has clearly collapsed and only a radical change can bring salvation.[4] But this implies that reason-guided search can at times, perhaps often, trigger creative imagination. One might go even farther and suggest that the desire to "solve a problem" that drives so much scientific and technological inventiveness and the methodology employed in previous problem solving become part of the process of creative imagination. (4) Some of imaginative creativity occurs in a group of people and not just in individual geniuses. Moreover, it occurs often over a long period of germinating, even though the breakthrough realization of shift may be sudden.

All this can throw light on the function of God's Spirit in history, especially its role in prophetism. It is in exposing the prophet to the unexpected "otherness" of the reality of God's self-revelation that God's self-revealing Spirit forces an abandonment of the regnant worldview and demands a shift from the status quo. The law *ecclesia semper reformanda* must be extended to *fides semper reformanda*. The worldview and ideology that have been guiding human social structures and activity are no longer a viable paradigm for the future. The "mind of God" translated into the process of "the reign of God" is the ultimate paradigm toward which successive paradigms for human life must move. God's Spirit is the eschatological impulse that drives human history toward its destiny as the achieved reign of God, a community of justice and peace.

It is important to remember that the divine creation of the new is not the destruction of the old but rather its transformation. It is for that reason that religious (and other) communities can develop traditions that honor both continuity and discontinuity. At times, elements that have been hidden or forgotten emerge transformed as part of the "new" vision. Understandings only vaguely grasped can gain new clarity as new contexts of "science" or new forms of experience throw light on them. But behind all this, the basic principle of continuity is the divine action of God's one Spirit. Ultimately, there is only one story, God's story.

One of the areas where honest creativity is most needed today is that of ethical judgments. Advances in science and technology have outstripped ethical reflection. Medical capabilities in particular have created both new opportunities for human betterment and questions about the moral acceptability of new procedures. Previous guidelines for acceptable application of new discoveries like DNA to genetic engineering are helpful but inadequate. Prolongation of human life far beyond what was possible just a few decades ago raises a host of questions about a person's choices regarding life and death. Much different but just as pressing are the issues concerning human labor in a new world of computerized automation and globalized trade.

At present, a great deal of the attempt to discover and apply appropriate ethical standards is framed in terms of debate: already existent rules and regulations are staunchly defended by those who insist on permanence of traditional moral standards; on the other hand, there is the pragmatic avenue of doing whatever works and seems to help people, even when this differs from previous ethical judgments. What is needed is more imaginative probing of the grounds of traditional reflection and more creative foresight into future developments and their applicability to human life within the bounds of ethical demands.

In this somewhat ambiguous and uncertain reflection, the tension we have already discussed, that between law and Spirit, is relevant. As new situations emerge, laws and regulations attempt to cope with the unprecedented potential and threat, to safeguard the one and avoid the other. However, the impulse of the Spirit working "instinctively" in the consciences of honest and informed persons will always extend beyond already existent laws and suggest unexplored paths of ethical behavior. This does introduce a certain element of relativity to ethical judgment and the danger of purely situational ethics, but the alternative appears to be a policy of "head in the sand." Unsettling though it be, there seems to be no avoiding "discernment of the Spirit" as ultimate law.

One aspect of Spirit as ultimate law reinforces the connection of Spirit with freedom and with creativity. To speak of the Spirit as divine force (which we have seen is basic biblical evidence) can create the image of the Spirit as an impelling, coercive power. Both the developing sequence of biblical thought and the testimony of mystics, however, indicate that it is more exact to speak of the Spirit's impulse as "invitation" to which humans must respond in free decision. Actually, such a view coincides with what I have earlier discussed about the creature as transcendental relation to the divine. Religiously, this impacts the debate about faith and good works, for it highlights the fact that the principal "good work" is to *accept* transformation/salvation by the power of God, to allow oneself to be saved. Moreover, it is in accepting the divine invitation that humans participate in the achievement of "the reign of God," in ministerial activity that is their "destined" role in human history.

9

The Power of Imagination

As we have seen in reflecting on creativity, the ability of humans to produce something truly new, to shape the future in ways different from the past, is rooted in the power of imagination. The need to examine further this intriguing human empowerment is specially relevant to this essay on power and God's Spirit because imagination plays an indispensable role in the enterprise of theology. As we have seen, theological reflection is grounded in the use of metaphor; without imagination, there could be no metaphor.[1] Even deeper is the connection of imagination to "spirit" in postmedieval philosophy. As the Romantic movement reacted to "scientific" attack on the notion of soul/spirit and to increased positivism in philosophical reflection on "the human," it was imagination that became the focus of attention. For poet/literary critics like Wordsworth and Coleridge, it was precisely the creative power of imagination that reflected humans' "spiritual" dimension.[2]

Most histories of theology or histories of the Church pay relatively little attention to the iconoclastic heresy that engaged Eastern Christianity in the eighth and ninth centuries.[3] Since as far back as Charlemagne, the West has tended to see iconoclasm as an odd and peripheral aberration, unaware of the central importance of the issues it raised and even unaware that it cropped up again in the Reformation struggles in Geneva in the sixteenth century. How could the question of icons and statues be considered to lie at the very center of Christian belief?

The response to this question is that the relationship between imagery and divine revelation takes definitive expression in the mystery of the Incarnation, the mystery in which the human, Jesus of Nazareth, embodies God's own revealing Word. As Roger Haight has detailed in his recent *Jesus, Symbol of God*, it is the very fact of human existing as spirit-manifested-in-body, that is, symbolic existing, that serves God's self-revealing intent.[4] So, it is not surprising that in the iconoclast debates the connection with Christology was immediately recognized by theologians like John Damascene.

Nor was the struggle over the images a purely theological debate. Instead, at the origin and the center of iconoclasm lay the power of images, the power to reinforce or to challenge the political regime of Byzantium. Study of this heresy points to the imperial effort to replace religious imagery with symbols of the emperor and his regime.[5] In the intertwined Church/State context of medieval Byzantium, the issue of imperial or ecclesiastical control was bound to be exacerbated by events and personages, as it was. What interests us here is the recognition of the sociopolitical influence exerted by symbols and the theological recognition that religious iconography is not to be confused with idolatry.

Basic to any study of the power of imagination is, of course, the understanding of what human imagination is. Without going into the different explanations given by philosophers, psychologists, and art/literary critics—and there have been many—there is a common understanding that between purely physical perception and human thinking there is a capacity to organize the manifold of sense impressions into a unified sense experience that involves sight and hearing and touch and smell. Besides this, there is the human ability to create images of what has never been, sometimes semiconsciously in dreams, sometimes in fully awake creation in painting, music, or practical inventiveness. *Homo faber* is an imagining being.

One can begin to appreciate the power of imagery to affect human experience when we reflect on the underlying images of time and space, which provide the context of consciousness that underlies all our experience of the world around us and of our location within that world.[6] The experience of living under a crystalline dome that would have prevailed at the time of Jesus was not that of existing in a "universe" constructed according to Ptolemaic astronomy, nor that of humans gradually growing accustomed to a Copernican heliocentric planetary system. In our own day the advances of astronomy have made us aware of the openness of space, but even that has been refined by the picture of earth taken from the moon, a picture of that blue marble floating unsupported and tiny in the vastness of space.

Kant's *Critique of Pure Reason* drew attention to the role of imagination in creating the subjective space/time construct in which all our experiencing takes place but did not point out the socio-cultural power of the manner in which we have assumed and still to a large extent continue to assume "space" to be a matter of up and down.[7] For centuries, the basic patriarchal culture has been embedded in this ladder imagery of reality, with "up" being seen as better than "down." God was "up in heaven," so prayers were directed upward, while "grace" and God's Spirit were imagined as descending. We have yet to see the radical shift in "power" that accompanies imagery of reality as "horizontal," with "community" and equality replacing patriarchal/hierarchical domination from above and replacing a social stratification that places important people "up" and the powerless "down." Apparently, such a radical shift to a horizontal image of "location" is today beginning to take place throughout the world, though the pace of shift is different from culture to culture.

Much of the power of this underlying imagery of space and time is tied to the fact that imagination is where sense perception and thought meet, where being spirit in the world is experienced in awareness of our bodiliness. How inextricably body and spirit meet at this juncture can be realized if one examines the extent to which a person's self-identity is linked with the image they have of their physical attractiveness. This has been tragically reflected in the destructiveness of current notions of what constitutes ideal weight for young women in our society. The ideal of an excessively slim body, proposed by TV and film, has led countless young women into anorexia/bulimia and resultant danger to their health. Strangely, an acceptable self-image seems to demand on the part of many women and men this unreasonable demand on their bodies. It is not just this extreme case—the billion-dollar cosmetic and weight-reducing industries testify to the extent to which millions of people depend upon beauty-enhancing products to bolster their self-image.

Perhaps the most basic and important aspect of imagination's power, more important even than its power to influence thought, is the fact that images lead to emotions, to passion, to affectivity, and then to action. Advertising agencies, preachers, politicians all work on the principle that "one picture is worth a thousand words." There are many examples one could give of this, but a frightening instance (to which I referred briefly earlier) was the clever and effective use of imagery as a propaganda device during the Nazi regime in Germany.

The huge gathering of the "faithful" in the Nuremberg stadium at the high point of Nazi domination of the country exemplified this. As the ceremony began, row after row of black-uniformed SS troops marched into the stadium carrying Nazi flags but carrying also standards that were a study in creative use of symbolism. The standards were like those used by the legions of Rome with one exception: the SPQR ("the senate and the Roman people") emblazoned near the top of the Roman standards was replaced by the swastika. The implication was subtle but powerful and reinforced the official rhetoric about the Third Reich as the new Roman Empire. To control images is to control thinking, emotions, affectivity, and action; it is the power to rule.

The movie "El Norte" that describes the tragic illegal immigration of a young brother and sister begins with a scene in Guatemala. Gathered together in the "kitchen" of a peasant home, a group of women page longingly through a well-worn U.S. mail order catalogue. How wonderful life must be in the great country to the north where each home has a refrigerator and dishwasher and microwave oven—to say nothing of the clothes and furniture and so forth. Half comical and yet half tragic, the scene illustrates the pervasive influence of advertising in today's world. In cultures worldwide, not just in the United States, it is difficult to find a more effective use of power than in the advertising industry. Aided incredibly by the advent of TV and the internet, which harness the motivational power of images, modern advertising leads people to decisions they would not even have considered previously and in many cases should not be making now. Advertising seeks to convince people that they need the advertised product or at least that life would not be complete without it.

Much the same goes on—and has for centuries—in bazaars or stores worldwide. Merchants use whatever means they can devise to make their merchandise so attractive that prospective buyers cannot resist. Instinctively, they are depending on what is basic to humans' nature: the attraction to what is perceived as desirable. So fundamental is the power of what is attractive that without it all human activity would cease. Not surprisingly, human reflection has for centuries pondered the character and the function of "the good": What is "the good"? How can it be attained? What things qualify as truly good? Linked with these questions have been the problems associated with human freedom. How free are people to seek the true good? What psychological dynamics and social location condition people's perception of "good"? What is meant by "free will"?

However, the power of images should not be focused on the exploitation of imagery like that just mentioned. On the contrary, imagination's expression in the arts has been an almost limitless spring of human refinement. Painting and sculpture have over the centuries brought to humans' attention the beauty of nature and especially the beauty of the human body. So also, in modern times, have films, television, and photography drawn humans into a deeper insight into their world, made them aware of both the joys and the anguish of human lives. The visual arts, when truly art, have perhaps more than any other influence helped to interpret the erotic dimension of reality and contributed to humans' attaining some measure of maturity in the area of sexuality.

Even more powerful than the visual arts in arousing human emotions and shaping human attitudes has been dance, more powerful but also more ambiguous. Humans have danced from time immemorial; dance may be the most ancient form of art. And dance has always carried with it powerful symbolic meaning. Traditional folk dances with their narrative overtones, ballet with its more sophisticated use of the human body to provide patterns of beauty in living and moving sculpture, modern dance that dramatizes and enhances music—all portray the power of human bodily beauty to move the spirit. But not all dance is artistic and positive in its effects; there is also dancing that is erotically suggestive, dancing that is meant to work people into frenzies of violence and hatred, dance that is demeaning and ugly.

Most mysterious in the realm of the arts is the power of music.[8] Nothing is a clearer reflection of human distinctiveness than the creation of music. Why music should so profoundly touch the human spirit is inexplicable, but it does. The film *The Mission*, which is based on actual happenings, shows how the Jesuit missionaries, hoping to evangelize the native people in what today is Paraguay, faced the dangerous encounter with the natives, whose language they did not yet understand, and created a bridge of understanding and acceptance through music. Quite different, though just as important, is the power wielded by MTV on the younger generations today. Its melding of music with visual imagery has created a culture whose perspective and values have had worldwide symbolic impact.

More pervasive even than human creations of beauty is the beauty of nature that still surrounds many people and enriches their lives, even when they scarcely or never advert to it. It is one of the worrisome features of human life today that with increased flight of people to some megalopolis, hundreds of millions no longer have the experience of nature, of its beauty, or of the profound effects it can have on the human psyche. What is the life of imagination and of the thoughts and feelings that flow from it for people who never see stars or butterflies or budding trees in spring?

Power of Beauty

Still, beauty is experienced to some degree by all humans, able to be shared with others, able to be created by art, but almost impossible to explain. Art critics or teachers in art classes can talk about beauty, in limited fashion explain works of art or music and why they are beautiful, but awareness and appreciation of what is beautiful can come only with developed aesthetic sensitivity. Capacity for aesthetic experience is linked with a person's overall refinement and "spirit." This has been recognized for centuries; whether one examines Longinus's treatise *On the Sublime*, Aristotle's *Poetics*, Ruskin's *Modern Painters*, or more recently Malraux's *Voices of Silence*, one can notice the same interplay between the beauty inherent in what is and the ability (or inability) of humans to discern and feel this beauty.[9]

Philosophical reflection on beauty has highlighted the close link of "the beautiful" to "the good." In metaphysical terms, they are practically interchangeable as transcendental aspects of being. Yet, there is a dimension of beauty that seems to defy inclusion within the boundaries of moral goodness. There are cases of great artists, like Gauguin or Wagner, for whom ordinary humans standards of moral behavior, especially in sexual matters, did not seem to apply. It was not only they who made such a judgment; common opinion, without judging such behavior to be good, also either accepted or was puzzled by the fact that artistic genius seemed to exempt one from ordinary moral strictures. Artistic genius provides a distinctive authority to express what it means to be a good human. This could be seen as an unusual instance of the tension between spirit and law.

Perhaps some of the reason for this strange judgment is that true art in its various forms has power to express and uplift the human spirit. This power builds on the power of beauty inherent in nature itself, reveals this beauty, draws attention to it, and in its own way enhances it. While a developed aesthetic sense intensifies the effect of beauty on a person, a certain level of beauty's uplifting affects even the dullest spirit. Music in particular has this ability; as the adage goes: "music has power to tame the savage breast."

In the daily battle of humans to overcome evil influences in "the world," beauty has a liberating role. There is an inexplicable pull (concupiscence?) toward what can be broadly termed "temptation," a fascination with the prospect of dangerous experimentation with life outside boundaries, a "hope" to avoid the responsibilities that beauty and law lay on one, an attraction to the vulgar and demeaning. Beauty challenges and overcomes this tendency to be untrue to oneself as spirit and to avoid maturity. While one can encounter such redeeming beauty in the arts and in nature's reflection of the creator's beauty, it is chiefly in relationships with people who are beautiful and mature as persons that vulgarity is experienced as undesirable and unattractive. As we will see in a later chapter, this is part of the power of love.

Theological Reflection

When we turn to theological reflection on religious imagery, we are faced with one of the more intriguing and little studied aspects of theological method. It is only recently that we have begun to appreciate the theological insights provided by the arts. I remember years ago, on the occasion of a conference at Marquette University on theology and the arts, an artist who was one of the participants correcting those of us who had—rather progressively, we thought—suggested that the arts could be helpful adjuncts to theology. Her remark: "To paint is to do theology."

Surprisingly, it is also a recent phenomenon that we have seen artistic use of imagery as a resource for studying the process of divine revelation or studying the historical evolution of a community's faith. Actually, careful investigation of the Bible makes it clear that tracing the development of key biblical images provides unique entry into the religious journey of the people who produced the Bible.[10] One might say that use of images to convey the belief and religious experience of the Israelite/Jewish community is the basic methodology that characterizes and links Israel's theologians. Israel's religious reflection is not so much philosophical as it is poetic—not surprising, because Israel's great prophets, they through whom the Spirit of prophecy worked to lead the people toward deepened insight into the mystery of God, were also Israel's greatest poets. That is not to say that the thinkers of Israel did not wrestle with the most profound questions faced by philosophy. They did indeed confront the same questions about humanity's existence, character, and destiny, but they did so with metaphor rather than logical categories, which means that their explanations were symbolic and open to unlimited depth of meaning. One can only speculate about the immense power that was exercised over centuries by Hosea's use of marital imagery to depict Yahweh's relationship with the people. There can be little doubt that it helped bring about a revolution in the people's thinking about their God, a revolution that led to the Deuteronomic revision of the Law itself. Through imagination's role in the religious experience of the people, the divine Spirit of prophecy worked to inject into Israel's understanding of its relationship to Yahweh the awareness of a personal bond of friendship. What implication would recitation of the Shema have had over the centuries if there were not implicit in it the Hosean imagery?

Using iconography as a resource in theologizing about the historical development of Christianity is only in its infancy; but it is already proving itself as a method. Studying the great medieval theologians like Aquinas or Bonaventure or Hugh of St. Victor allows us to glimpse the action of God's Spirit in the faith of that period. Reflecting about the influence on people's relationship to God that was exerted by the windows of Chartres Cathedral may lead us even deeper into the religious experience of that age. What would be theologically invaluable, if it were possible, would be to recreate more fully the sensible surroundings that provided the context for Christians' experience of encountering God in their eucharistic gathering.[11] Père Chenu has detailed the way in which the Middle Ages were a time of symbolic existing and pointed to the power that images had to shape the entire culture.[12]

The deepest levels of imagery's effect on Christian theology pertain, of course, to the rich symbolism of human bodiliness as that relates to the mystery of the Incarnation. Christian belief that Jesus of Nazareth embodied in his human existing God's own self-revealing Word draws into itself all that I have said earlier about the symbolic power of human bodiliness. From the very beginning of Christianity, there have been attempts to avoid the bodily dimensions of this belief. Docetism and Gnosticism tried to reduce the divine intervention in Jesus to a purely spiritual action. But the Christian Scriptures are unwavering in their insistence: "the Word was made flesh." Jesus' own bodiliness and his concern for the bodily well-being of others were intrinsic to the divine revelation that he was. Some religions have viewed the world as the dance of the divine; Christianity might add that Jesus was the dancer par excellence. Christology absorbs and deepens all the imagination-based insights of the Hebrew Bible.

So strong was the Jewish understanding of bodiliness being intrinsic to human existing that when attempting to grasp the implications of Jesus' resurrection, St. Paul could only describe humans' sharing in risen life in terms of a "risen body," a spiritual body. In some unfathomable way, the salvation of humans absorbs the salvation of their bodiliness; but the nature of this salvation remains beyond understanding. Paul himself acknowledged this when in I Corinthians 2:9 he cites Isaiah 64:4: "What no eye has seen, nor ear has heard, nor the human heart has conceived, God has prepared for those who love him." Popular notions of a final "rising from the dead" when earthly bodies will be restored do not stand up to careful reflection, but the question remains: what then is involved in Christian faith in resurrection? No doubt it has something to do with Christian belief that one does not lose individual identity with passage into afterlife; but what replaces the function of earthly bodiliness in establishing individuality is a great unknown. Christians, like others, must live in hope.[13]

In the vision of Luke, the Spirit's "creation" of Jesus' humanity and ministry continues in the Pentecost mystery of the Spirit's creating, animating, empowering, and sustaining the Christian people. Like Jesus himself, Christians have the prophetic mission of manifesting to the world the God revealed in Jesus; they are a prophetic community. Acts 2, describing the Spirit's empowerment of Jesus' first disciples, clearly sees the Spirit's activity in terms of the effect on human imagining. Referring to the prophecy of Joel, Peter says that the Spirit will lead young and old, women and men, to dream dreams. Dreaming, whether it occur in humans asleep or awake, is a matter of images, images of things yet to be, at the root, therefore, of creating the future. Dreamers may not often be thought of as powerful, but their dreaming has the power to shape history. Such dreaming is a sacramental manifestation of the eschatological Spirit's embrace of human history.

PART IV

Symbol

At first glance, it might seem that turning from the power of office to the power of nature and then to the power of symbols represents a complete shift of perspective. However, recent study of the public impact of symbolism and in particular of language makes it clear that these two aspects of power are inseparably intertwined. Still, the distinctive nature of symbolism's power requires a separate consideration. That will be the purpose of this unit, which begins with a longer essay on the power of word/symbol and then continues with chapters on the power of thought and of ritual. Situating reflection on imagination in the previous unit so as to connect it with creativity was arbitrary since it could just as easily have been part of this present unit. As will be indicated in the book's conclusion, such overlap points to the integrating influence of the all-encompassing Spirit of God.

IO

The Power of Symbol/Word

Few, if any, periods in history have seen as much interest in and reflection about words as today. This is not confined to the technical discussion of literary critics, sociologists, or philosophers. Newly developed communications media and commercial dependence upon advertising have amplified the power of words to influence minds and decisions. Words, however, are only one facet of the broader issue of the character and power of symbols, and study of language is but one element in current examination of symbols' role in relating humans to reality.

Interest in symbols is, of course, nothing new. Plato's wrestling with the relation of words to ideas, Pythagoras's interest in the nature and influence of numbers, and Aeschylus's dramatic questioning about the deeper significance of human activity have continued to be influential over the centuries. Medieval culture, as Chenu has so brilliantly described,[1] was fascinated by the symbolic aspect of experience; people of that epoch lived in a world of symbols. Still, with modernity and the seminal influence of Immanuel Kant, a new phase of the study of symbols has emerged.

Kant can be read as a step in the refinement of Plato that has led in some instances of contemporary postmodern thought to a practical denial of any reality beyond individual opinion, an intersection of interpretations.[2] What the *Critique of Pure Reason* did, in effect, was to take a major step beyond the regard for symbolism that had preceded it. Whereas medieval dealing with symbols had always presumed that there was a reality that was being symbolized, a hidden *res* being revealed in the sacramentum, Kant's phenomenal world tended to substitute for, even bar, cognitive contact with the "world beyond." Developed to provide a criterion of certitude for Newtonian physics, Kantian thought provides equation between knowledge and the world known by regarding the scientific knowing itself as "the world."

However one wishes to interpret Kant, it is difficult to deny the immense influence he has had in drawing attention to the process of symbolizing. Freud's work on the interpretation of dreams as key to the "reality" of a person's psychic existence is one example of this influence. Another is the Neo-Kantian philosophical school, whose proponents like Ernst Cassirer and Suzanne Langer have spelled out the symbol-making character of human nature and laid the ground for more recent study of the creative dimension of human experience.³ Most recently, the debates, in both social sciences and linguistic analysis, between structuralism and deconstructionism, between Enlightenment liberalism and social construction theories of human society, illustrate the not-too-successful attempt to deal with the Kantian heritage and move into a period of true postmodernism. Perhaps most important, the Kantian perspective led to the focus on methodology that has for several decades absorbed technical discussion in practically all disciplines of knowledge.

All this ferment bears witness to the immense power of symbols in human experience. While it is obvious that symbols of various kinds have always been and are still employed to express human thoughts, emotions, and intentions, we have become increasingly aware of the power of symbols to create the reality of human experience. We experience what we think is happening, and symbols play a key role in interpreting this. One could say that the central purpose of education, especially higher education, is to help a person develop a more accurate hermeneutic of experience, a mastery of the symbolic structures that constitute methodologies like psychology or sociology, which make one critically aware of the symbols that enter into experience.

Not only do symbols function to shape one's understanding of one's self and the surrounding world, but they are also a powerful force to shape desires and decisions. No one knows this better than those who devise the advertisements that convince people that they need what they really don't. As we saw earlier, the creative power of symbols can be misused, as it was by the Nazis during the Hitler era. More than one civil power has legitimated itself by relating its ideology to the regnant symbols of a culture. One of the most instructive instances of this occurred in the ninth century when the iconoclastic Byzantine emperors sought to replace icons of Christ and the saints with imperial symbols.⁴

Of the various symbols that both express and create human experience, ✶ language clearly holds a primacy. Clarifying this fact has been one of the more important contributions of recent philosophy and behavioral science. In a true sense, it can be said that for one to exist humanly is to use words. As one develops in infancy toward formalized thinking, it is the words of one's mother tongue that structure experiences and shape thinking; and this process continues throughout one's life as the character of new discoveries is described by words. Possession of a broad vocabulary and exposure to more than one language enable this describing to be more subtle and more accurate.

Modern times have dispelled some of the ancient belief in the magical power of certain words or formulae, but there still remains a certain magical aura to language. No longer is there the old feeling that somehow the proclamations and commands of a ruler embodied and made present the power of that person, even if he was far away; but there is an awe that attaches to the statements of those in high places, be he or she Pope or President—or TV pundit. One ancient belief, however, has found no present-day parallel (except perhaps in the novels of C. S. Lewis): the power intrinsic to a person's name. To invoke the name of a powerful person like a king was to tap into the power exercised by that person. This was even more the case when one in religious ritual used the name of some divinity. An instance of this in Christian ritual is baptizing in the name of the Father, Son, and Holy Spirit—"in the name of" implies "through the power of," that is, the power of God is made present and effective through the invocation of the name.

Linked with the power of a person's being present in their name was the iconic presence of such power in an image. While we are most familiar with that notion when it is exemplified in the religious icons that play such a prominent role in Byzantine art and religion, it lay behind the use of a ruler's image on the coinage used during or after his or her rule. In more modern times, a ruler's image on coins or postage stamps no longer carries the depth it formerly possessed, but it still functions to reinforce the assumption of that ruler's power.

One of the most important cases of such iconic presence has had to do with the manner in which the consecrated bread from Mass and the eucharistic action itself became static objects of veneration. Rather than Eucharist being for people an experienced ritual that transformed those attending, it became a spectacle performed by an ordained celebrant and observed by the congregation. Obtained through the "transubstantiating" act in the Mass, the consecrated host was then enshrined visibly in a monstrance so that it could function symbolically to make Christ present as the object of adoration.

Another aspect of the power attached to words is the connection of language to thought. Present-day studies of child psychology detail the way in which the proliferation of sense experiences is given patterning and intelligibility through the infant's being taught to identify "objects" through naming them.[5] Ancient philosophy laid the groundwork for such views by intimately linking words and rationality. Greek thinkers and their Roman successors used the same word *logos* to signify both word and reason. There was no more prominent nor basic term/idea in Greek thought, especially in Platonism and Stoicism, than *logos*; it was considered the ordering principle in language, thought, morality, and even the world of nature. But neither human life nor nature itself was completely reasonable, so *logos* personified in Apollo was traditionally matched with "disorderly" spirit (*thumos*) personified in Dionysius.

Still another aspect of words' power that is clear even in today's use of language is the ability to create "reality." Though it does not bear the implication of basic physical creation that one finds in Israel's prophetic tradition (which we will examine shortly), use of words is causative of social reality. Attaching certain terms to people or movements gives them the identity that functions in people's estimation of them. To refer to a group of persons seeking their rightful political independence as "revolutionaries" immediately arouses images of gun-toting terrorists and judgments that they are undisciplined and dangerous. Feminist scholars have studied the manner in which use of masculine pronouns in a generic sense has subtly but effectively created the notion that men are superior and the norm of humanity.[6] In today's political climate, the word "liberal" has power to influence popular opinion and elections. Social construction of reality is a widespread and verified phenomenon, and use of language is at the heart of the process.[7]

Hugh Duncan, in his *Symbols and Society*, describes the function of certain basic symbols as the "engines" driving and shaping cultures. Imagery plays a major role in this symbolic underpinning of a given culture, and to a large extent these images are given shape and impact through the classical literature of that culture. However, there is a pervading notion that the power of this literary use of words comes not only from the words as such, but also from the author's inspiration. Secular explanations attribute this inspiration to an author's muse; a religious interpretation of sacred literature is that the text is attributable to inspiration by God's Spirit and is therefore "word of God."

Certain key words, like the "Liberté, Fraternité, Egalité" used by the French revolution, have played and still continue to play a powerful role in creating a Zeitgeist. Clever propagandists, like the Nazis in the 1930s, have learned how to extend this into a few slogans that influence profoundly the attitudes and worldview of entire populations. In a somewhat more limited and specified way, effective advertising accompanies images with slogans such as, "A meal without meat means nothing to eat."

Modern philosophies of language and socio-psychological studies of culture have uncovered the power of words to shape thought and activity and human existence more broadly. In the past few decades, considerable attention has been given to the power of narrative, to those accounts, fictional or "historical," that individuals or groups use to give an account of themselves.[8] It is these narratives that provide, in concrete rather than abstract analytic fashion, the ideologies that pervade and influence a culture. All this suggests that they who master language have considerable power to master human life. There is considerable truth to the old adage "The pen is mightier than the sword."

Theological Reflection

Ancient Israelites were no exception to the centrality of "word" in their thinking and activity. At the same time, theologies of word take on a distinctive character in Israelite faith. While there unquestionably was some influence coming from surrounding cultures, especially from Egypt with its strongly magical understanding of language's effect, there is little if any indication that Israel's concept of "word" resembled or was affected by the Greek perspective, at least until the wisdom literature. No doubt, in the period prior to written accounts of its origins, oral traditions were cherished and effective in shaping and preserving the covenant people. Already then the word/commands of their god, Yahweh, were viewed as carrying authority and power. However, it was with the great prophetic movements of the eighth to fifth centuries that a formal and sophisticated theology of Yahweh's word was created. Isaiah 55 (from the period of exile) reflects in a few lines the sequence of thought on "word." Centuries before, Elijah had dramatically preached that Yahweh, not the Baal, provided the rain that brought needed life to the earth and its crops. Now in Deutero-Isaiah, God's *word* is seen as the power that sources all life. This is not a new insight, for already with Jeremiah and Ezekiel the word, Yahweh's word on the lips of the prophet, was believed "to build or destroy, to plant or uproot" (Jer. 1).

At the same time, a parallel thought development was happening in the priestly tradition. Perhaps connected with the view that the Jerusalem temple was an oracular situation with privileged priestly proclamation parallel to that of the prophets, a theology of the word emerged that controled the priestly description of creation. Deceptively simple in form, the account of creation at the beginning of Genesis is noticeably sophisticated when compared with other ancient creation myths. There is no slaying of monsters or gods emerging from the primitive mud, not even the anthropomorphic shaping of things that one finds in the Jahvistic account of Genesis 2–3. Instead, the divine action is simply one of speaking, of command. Yahweh's word is the power at the heart of the world's existence.

Even though the later strata of Second Temple Jewish thought center on the influence of divine Wisdom and especially on that Wisdom as expressed in the Law, this does not imply the loss of insight into the power of the divine word. Wisdom needs to be taught, indeed, Wisdom herself is imaged as a teacher, and the Law needs to be proclaimed and scribally explained. So, words remain the power that shapes the faith and ritual and religious practice of Judaism and that the Jews believe to be the power that creates and sustains all that exists.

 However—and this is crucial for the thesis of this book—"word" never functions apart from "spirit." In oversimplified fashion, one could say that Spirit is the power within word that brings to being what word states. Prophets are the privileged bearers of Yahweh's Spirit; moved by God's Spirit, they see visions and speak for God. That Spirit continues to work in the schools of prophecy that finally produce the biblical collections of prophetic tradition, which means that these writings are "inspired word of God." So intimate is the relationship of word and Spirit that in the wisdom writings one can almost identify Wisdom and Spirit; God's influence on human life is the divine self-communication in sharing Wisdom and Spirit.

Roughly parallel to other ancient literature, the "classics" of Israelite/Jewish writings that constitute the Hebrew Bible are viewed as inspired writing. However, the character of their "inspiration" is distinguished by the attribution of that inspiration to Yahweh's Spirit. The effectiveness of that writing comes not from its literary effect, though Israel's prophets are also its great poets, but from the transforming power of God's Spirit communicated through word.[9] Moreover, in one way or another, the word of Yahweh continues always to be what it was at the very beginning, a word of command requiring a basic conversion of the people's life.

Word and Spirit in Early Christology

Christian Scriptures not only inherit the Jewish outlook on God's Spirit, but their depiction of Jesus of Nazareth devotes even greater and more explicit attention to the Spirit. Within a century of Christianity's beginning, the focus of Christology, under the influence of the Johannine prologue and Greek philosophical fascination with Logos, will shift almost exclusively to Christ as incarnate Word. This theological focus on Word will continue to characterize Christian understanding of Jesus up to the present time, especially in the West. Initially, however, this was not the case, so much so that an argument can be made—and is now being made by some theologians—that "incarnation" can be applied to both the Word and the Spirit.[10]

Luke's theology in particular, though not exclusively, speaks of the Spirit's role from beginning to end in the life and career of Jesus. This is, of course, inseparable from Luke's theological explanation of Jesus as the eschatological prophet. Even before Jesus enters the scene in Luke's narrative, the Spirit is mentioned as inspiring Zachary, then Mary and Elizabeth, then Simeon and Anna, and finally John the Baptist. Jesus is led by the Spirit to baptism by John, then led into the desert to be tried, then led out of the desert "in the power of the Spirit" to begin his prophetic ministry. Empowered by the Spirit, he is able to teach with authority and to heal—in fulfillment of Isaiah 61, which speaks about the eschatological prophet of Wisdom ("The Spirit of the Lord is upon me . . ."). Though in different ways, he can be said to embody both the divine Word and the divine Spirit.

One aspect of this link of Jesus and Spirit may need to be emphasized, for it has received little attention in the discussion up to this point. Not only is Jesus empowered by the Spirit; he is *as embodied Word* the agent for the communication of God's Spirit to others. To reveal the God he knows as Abba is automatically to communicate Abba's Spirit, the mind, the will, of God. In a certain sense, there is greater ultimacy to Spirit; communication of Spirit reaches deeper than communication of word. In his prophetic ministry, Jesus desires to bring the spirit of his hearers into agreement with the Spirit of God. This is the final stage of their conversion, not only conversion of understanding but also conversion of heart. The Spirit that Jesus conveys is the Spirit of truth and God's profoundly loving will and command.

Word and Spirit in Early Christianity

Though Jesus' own prophetic activity remains paradigmatic for Christian ministry, prophecy did not cease in the community of disciples at Jesus' death. Acts 2 suggests just the opposite. Quoting the prophecy of Joel, Peter is described saying that from now on the prophetic Spirit will be poured out on all, young and old, women and men, slave and free. This Pentecost event is the last stage in Luke's unfolding journey-narrative that began with the scene of the Transfiguration. On the "mountain top," Jesus is enveloped by the bright cloud, symbol of the Spirit; and thus "reempowered" by the Spirit of his baptism, he sets out on his exodus during which he teaches the new Torah. Arrived at the final promised land of resurrection, having remained faithful to the indwelling Spirit despite the "temptation" of death, he shares this Spirit to empower the community for its proclamation of the word.

Conscious that a treasure, longed for from generations past, was theirs in the experience of Christ and the Spirit, Christians from the beginning undertook the fundamental ministry of evangelization. Theirs it was to share, with all who would hear, the good news of a God who loved unconditionally, a God of compassion and forgiveness who shared with humans the divine creative Spirit that enabled them to reach their human destiny. Like the risen Christ in their midst, they were empowered to share with others the Spirit of truth and love that was God's own and theirs. They understood themselves moved by Christ's Spirit to do this.

Some would be specially anointed with this Spirit of prophecy, charismatic prophets in the midst of prophetic communities whose prophetic ministry they would enable. But this raised and raises certain questions that endure to the present. How is the community to discern the genuine prophetic voice? Is the prophetic charism attached to those holding ecclesiastical office, or perhaps to the office itself? Is selection for and ordination to official roles in the Church done by the Spirit, or perhaps endorsed by the Spirit in an ordination ritual? How are Christians to discern the "will of God" when a genuinely prophetic voice is in conflict with the authoritative voice of ordained officialdom? And does ritual anointing give special effectiveness to the words of the anointed when they evangelize (or pray) specifically because their words are "official"? For the most part, the historical record suggests that officialdom has generally won the argument, but it may be that it is not a debate to be won but a dialectic built into the very nature of the Christian community (and for that matter into human social existence), which can be "resolved" only by respectful and loving cooperation in community between both elements of the dialectic.

Medieval Symbolic Thought

Chenu's book on twelfth-century Europe, *Nature, Man, and Society in the Twelfth Century*, lays open the immense richness of medieval theology in that and the following century. The twelfth century still lived with the complex symbolism that marked the emergence of medieval culture, and its great classics, like Bernard of Clairvaux's commentary on the Canticle of Canticles, the visions of Hildegard of Bingen, or the *De Sacramentis* of Hugh of St. Victor, witness to the dominance and power of symbolic thought. So, too, do the great cathedrals like Chartres and Lincoln and their marvelous windows. However, by midcentury and then increasingly into the thirteenth and fourteenth centuries, another trend developed as a result of Aristotelian philosophy and Roman legal thought being "rediscovered." This meant a new respect for and employment of logic, epitomized in the brilliant career of Abelard (which aroused an instinctive negative reaction from Bernard), the beginning of search for empirical evidence, witnessed to by the experiments of Roger Bacon, and formalized legal training along with codification of laws at the universities of Padua and Bologna.

Thus began a centuries-long struggle between on the one hand the _symbolic/mystic consciousness_, which spoke of two great books that God had given humans, the book of scripture and the book of nature, both of which needed spiritual interpretation, and on the other hand _orderly rational thought_ which prized clarity and logical consistency. The continuing existence of the Bible as privileged guide of Christian faith and the celebration of sacramental liturgies as the structure of time meant that the defeat of symbol was far from total. Throughout the thirteenth century, the *explicatio sacrae paginae* would persist as the central task of the professor of theology. But ineluctably, the method of theology became more "scientific" until it was overtaken by nominalism in the fourteenth and subsequent centuries.[11] As for liturgy, neglect for the intrinsic symbolism of the ritual actions led to its being overshadowed by the more "intellectual" allegorical explanations that had already appeared in the Carolingian period.

Before leaving medieval developments, we need to ask an intriguing question respecting the view at that time of "word" and its power. As Aristotelian categories of "matter and form" were applied to explanation of sacramental rituals and their mode of instrumental causation of "grace," words were viewed as the "form" of the sacramental symbol.[12] That is to say, the words that made up the accepted sacramental formulation were the more important element of the symbol, the element that specified the character of the effect to be caused. Now the question: were ritual words seen to have such efficacy because they worked instrumentally (or semimagically) to bring mystery realities into existence, or was their effectiveness due to the fact that they spoke the faith of the celebrating community, a community living and acting by the power of the Spirit?

With the cultural move toward modernity, the balance between symbolism and rationality shifted increasingly toward the latter. In the period of medieval decline, this shift was abetted by the emptiness of much ritual performance. Even when sermons were given—and this was largely confined to the cities—

they tended to be scholastic preaching rather than homilies explanatory of the liturgical ritual and its incorporation of Scripture. Unaware of the intrinsic symbolic character of what was being enacted, most people attended the Eucharist as a cultural activity or out of fear of mortal sin or, if they were more devout, as an occasion on which they came into more familiar contact with Christ and gained grace. Liturgy ceased to be ritual that Christians performed and became increasingly a spectacle they witnessed. Still, a caution needs to be added: in the faith awareness of people, there remained a link of the Eucharist, the sacrifice of the Mass, with the atoning efficacy of Jesus' death. The allegorical interpretations themselves, despite their artificiality, focused on this link.

The sixteenth-century reaction to all this was mixed. Although Luther, himself a professor of Scripture, represented an attempt to recover the more symbolic, less abstract, theology of Gerson and the Cistercian writers, another wing of the Reformation headed toward increased rationalism. The chief proponent of this latter trend was Zwingli. His rejection of ritual and focus on preaching gave a primacy to word that gradually moved the Reformed tradition beyond Calvin's own scholasticism. Zwingli himself was not that extreme, but some of his allies in Zurich turned to actual iconoclasm, revealing the antisymbolic character of this starkly evangelical position.

In England, where the normal conduct of Christian life remained largely unchanged in Anglican circles, this was challenged by attempts to replace it with Reformed theology. In both camps, though, there was an underlying if reluctant respect for the ritual power of the Mass, a respect that expressed itself in the vicious attempts to uproot any Catholic celebration of the Eucharist. Ultimately, the strength of the Protestant party declined in England, but in Scotland, from John Knox onward, Reformed theology with its rejection of ritual and of symbols more broadly became solidly entrenched. In both situations, and on the continent as well, whatever remained of the symbolic world of medieval centuries would be profoundly undermined by the secular rationalism of the Enlightenment. Even when they continued to be performed in supposedly Catholic circles, as at the court of Louis XIV, sacramental liturgies were often little more than civic activities whose religious depth and ritual effectiveness were minimal. The Eucharist itself became a civic symbol. Among the ordinary faithful, especially in the countryside, the celebration of Eucharist remained an important religious act, but it was increasingly supplemented by a range of devotions, particularly to the Blessed Virgin. More than that, eucharistic devotion directed to the reserved species often overshadowed celebration of the Mass itself.

As positions hardened in post-Reformation debate, a false opposition of word to ritual came to be taken somewhat for granted. Catholicism was characterized as "sacramental" and opposed to the evangelical/biblical stress of Reformed churches; and on the other hand, the heirs of the Reformation concentrated more and more exclusively on the power of the biblical/preached word and regarded sacramental rituals as "idolatry." Such characterizations proved to be self-fulfilling. Use of and regard for the Bible declined in Catholic circles with the result that ritual's rooting in tradition was diminished, and in Reformation churches deprived of ritual the Bible itself became a sacramental icon.

None of these religious/theological developments would have occurred as they did if it had not been for the way that intellectual life developed in more secular contexts. Even though increasingly "secular" and "pagan," the Renaissance still retained much of the symbolic world of the Middle Ages. However, as it progressed and then gave way to modernity, what was regarded as "science" (i.e., mathematical mechanics) became more prominent, the Cartesian search for clear and distinct ideas dominated, mathematical precision became the ideal, and reason came to be "divinized." The triumph of word over spirit was apparently complete. Yet, Dionysius was not to be denied. Romanticism, sometimes formally antinomic as in Wagner and Nietzsche, arose to preserve spirit and symbol, poetry, and music. Along with it came "liberal Protestantism" with romanticized anthropology and sentimental understandings of religion. Against this humanistic Christianity, there emerged the revolt of Barth and dialectical theology.

It would be a caricature to reduce as complex a theology as Barth's to one central position, but certainly his understanding of Christianity focused on the word of God. To what extent Barth would exclude sacramentality from the interpretation of divine activity is not clear, but his view is definitely a "down from above" understanding. Salvation derives from the irruption into human history of God's word; reception and proclamation of that word is the basic responsibility of discipleship. It is ironic that Bultmann, whom Barth opposed because he considered him the heir of liberal Protestantism, also grounds his soteriology in the event of proclaiming and hearing the revealed word of kerygma.

To confront the supposed opposition of Protestant focus on word and Catholic focus on sacrament, Karl Rahner, in his essay "Word and Eucharist,"[13] developed a position that bypassed the classic problematic. In summary, it stated that revealed/biblical word and ritual proclaiming of that word were and had always been intrinsically inseparable. On the one hand, the Bible had grown out of and had been historically interpreted by Christian ritual. On the other hand, Christian ritual had always been a proclamation that drew from and cherished the tradition embodied in the Christian scriptures. Rahner's essay was a revolutionizing contribution, and though it did not deal with the underlying issue in terms of God's Spirit animating both Bible and liturgy, dynamically transforming both individuals and communities into Christians, it did the equivalent by linking the efficacious word of God and the operation of prevenient grace.

Central question of pneumatology

That is not to say that Rahner neglects the issue of pneumatology. His reconsideration of trinitarian theology was a major catalyst in moving Christian thought into a post-Chalcedonian context; and so necessarily, he raised questions about the prevalent understanding of the Holy Spirit as "a person."[14] He was aware of and involved in mid–twentieth-century debates about "proclamation theology," understood theology itself as a service to the proclaimed word, and accepted the transforming power of word and of grace. Still, his relating Spirit-power to Word-power remained undeveloped, though his theology invites such development.[15]

Theological Conclusion

If anything is clear about the biblical and traditional Christian understanding of God's word, it is that it is a word of power. It does instruct, it does comfort, but it goes beyond that; it creates. While the centuries of Christian experience of and reflection about this power have never denied the link with Spirit, deeper explanation of this link remains as a task for theology. But not only for theology: ultimately, insight into the reality of God's Spirit, precisely because it is spirit and not word, cannot come from word alone. It must come in experienced symbol activity, that is, in ritual. Until there exist ritual celebrations in which Christians become aware, in the lived symbolism of the action, of God's creative Spirit transforming them into community, neither the transforming character of God's Spirit nor the transforming character of God's Word can be known as they should because they are inescapably interdependent.

Thomas West has summarized this succinctly. "Shared meaning without power is simply agreement in belief. But communal life at its deepest is shared emotion and not just shared belief. This same emotion moved Christians to act in a certain way. To put it another way, it is the emotion and directive power of God's Word that binds Christians into community. This power is the Holy Spirit. It is no accident that through the centuries the Spirit has been closely linked with the formation of community and church."[16]

Communication to humans of divine selfhood, achieved in the mystery of God's Word embodied in creation and especially in Jesus of Nazareth, is a process of word-power. However, the very communication of this creative divine Word has as its objective to share with humans God's own Spirit, God's compassionate mindedness toward humans, God's love creative of their personhood. Proclamation of God's Word carries that Spirit and conveys it, or else it is spiritless and abstract "revelation" without power.

thought → interp. of symbol/word in social context →
→ perception of the desire object of. eros
→ control of imagination disempowers irrational fear
→ become the self-giving servant of love (nonviolence
disempowers force
+ physical strength)

II

The Power of Thought

Symbolism is inherent in each thing in the created universe, for each possesses meaning beyond itself. Discovering and clarifying that meaning comes through human thought that is therefore intrinsic to the power of symbol. The meaning of a given symbol and *thought* hence its power is dependent on the interpretation given it and the communication of this meaning. In religion, this is the power of exegesis and catechesis.[1] So also is the power of creative thinking that accompanies creative imagination and gives substance and context to it. Clearly, thought has had and still has the power to shape social structures, attitudes, and motivations. Therefore the need of "rulers," whether civic or religious, parental or pedagogical, to control or direct the thinking that can have such social impact.

While focus on "power" in study of human experience and specifically in study of human thought is quite recent, it has long been recognized that ideas are powerful. True, in more modern times, there have been a number of attacks on the "objectivity" of human knowing, questioning the power of knowing to bring humans in contact with "reality." More recently, attention has been drawn, particularly by Michel Foucault, to the extent to which power interests have shaped people's outlooks and attitudes. However, in its own way, such suspicion witnesses to the power exerted by thought in human affairs. At times, this power has been exaggerated, as it was in the illusion Plato had that philosophers should be kings—that is, that possession of knowledge was the essential endowment that equipped one to exert political power. At the same time, the wisdom movements that stretched from China to Greece, roughly a half millennium prior to the Common Era, realizing that <u>wisdom is more than knowledge alone,</u> recognized that understanding was an indispensable element in the processes of <u>judgment that eventuated in justice</u>—so Isaiah 7 and 11.

There is no need to make the argument that ideas are powerful. Thinking is basic to all human activity; people can only do what they are aware of doing. Even in the cases of psychological disturbance, thinking is taking place, though it be seriously misdirected. <u>If one can control another's thinking,</u> one can control that <u>person's actions.</u> This is the underlying assumption in all advertising, in governmental programs of propaganda and brainwashing, in newspaper editorials, in all debates about public policy.

Recognition of this ability of thinking to influence behavior is reflected in today's concern about and discussion of "the freedom of the press." If communications media—and in today's world, that means books, newspapers, radio, television, the internet—are controled so that information and opinions are limited to what is desired by governments or special interests, the very possibility of people making free decisions vanishes. One cannot choose what one does not know about. Despotic dictators do not wish their "subjects" having ideas of which they themselves do not approve, ideas that could prove to be subversive.

A broader assertion of this same reality is that <u>ideologies are basic to cultures.</u> In any culture, the processes and institutions of society are the expression of the worldview of people. Culture, of course, is always complex; many different kinds of people, many different insights into human life, many differing objectives compose a given cultural context. This means that there is not a simple worldview or ideology that is espoused uniformly by everyone. However, <u>there are certain ideological elements that are dominant, that are</u> the "engines" of the <u>culture; these make up an interrelated web of understandings</u> that are expressed in <u>the control mechanisms/institutions of the culture. To change these understandings is to change</u>—sometimes perhaps rather slowly— <u>the culture.</u> Not only is there a variety of worldviews to be found in any large-scale group of people. Even in the basic understandings that apparently are shared by everyone, there is a <u>range of acceptances of those understandings.</u> Some will accept them enthusiastically because they foster their own self-interests. Others will accept them "politically," knowing that for the present there is no better practical option for obtaining their own diverging goals. Many others are just too apathetic to bother examining these understandings, much less challenge them. As a result, there is a temporary social unity based on consensus rather than a genuine ideological homogeneity. The stability of the culture in question will depend upon the extent to which unified insight and agreement, a commonly accepted understanding, underpins the social contract. Hence the power of ideas as a bond or a disruption of human societies.[2] ❧

Some disruption of societies is inevitable because change is built into human existence. We are historical beings. Much of this change, especially more identifiable change, is associated with the introduction of new ideas. This has been well documented in the case of Copernicus where the fundamental human perspective of being at the center of the universe was challenged, or when the evolutionary character of creation and history was proposed by Darwin, or when the supposed regularity of physical laws was qualified by Einstein's theory of relativity. Not all revolutionary shifts in understanding are this quick and attributable to an individual genius, nor do they occur at an identifiable time. Rather, like the gradual surfacing of the notion of "democracy" as we have come to understand it in today's world, these life-transforming ideas come to influence along with centuries-long shifts in technology, economy, and literacy. Even more difficult to chart would be the long process by which in "advanced" societies we have come to understand that each and every human is not just an individual in a multiplicity making up "the human race" but is a distinctive person. Incidentally, this would be a good example that not all the shifts in understanding have yet been fully appreciated or fully respected.

Because growth and shift in understandings are so influential, it was assumed a few decades ago that an ideal way of tracing the deeper currents of human history was to study the history of ideas.[3] Clearly, great benefit came from this methodology; to examine the sequence and reciprocal influence of ideas does throw a good deal of light on the patterns of human thought and life. However, in more recent years, we have become more aware of the influence that power interests of one sort or another have on the emergence or suppression of new ideas and of the societal structures to which they lead. Precisely because ideas have power to influence human behavior, those who wish to gain or to retain control work to nurture those understandings that will augment their power.

It would be a mistake in studying the culture-changing power of new ideas to overlook the role played by the arts. In subtle but important ways, the evolution of art forms, whether painting or sculpture or music or poetry, forecasts—almost in a prophetic way—and helps create new cultural movements and societal developments. Certainly, the theater has played a key role, almost a religious role: holding up a mirror to society, challenging its mores and values, revealing the deeper currents of motivation that drive it, suggesting a conversion to more authentic humanity. With the current explosion in communication media, the extension of the theater into film, television, and the internet promises to be one of the principal forces in the societies of the future.

Clearly, new ideas can be dangerous. Of their very nature they are subversive, for they demand change. New ideas inevitably bring about a noetic dissonance with established understandings of humanity, the world, or God; and this dissonance spreads to ethical attitudes, and socio-political judgments, and institutional structures. The wine sacks that "translated" and externalized old ideas cannot hold the "living" wine of the new ideas. Because they are such a threat, new ideas consistently face opposition. Attempts are made to negate or discredit them; when that fails, the agencies under threat attack those disseminating these ideas, ridiculing them as naïve or discrediting them as disloyal; and when all else fails, they "burn the books." Despotic dictators pay tribute to new thinking by always keeping a wary eye on universities, not infrequently keeping them under observation by their secret police. The reason is obvious: ideas have power.

Power of Education

But the worry about universities is not just a paranoid reaction to "new" thinking; it points beyond that to the power possessed by education.[4] Clearly, education extends beyond formal schooling—parents educate their children in a variety of ways and with more or less conscious intent; worthwhile conversations on serious topics are a life-long process of education; reading and watching television, films, or stage plays can be valuable sources of ongoing education. There is no question, however, that structured education carried on in schools, from kindergarten to doctoral programs, is—or at least should be—a key to education. Modern times have been shaped to a great extent by the increased possibility of formal education, even for classes of society that previously were deprived of such schooling. The shifts in social structures and possession of power, especially among women, can be traced to a considerable extent to increased opportunities of higher education.

If education is such an influential aspect of life today, it follows that teachers and administrators of schools possess great power and bear great responsibility. It is critical, then, that the character and source of that power be identified and respected. Intrinsically, educational administration is for the sake of effective teaching, learning, and research, which means that the power question focuses on teaching. However, one would be naïve to overlook the extent to which other kinds of power—political, economic, social, religious—play a role in the actual exercise of administrative power in academia. Granted this, the kind of power peculiar to the educational process has to do essentially with teaching. This includes the role of research, which provides the cutting edge of the insights that teaching is meant to transmit.

Basically, a person has the authority to teach if he or she has knowledge of what is shared in the teaching situation. The old adage *Nemo dat quod non habet* (No one gives what they do not themselves possess) has obvious application here. Other things being equal, the greater the knowledge a teacher has, the greater is that person's authority. Generally, some recognition of this is provided by the ranking accorded a teacher—in college and university circles by promotion to "professor." Another element of a teacher's authority is more subtle and difficult to measure, that is, the teacher's ability to communicate, to lead the student to accurate understandings and an enthusiasm for learning. A woman or man who has both superior understanding and skill in communication can exert a most important influence on others' lives and through helping shape those lives to influence society.

Teaching has an awesome power whose exercise demands from professional teachers and the institutions that structure the context for teaching a balanced and insightful examination of the manner in which education is actually conducted in a specific situation. Genuine education, while it takes respectful account of previous ideas and the teacher's own knowledge, is meant to go beyond that and as far as possible bring the student into contact with the reality that lies beyond the teacher's understanding of that reality. Good teaching should be a joint effort at understanding by teachers and students.[5] Knowledge of reality itself, not knowledge of the teacher's knowledge, should be the objective and norm of learning. The more basic power of education lies in the student's own thinking; the teacher acts as midwife.

This leads me to remark on what is often overlooked in discussion of power, namely, the power of carefully crafted thinking to produce new understandings in the thinker. For centuries this has been recognized: in the medieval reflection on the mediation of reason (*ratio*) in leading a person to new insight (*intellectus*), in postmedieval study of rhetoric, and in modern attention to methodology. What one is confronted with here is the reality of thinking as a life process and therefore with a form of life-power distinctive of humans. In today's world of critical thinking, disciplined intellectual activity has power to lead from one level of awareness, naïve realism, to a "higher" level of critical realism.[6]

It is an educational truism that formal education is meant to prepare students for life. Too often, though, this is understood only in terms of equipping a young person with the practical training that will lead to a successful career and/or financial well-being. To facilitate achievement of such practical goals, a student is taught how to fit into society's already existent structures and practices. Success is achieved by not rocking the boat, by efficient support of the status quo. A vibrant society requires, however, that at least some of the students are learning how to enrich their own life experience and personal growth and how to challenge and better the society in which they live. To do this, education should enable students to interpret more carefully and correctly what is happening in their world and in their own inner being; education should be directed at students acquiring an accurate hermeneutic of experience that enables them to discern and critique the values, procedures, and goals of society, even those reflected in the academic institution itself. The ideas and wisdom imparted in a good education provide irreplaceable empowerment. Such is the power of a teacher.

Theological Reflection

It is obvious that the kind of power exerted by teaching functions importantly in a revealed religion such as Christianity. The notion of religious faith and belief is correlative to the notion of revelation, that is, the communication by God to humans of privileged and otherwise unavailable understandings. In principle, this revealed knowledge surpasses all other understandings since it represents divine knowing as far as that can be transmitted to humans' limited intellect. Moreover, since divine knowing along with Spirit is creative of the universe and of history, to "tune in" on God's knowledge is to learn the secrets of the universe and of human destiny. It is only a short step to realize the immense power possessed by those in any religious context who claim that they are the special subjects and guardians of that revelation and entrusted to communicate and interpret it to the faithful. Not surprising, there has been an enduring conflict between those who claim such knowledge because they are officials and those who claim it because they are prophets.

That dispute has acquired new dimensions in recent times for several reasons. For one thing, the very possibility and character of "revelation" have been questioned.[7] How can any authentic communication from God to humans occur since divine knowing itself is radically different and uses neither words nor ideas? On the other hand, revelation is inseparable from, impossible without, words and ideas. One can respond by saying that God communicates through the special events in history, like the exodus, that express the divine intent in history—but what justifies a group of people interpreting events in this way? Perhaps the answer lies in the immediacy of prophetic experience of

God, but who is to judge the true prophet from the false? "Revelation" is a highly complex and continuing occurrence involving a number of interacting agents, none of which by itself can claim normative control of revealed knowing.

Vatican II's document, "Dei Verbum," opened up the view of revelation and freed it from the static notion that revelation ended with the death of the first generation of Jesus' disciples. That inevitably intersected with today's more dynamic and nuanced discussion of "tradition" and the power of memory to shape faith and the formation of community.[8]

Revelation never happens apart from a specific cultural context that conditions the understanding of the divine "word" and provides only limited instruments for expressing it. It may even be that the culture itself is part of the revelation since the humans that compose the culture are themselves sacramental and make up part of "the word." This means that technical insights into the culture must be part of the "equipment" of those who will interpret and explain the revelation. To a limited degree, deep religious insight through prayer or a high degree of individual intelligence can compensate for a lack of technical understanding, but sincere belief cannot replace careful scholarship.

This is not to say that scholarship replaces faith and belief. Religious faith is a distinctive way of knowing. While it takes account of verifiable evidence and is reinforced when such evidence exists, it itself is grounded in one's religious experience and in trusting acceptance of others' witness to their religious experience. Because of this second element, faith begins and develops within one or another community of believers. While they do involve assent to the basic formulations of belief cherished by that community, faith and belief are a special way of knowing the reality expressed by those formulations.

Most Christians do not in their theoretical knowing grasp much of the official teaching about the divine Trinity; the awareness of the divine as they pray deals with God beyond the boundaries of such trinitarian speculation. Such knowledge of God may appear vague and ungrounded, but history indicates that it has exerted and continues to exert unparalleled power in people's lives. Millions have been engaged in crusades of one sort or another on the basis of their religious beliefs. Powerful governments have had to take serious account of the religious adherence of their populations; neglect of this has led to the fall of more than one regime. In recent decades, a striking example of this came when the overthrow of Soviet domination in eastern Europe was spearheaded by religious leadership.

Historically, religious beliefs have originated in the experiences and insights of prophetic figures, experiences and insights then communicated with disciples and gradually spread to a broader community of believers. Christianity's beliefs are, of course, grounded in the religious "revelations" of the great charismatic prophets of Israel and then of Jesus of Nazareth. St. Paul attests to the existence in earliest Christianity of prophets whom he considers to be the foundation stones of the Jesus movement. This directly involves the action of the Holy Spirit since in both Israelite/Jewish and Christian tradition the divine Spirit is seen to be the power working in the prophet—the Spirit is the prophetic Spirit. Hence, it is this Spirit that is the divine agency of God's self-giving revelation.

However, if Paul sees prophets as charismatically endowed by the Spirit, he sees the same thing to be the case with teachers (1 Cor12:8–10). Teaching that explains the gospel is more than a purely human transmission of knowledge. Though not technically identical with evangelization, it is part of the process of making known to people "the good news."[9] Teaching about God's action in Jesus is part of the Spirit-guided and Spirit-empowered activity of ongoing revelation. This would seem to indicate, then, that *magisterium* is a broader reality than the teaching of the episcopate, that it is grounded in a charism other than governance, that it is a distinct ministry with its own empowerment, responsibilities, and divine guidance, that it is not opposed to but instead includes and complements the word of Church officials.

Divine revelation, channeled through prophets and teachers, is by definition a new way of thinking that challenges other human understandings. It is not essentially informational in character, though it intersects with "secular" information. Instead, it is wisdom knowing, insight into the meaning and purpose and destiny of human existence. It is the ground of ethical norms because it clarifies what is "the good" for individuals and society. The revelation that flows from the prophetic experience through the teaching and experience of charismatic teachers to create the religious experience of believers is knowledge about God-for-us and also a new anthropology. Openness to and acceptance of this revealed word leads to a unique kind of knowing that, though grounded in the witness of other believers, is not just a blind and unjustified agreement with official teaching. The authority and power of this belief flows from the prophetic Spirit.

The authority of an individual teacher, be he or she official or not, is based on the knowledge of that teacher as well as on the Spirit's charismatic endowment (1 Cor). This principle is particularly important to recognize today when emphasis is laid, rightly, on experience as the starting-point of theological reflection. Not all experiences are equal in insight and value. Interpretation of past religious history and of the "texts" that bear witness to it is difficult and demands educated capabilities. The norm of present-day faith is not what we imagine was the faith of earlier generations but what that faith truly was.

Truly authoritative teaching is a joint effort by several voices within the Church. Christian belief and teaching are grounded in the historical happening of Jesus, especially of his death and resurrection. So, the witness of the episcopal college whose responsibility it is to witness to that grounding event is essential. Without the reality of Jesus, there is nothing distinctive that Christianity has to teach. In addition, because Christian belief is a tradition evolving through the centuries, one who teaches that tradition needs to be accurately informed about that process and be able to understand the tradition's relevance to present-day believers. This involves two interacting ministries: theology and communication, each of which has a distinctive base of authority. It is all these distinct voices acting in concert, though sometimes with some tension, that constitute the authoritative teaching of the Christian community and *together* possess power to shape the faith and life of believers.

Given the two millenia of its existence and the diverse cultural contexts in which the faith of its members has found expression, Christianity faces a special form of the question of "the one and the many." In the midst of the diversity of cultural experiences and formulations of the Christ-mystery, what elements of the teaching provide for unity in faith? What is the process of "tradition" by which the basic faith experience of relationship to the risen Christ is transmitted across generational and cultural boundaries? The recent spate of writing on this topic suggests not only the valuable rethinking that is occurring but also our still unsatisfactory responses to these questions.[10]

Though no verbal or ritual formulations can sufficiently express the community's faith, certain writings and rituals have acquired normative authority, have become the community's "classics,"[11] a canon of literature and liturgy that function as a central guide to teaching. Clearly, the Bible has occupied a privileged position along with eucharistic celebration; but both have needed and found interpretation by councils like Nicaea and Vatican II, by theological reflection in a variety of philosophical contexts, and by the "lives of the Saints," those Christian lives in which faith has found heroic translation as it has with the martyrs of El Salvador in our own day. Together these form the "wisdom tradition," whose transmission to succeeding generations is the Spirit-guided role of the magisterium, the teaching activity which in different ways the entire community shares.

What emerges, then, as the intellectual life of the Christian people is an ongoing infusion of understanding from the Spirit of God, an understanding of human life unfolding within the saving presence of God, a presence flowing from divine revelation, a revelation of Godself in relation to humans and concomitantly a revelation of humanity in relation to God. Embraced by God's Spirit, Christians—along with others who do not refuse the demands of "reality"—understand themselves and their world with a transformed hermeneutic of experience.

Given the fractured (some would say "chaotic") character of human thought at the present time, it may be that only the universal influence of the Spirit of God can provide a principle of unity that will respect the diversity represented by divergent cultures and ultimately by distinctive human persons. If so, this would represent a direct challenge to the theories of "decentering" that are a feature of some of today's atheism.

Although implied in what I have already said, a word needs to be added about the power of truth. As Geiko Mueller-Fahrenholz has stressed in his recent book,[12] it is basic to Christianity, as to other great religions, that people strive to live in truth. This means that truth is much more than not telling lies; it is more than accuracy of understanding or certitude; it is all that but also the attempt to respond authentically to the circumstances of life as they unfold. It is to accept humbly what is instead of trying to pretend or to create what I would wish it to be. It means accepting my virtues and gifts and also my mistakes and sins. It means being patiently aggressive, neither exaggerating my role in society nor pretending that I am not as gifted or successful as I actually am. Perhaps most important, it means accepting our human dependence upon one another, accepting responsibility for others, for the "neighbor," at the same time that I acknowledge gratefully the necessary support received from others. Another way of approaching this is to reevaluate the meaning of "obedience"—one is obedient, not just to formulated laws, but to the demands of reality as one encounters it.

There is a strange power to truth, hard to describe but almost palpably evident.[13] It is not accidental that the Last Discourse refers to the Spirit as "the spirit of truth." Though they may suffer—and often have suffered—for it, those who have witnessed to the truth have ultimately triumphed, beginning, of course, with Jesus of Nazareth. On the contrary, those who try to maintain control by lying or muzzling the truth legitimately fear the power of the truth and of those who witness to it—why else would they go to such pains to conceal it? Two things are clear: human powers of thought are meant for truth as their proper object, and genuine humanism cannot flourish in a context of systematic obscuring of truth. Human society, true community, is absolutely dependent upon truth—truth in communication, truth in behavior that corresponds to declared ideals, truth in people's relations with one another. The condition of living in truth is to realize and accept the fact that living fully in truth is impossible without the influence of God's own Spirit of truth—the opposite is Pelagianism. God's Spirit is a power drawing a person to exist with personal openness and genuineness that is, free from fear and false self-knowledge.

12

The Power of Ritual

Perhaps the most influential instance of symbols' power to affect societal structures and processes is ritual. For both those with academic and those with pastoral interests, ritual has been a major object of discussion during recent decades.[1] Social scientists,
particularly cultural anthropologists, have investigated the character
and practice of rituals as a key to understanding the ideologies and
the power structures of cultures. Religious groups, particularly those
in the "catholic" tradition, have worried about the apparent ineffi-
cacy of traditional rituals and the sharp decline in regular participation in these and have studied means of reanimating rituals such as
the Eucharist. One factor of historical development that plays an important role in such studies is the modern split between religious
and civic rituals that has accompanied the increasing secularization
of society.

Attention has been drawn—perhaps not sufficiently—to people's actual experience of religious rituals because of the evident decline of participation in traditional religious practices. Moreover,
even among those still regularly "attending church," there is growing dissatisfaction with what often seem to be empty liturgical celebrations. Instead, evangelical services of various kinds attract large
crowds and suggest a felt need of people to discover, nurture, and
express some kind of belief about the meaning of life. This has been
particularly noticeable among "pious" immigrant groups like the
Mexicans coming to the United States—when they are detached

from the cultural situation in which they had become accustomed to certain routine liturgical activities as a meaningful part of their life context, they do not find an affinity with those same liturgical rituals when performed in perfunctory fashion in the new environment. To put it simply, studies indicate that believers apparently wish to become engaged in some shared ritual rather than simply witnessing a religious spectacle performed by an official "expert."

This has led some scholars, notably Catherine Bell, to move from focus on rituals' forms to the examination of people's actual ritualizing. *What* do humans commonly ritualize? *How* do they do this and *for what purposes?* In what way does such activity fit into people's religious beliefs and commitments? What is the effect of this ritualizing on the power alignment in a group? This emphasis on the action of ritualizing has the benefit of honoring the intrinsic reality of rituals as shared actions of a community, maintaining the concrete distinctiveness of any given ritual action while suggesting the "communitas" that rituals create.

Probably no one has more broadened the notion of "ritual," extended reflection to secular as well as religious ritualizing, and stressed the fluidity and complexity of the power relationships involved in ritualizing than has Michel Foucault in his study of the patterns of regularized public activity. In doing so, he has drawn attention to a central element of power, to rituals' influence on the various expressions of power in structured human relationships. Not illogically, his influence has intersected with the postmodern discussion of language and symbolism in general, which indicates the central role played by ritualizing in humans' societal existence.

What, then, is the power exercised by ritualizing, a power that is distinctive but to some extent is shared with other forms of symbolizing? To all appearances, one of the more obvious effects of ritualizing is expressing and causing the participants' identity, as individuals and as a group. However, because a given act of ritualizing can involve a number of interacting relationships and people's inner consciousness as well as their external activity, an individual's identity may not be as clearly expressed as it appears to be.

Individual distinctive identity, a person's awareness of being this particular self, though pervasive as a human experience is at the same time one of the most elusive. Phenomenological reflection has drawn attention to the fact that the perception of self is not the perception of an object of knowledge; rather, it is an implicit but given element in all perception. One cannot know something, the world of experience, the Other, without being conscious of being a knowing subject, though that is seldom adverted to. One can, of course, also know oneself as an "object"; this occurs whenever one explicitly examines one's behavior, attitudes, or states of mind. But this is different from awareness of oneself precisely as a "self." It is only in knowing an "other" that *self*-awareness occurs, for this is what it means to be a self, a person and not simply an individual in the species *homo*. Awareness of self, a self-identity that is both discovered and chosen, is the distillation of innumerable implicitly observed relationships to a manifold Other. The situation of the person in this network of relationships is unique; to be the pole of these relationships is what it means to be this particular self.

It is in activities of ritualizing that the person, by bodily gesture as well as by spoken words, is involved in accepting or quietly rejecting or politically assenting to a certain group of such relationships. A family meal, for instance, can be the occasion on which the very "body language" of a child can implicitly agree with the "traditional" ritualizings that express the family's self-image or it can be a scarcely recognized protest.

Much more complicated is the ritualizing that takes place in a public protest, for example, in Seattle in 1999 against the World Trade Organization. Many persons engaged in the action became increasingly identified personally with the antiglobalization movement as a result of publicly demonstrating; and the action itself became a movement and not just an isolated event as at least some of the participants discovered themselves to be a community of shared outlook. In many instances, a person will be "thinly" participating in a common ritualizing, such as going to Sunday religious services, with a mixed recognition or nonrecognition of the dynamics of the action, with a mixed acceptance or rejection of the ritual's intrinsic implications, with a mixture of belief and doubt. Even in such instances, the very sharing in bodily gestures, such as sitting quietly during the sermon, kneeling at certain moments of the liturgy, bowing the head as the ordained presider prays, feed into a self-identity as a member of the religious community.

One of the most complex, indeed baffling, aspects of such ritualizing *despite* awareness is the shared understanding of being a community. In any given act *difference* of ritualizing, there is always some *communitas* in the midst of diversity, though true unity and homogeneity are two quite different realities.[2] Certainly, some elements of this communitas can be easily recognized—the protesters at Seattle were all opposed to globalization; but the precise nature of this opposition differed greatly from one person to another. At times, such ritualizing brings about a rather deep and lasting human bonding as people develop a respect and even an affection for one another—but this does not clearly state what it is they have in common.

Members of a group engaged in some shared purpose, such as teachers in a school or a Marine platoon in battle, can develop a strong esprit de corps in which individuals are genuinely identified with one another, a true community; and certain ritualizing, like the ceremony of inducting new members, can make an important contribution to this sense of community.

On the other hand, despite ongoing sharing in the public rituals of a group, this sharing can play a minimal role in a person's self-identify. Studies that have been made in the United States of the priorities in people's self-identity indicate that adherence to a particular religious denomination is far down on such a list, though most of these people would wish to think of themselves as "spiritual." Probably they are identifying themselves as "respectable." More likely, they have little understanding of what it means to participate in a ritual; for many of them have been educated to think of the Sunday service as a religious spectacle that they are meant to attend and the Church as an organization to which they belong.

In the case of a genuine celebration of ritual, the group involved becomes more aware, or at least is reminded again, of the purpose for the group's existence. This purpose need not be some specified external activity. In the case of a family gathered for Thanksgiving dinner, the purpose of the group as such and of the ritual being performed is to reinforce the personal relationships among those participating and so enrich their individual lives. Awareness of a group's purpose is, of course, an aspect of the group's self-identity and to some extent of the individual members' self-identity. However, in a group of any size, the purpose may be complex and require that different members perform a range of activities—this also is expressed in the ritual. The ritual, though, is not simply an acknowledgement of the group's purpose; participation in the ritual, even though for some it is reluctant and minimal, is a *commitment* to work for achievement of the group's purpose. This enthusiastic or only "negotiated" commitment is implicit in the bodily gestures in the ritual as well as in any explicit verbalization. Ideally, the ritualizing activity itself will have persuasive power to induce in the participants a stronger identification with the communitas and a deepened commitment to the group's goals.

Various groups are distinguished by their specific reason for existing, and that is reflected in the "shape" of the group. Much of the arrangements of organization and activity of a group can be the result of explicit planning. However, ritualizing can function not only to reinforce those formalized arrangements, but also to deal with many of the more subtle personnel issues that any group encounters or to bring into people's awareness elements of identity or purpose of which they had not previously been aware.[3] This becomes more important as a group continues in existence and encounters happenings or needs it had not anticipated and to which it now must make a more unplanned response. As this happens, the shape of the group can change, sometimes quite drastically. A classic exemplification of this which has frequently

occurred in the course of history is that what originated as a movement gradually becomes an organization, at which point, both the self-identification taking place and the actual goals of much group activity are changed from the
primal situation of the group. When this occurs, the forms of ritualizing that
genuinely and effectively functioned at the beginning are no longer relevant to
the changed social situation. Unless the ritualizing itself is transformed, it
becomes an empty performance with little effect on the shape of the community in its new context. Still, ritualizing has a certain undeniable effectiveness, and if a group's ritualizing is "out of synch" with the social context in
which it takes place it can contribute to making the group itself irrelevant.

If a community is of any size and regularly ritualizes its identity and purpose, this ritualizing will inevitably interact with the regnant ideologies of the
culture to which the group belongs, reinforcing, refining, or challenging them.
While one can speak generically about the ideology that underlies any particular culture, it is good to bear in mind that in the concrete there may well be
in a society a number of somewhat competing ideologies at work. In addition,
the apparent acceptance of the dominant ideology by a minority group may be
little more than a negotiated consent for practical reasons or in some cases a
veiled opposition that it is judged not profitable to manifest.

What ritualizing can do is to create over a period of time, often without
people becoming aware of it, an ideology that reflects the identity and purpose
of the group. A classic example would be the ongoing religious process that
was early described by Prosper of Aquataine: *lex orandi, lex credendi*—a Christian community is essentially a community formed and shaped by the ritual
expression of shared belief. The exact character of any particular community's
belief is shaped, perhaps more importantly than by any other influence such
as catechizing, by the ritualizing of belief that takes place in liturgical celebrations. One of the interesting aspects of the doctrinal evolution that led up to
the trinitarian and christological creeds of Nicaea and Chalcedon is the way in
which, by way of grounding the theological position they were taking, some
theologians appealed to what was done in sacramental rituals such as initiation.

In Christian liturgical ritualizing, the central ideology, the gospel, is meant
to confront and challenge the "secular" ideologies of the assembled believers.
Public Christian rituals, inseparably intertwined as they are with the canonical
scriptures, are basically prophetic proclamation that demands conversion.

Ritualizing is an interesting and instructive example of the interplay of
various kinds of power. Probably no aspect of ritualizing has been more studied
than the influence this activity has on identifying and grounding the power
structure of any given community. Ritualizing has power of its own, the ability
to empower those in a community who exercise roles of organizing, directing,

of even controling the members of a community and their various activities. Ritualizing has been used to legitimate officials' domination; but it has also been used to challenge illegitimate domination. In today's world, the liturgy of street theater has often proved to be an effective strategy used by those without recourse to military or police might in their efforts to challenge unjust official activity.

In any given instance, the precise manner of defining, reinforcing, or confronting a community's power structure may be very subtle and consist in a long process of ritualizing whose effectiveness is exerted only gradually and over a length of time. It took centuries before the ritualizing of chivalry transformed medieval warriors from savages to knights. On the contrary, ritualizing may celebrate and feed into a sudden and unexpected shift in political power, as it did at the French Revolution with ritualizing like the enthronement of "Reason" in Notre Dame Cathedral. Again, the regularized ritualizing connected with the inauguration of an American President gives formal recognition to a transfer of political power, but it also helps effect national acceptance of the transfer of power, as it did in the disputed election of George W. Bush.

Theological Reflection

To apply this to the realm of religious ritualizing: as is well known, the Second Vatican Council through its document on liturgy initiated several changes in the ritual form of the eucharistic action. The effect of some of these changes was immediate and quite apparent, for example, the use of vernacular languages instead of Latin. But the effect of other changes was less obvious and to some extent is only gradually being felt. Turning the altar so that it faced the people clearly meant that the people could now have a new experience of the liturgical action. However, it also altered drastically the power position of the ordained leader, who previously was considered by himself to be the celebrant of an action upon which the others were dependent.

Significantly, the former "celebrant" is now being named the "presider." The ritualizing of Eucharist is now beginning to be experienced as a shared activity of the entire assembly, including the ordained presider. In many circles, the presider no longer is regarded as one with sacred power to channel God's grace to the community; his role is that of animator/facilitator rather than mediator. Formal recognition of this power shift is far from being universally realized, least of all by many of the ordained, but has already had the result of creating in many of the ordained an identity crisis—what precisely is their role and their power in this "new Church"? From the point of view of our study, what is important in this instance is that the new understanding and community realignment is not coming because of theological clarification but rather through the actual ritualizing that is taking place.

Holy Spirit and Christian Ritual

In studying the history of pneumatology, one cannot but be struck by the very early association of the Holy Spirit with Christian ritualizing. By the year 80, if not earlier, baptizing was already being celebrated in some areas in the name of Father, Son, and Holy Spirit. The use of the word "Holy" is significant because this was clearly attached to the notion that the Spirit of God/Christ was the source of "holiness"; and the linking of the Spirit's power in initiation with that of Father and Son, both of them clearly being considered divine, already reflects belief in the divinity of the Spirit. Again, as early as Jesus' own prophetic teaching, the Spirit is linked with the forgiveness of sin; and from the beginning, Christians believed that they, too, possessed this divine empowerment over evil—"Whose sins you shall forgive . . ."—even though for the moment there was no formal ritualizing of such reconciliation. By mid–second century, the ritualizing connected with episcopal ordination invoked the power of God's Spirit to empower the ordinand for ministry.

The Spirit's influence in such ritualizing, especially in the case of baptismal initiation, was characterized by the second century as a "sealing." Just as the use of a signet ring by a person left on the hot wax the recognizable imprint of the ring and signified that the document in question came from the owner of the ring, so the Spirit left on the initiate the imprint that marked him or her as Christian. Within a short time, this had led to the theological teaching regarding the "sacramental character", a teaching which persisted until the twentieth century and which, developed by medieval theology into the *res et sacramentum*, provided the key response to Donatism.

Perhaps the most important association of the Holy Spirit with Christian ritualizing has to do with the central ritual of Eucharist. While there is no clear evidence of invocation of the Spirit in the very earliest eucharistic celebrations, there are a few intriguing suggestions for some linkage. In the *Didache*, for instance, the proclamation of the eucharistic prayer was seen to be a prophetic action, so much so that, if a community did have a prophet, that individual was the appropriate person to proclaim the eucharistic prayer—and prophetic proclamation was believed to flow from special empowerment by the Spirit. Again, Acts describes a number of occasions when during gatherings of a community, there were extraordinary manifestations of the Spirit (e.g., chap.

13). However, by as early as the third century, the epiclesis appears as a prominent element of eucharistic rituals.[4]

A radical development has occurred in the twentieth century regarding the Spirit's role in eucharistic ritualizing, a development that is only slowly being realized and honored in practice. In mid–twentieth century, a breakthrough occurred in theological understanding about the intrinsic reality of Jesus' resurrection and, consequent to it, a recovered awareness of the presence of the risen Christ to the community. This implied that "eucharistic presence," though it does touch the transformation of the symbolizing elements of bread and wine, pertains most importantly to Christ's presence to the assembled believers.

Along with this came the realization that the risen Christ is the principal celebrant of Eucharist and is enabled to do this because the assembled Christians embody him. Christ continues still to function as prophet and Word of God, communicating to humans the divine self-gift and self-revelation, which he does by sharing his own prophetic Spirit with those of faith. This involves, at least in theory, a rehabilitation of the epiclesis in Western eucharistizing, for it is in sharing with the assembled Christians his own Spirit that the risen Christ becomes present to them. Moreover, the Spirit invoked in Eucharist is not an absent Spirit coming anew to the community; rather, this Spirit already abides, as does the risen Christ, as the promised gift of "another Paraclete."

Invocation of Christ's Spirit to increasingly transform the community into "body of Christ" points to the eucharistic act as *conversion*. Christ's Spirit is a divine ideology in tension with the prevailing cultural ideologies that the assembly possesses. The "mind of Christ," which the Spirit is, must replace the "false spirits" of the world so that the community can become truly a faith community. In this way, the action of eucharistic ritualizing is meant gradually to shape the assembled believers into a community of faithful discipleship.

It would be a mistake to confine the action of the Spirit in Christian ritualizing to eucharistic gatherings. Since Christ's sharing of the Spirit results in an abiding presence and enlivening by that Spirit, the influence of that Spirit flows into the diverse forms of ritualizing that mark the lives and celebrations of Christians. Eucharist enjoys place of honor, but there are any number of symbolic activities that contribute what one can call "folk religion" and that truly deserve to be considered authentic Christian ritualizing. Indeed, in situations where frequent eucharistic celebration is impossible, the burden of sustaining and nurturing Christian faith may well fall on these alternative rituals.[5]

Medieval theologians in their theological reflection on the Eucharist were in agreement that the *res*, the grace effected through eucharistic ritualizing, was basically the deepened transformation of the assembled Christians into a community of faith. This is, of course, the precise petition involved in the epiclesis; and it is entirely appropriate that this grace should be attributed to the Spirit. That attribution, however, throws considerable light on the character and role of Christ's Spirit. God, who is the principal agent of the eucharistic transformation as well as the object of the Eucharist's prayer of grateful praise, reaches out through the mediation of Christ's risen presence to reveal self and thereby invite the assembled believers into deeper covenant relationship. This God does through the "sending" of divine Spirit, the infinite creative power of divine love. Acceptance of this covenant invitation is a matter of the free decision of those who are gathered, and so it involves their individual transformation as well. As this occurs in ritualizing, there is the creation of *communitas*, a dynamic communing in faith, that brings into being the shared identity and purpose that characterizes the assembly as a Christian *communio*.

Students of power point to the universal presence of conflict in power relationships. The exercise of power by the "dominator" is met in one form or another with the resisting power of "the dominated." In relationships of love, one can observe conflict, or at least tension; but clearly, this is a very distinctive form of conflict that is positive and creative and, at least ideally, is without "dominator" and "dominated." Self-giving and self-abandonment coexist with self-assertion and demand for recognition of one's distinctive identity and worth. Religious ritual is meant to be the external enacting in bodily "dance" of the inner, never resolved dialectic between God's loving and human freedom—a special kind of "conflict" upon which many other "powers" impinge, a conflict that is not oppressive but lovingly welcomed, a creative tension that is perhaps best sacramentalized by lovers' intercourse.

PART V

Love

This final unit will lead to a reflection on love, human and divine, as the ultimate power operating in human life. It will, I hope, move focus on "power" as domination and control to focus on empowerment. Though in human experience it is impossible to isolate eros and agape, the first chapter in this unit will examine "eros," the power it exerts, and its relation to the Spirit of God. Giving this distinct treatment to eros is intended to draw attention to its positive relation to the Spirit's work of human transformation and at the same time make clearer the distinctive power of love that will be studied in the second chapter.

Following these two chapters, the concluding chapter of the book will propose a basic metaphor for the power of divine "reaching out" that is the Spirit.

13

The Power of Eros

A few key insights have had unparalleled influence on the shape of human history. One of these has to be Gotama's realization that human suffering is rooted in desire, an understanding that has underpinned Buddhist thought and life for two and a half millennia. If only humans could free themselves from attachment to the objects of their desire, there would be no frustration or disappointment, no pain of loss, no defeat or failure, no fear of suffering or death.

In a negative way, this points to the immense power of desire. It is desire that moves persons and nations to strive for goals and achieve greatness. It is passion, that is, intense desire, that drives women and men to devote their time and energies and at times their lives to obtain "the pearl of great price." Without passion, nothing of moment happens. Lives lived with apathy, without enthusiasm or commitments, end up without meaning or purpose.[1]

We already saw, in treating the power of nature, that there is a fundamental eros that permeates the entire universe. This power that drives the galaxies, that moves atoms and molecules to combine and interact, that makes continuing cosmic evolution an explosive event, that leads living things to reproduce and preserve their kind, is none other than desire. The quest for their appropriate good is the finality intrinsic to their very existence.

Humans, too, share this thrust toward "the good"; it is at least half of what it means for them to be persons. In their case, however, it is the good *as they perceive it* that they desire; and this perception can be accurate or erroneous. This means that the desires harbored by women and men can be misleading, even dangerous and destructive, as well as laudable and ennobling. Humans can desire what is bad for them, even when they know that this is the case. Desires can lead them to steal, to betray, to kill, all in order to obtain something thought to be "good." But desire can also motivate persons to sacrifice their lives and their wealth in the effort to better human society. Desire to serve others as a physician or a social worker or a teacher can motivate a young person to spend long years of preparation in the course of which many other desirable things are foregone.

There is no need to expand on the omnipresence and power of desire in human life. Centuries of literature and philosophical reflection on the nature and desirability of "the good" make the case. What, if anything, does this say about the reality and influence of God's Spirit?

Theological Reflection

A leading question is: can one speak of "eros" at the divine level? Clearly, in polytheistic belief like that of ancient Greece, eros is very much in evidence among the heavenly beings—in fact, it is accentuated. Zeus was famous for his amatory exploits, male and female. However, in a monotheistic context, eros seems incompatible by definition with the being of "God." Monotheism implies that the being of the Transcendent requires infinity, and infinity rules out desire, for desire means that there is limitation, something not yet possessed that is sought. Infinity leaves no room for such a lack of completeness. Process thought, of course, reacts against the static character this suggests for the Transcendent, but how to combine true transcendence with the movement toward further fulfillment that desire suggests remains an enigma. Christian theology would qualify that last statement: we are involved, not with an enigma but with a mystery.[2]

mystery
of desire
in
Monotheism

Already in the Israelite antecedents of Christianity, God is described as desiring—wanting the obedience and loyalty of the people, looking unsuccessfully for justice and mercy in the covenant people, awaiting in vain an abundant vintage from the "vine" planted in Jerusalem. Yahweh patiently hopes and looks forward to the day when the chosen people will worship in honesty and fidelity. Like a spouse who has been betrayed, the God of Israel so desires the response of love from his beloved that he is willing to forget the infidelities of the present, remember the dreams of the past, and begin anew his courtship of the people.

With the advent of Jesus of Nazareth, the evidence for divine desire takes

a radically new dimension. Jesus' most basic experience of God, which incidentally establishes for him his own personal identity, is the experience of
being unconditionally loved. The God of Israel is his Abba. The relation between them is that of unparalleled friendship. As friendship, it is a two-way
relation; Jesus' loving response in the one Spirit they share is not a matter of
indifference on the part of Abba. If Jesus "does always the things that please"
this means that "being pleased" is not a matter of indifference to his Abba.
Once the relation between humans and God is placed in the context of intimate
friendship—which Christianity claims occurs in a distinctive way in Jesus—
the compatibility of transcendence and desire remains a mystery but an undeniable mystery.

Recent theological reflection has formalized the idea that Jesus is a sacrament, in a special way the observable symbol of the presence of God. His
attitudes toward others, his concern and sympathy, his desire for and human
need for friendship—all this is sacramental. All this points as a word of revelation to the mysterious reality that the Transcendent is not without something
analogous to human desire, a desire to receive from humans an acceptance of
and gratitude for the divine offer of love.

Christian tradition, particularly the tradition of Christian mysticism, has
always spoken of the Spirit of God as being connected with divine loving, as
the outreach—some have called it "the overflow"—of God's own superabun-
dant love. At the same time, there has often been the tendency to insist that
this love, and even "pure" human love, is agapic, that is, completely without
any self-seeking, completely one-directional. Though it has never been described explicitly that way, God's loving is believed to be creative, outgoing, all-
powerful, and without need for return, like a mother's love for a newborn.
Jesus did not sacramentalize divine loving in that way. Though he certainly
loved unselfishly and unconditionally, continued to love even those enemies
who hated and murdered him, he was deeply grieved by Jerusalem's rejection,
grieved by Judas's betrayal. He desired his hearers to accept his message, to
accept him, and above all to accept his Abba. Jesus was in no way like a Stoic
sage, living with calculated indifference to the world around him; he was a
profoundly passionate human person. In all this, he was moved by and embodied the divine Spirit; the divine loving sacramentalized in him and thereby
revealed a God who was "erotic."[3]   2-way love, desire for requittance

But does this mean that the Spirit creative of the universe is to be identified
with the internal eros of that universe? Is it God's own desire that is the force
drawing all things to their divine destiny? To say "yes" would lead to pantheism.
Rather, God's Spirit is the invitation to loving union that expresses God's desire; for what meaning would an invitation have if it awaited no response? The

eros of creation and particularly the fundamental eros of humans is the response to God's Spirit; creation is drawn to the divine, but the being drawn is an internal power triggered in response to the divine invitation. There is an almost instinctive realization of this reality; the saying of Augustine of Hippo is widely recognized as "true" even when it is rejected: "Our hearts were made for you, O God, and they are restless until they rest in you."

The profoundly mysterious relationship of divine to human in Jesus extends beyond him as the very heart of Christian spirituality. One can speak of "spirituality" in terms of the refinement and growth of the spirit dimension of humans and describe the methods through which this spirit aspect can be nourished by practices such as meditation. Clearly, this is something good and worth encouraging. However, though it is a valuable underpinning for Christian spirituality, it is not itself Christian spirituality. Christian spirituality consists essentially in humans' outlook on life, prioritizing of desired "goods," evaluation of and relation to other persons relating positively to God's Spirit. To put it more simply, Christian spirituality is the living out of the love relationship with God to which one is invited by Christ's (and God's) Spirit. Though sinful activity is inimical to this relationship, Christian spirituality is much more than the avoidance of sin. A person could avoid doing wrong by doing nothing; but that may well be the worst situation. "Because you are neither hot nor cold, I have vomited you out of my mouth" (Revelations 3:16). True Christian spirituality is a passionate lifelong dedication to furthering the reign of the God one loves. It is making God's Spirit one's own spirit, making God's desires one's own.

Life lived in this manner is the essence of evangelization, for it goes beyond proclamation or explanation. It bears witness to a person's belief that the God revealed in Jesus is the ultimate good; friendship with God is "the pearl of great price" for possession of which one willingly foregoes all else, if that is needed.

In the way in which it deals with eros, Christian spirituality is radically different from two other great "spiritual" movements, Buddhism and Stoicism. Both regard eros with suspicion; passion and desire are viewed as blocks to authentic human living. The truly wise person in their view is the one who can go through life unencumbered by the disturbance that desire inevitably brings. There is, of course, a great difference between these two ethical systems; for one thing, Buddhism is characterized by compassion and concern for others, whereas Stoicism tends to avoid any involvement that will disturb the sage's psychic tranquility.

In the course of its history, however, Stoicism has exerted a constant attraction for committed Christians and been a major force in shaping Christian moral theology. Asceticism, even extreme at times, is at least as old as the desert monks of the second century, and in many circles, great asceticism has been regarded as an ideal expression of Christian virtue. Without question, Christian ascetics have correctly assessed the power of human desires and legitimately feared their ability to mislead and corrupt humans. Desire for one or other form of "the forbidden fruit" can warp human moral decisions and has often done so. Temptation by the attraction of earthly goods is part of human experience, as it was for Jesus himself.

against ascetic influence in Christianity

Still, desire is not itself an evil inclination nor is pleasure intrinsically wrong. While they are replete with condemnations of humans' capitulation to temptation and abandonment of God for the pleasure of lesser goods, the Hebrew Bible and the Christian Scriptures depict a God who appeals to humans' eros by promises of pleasure. The Israelites are motivated to undertake the exodus, endure the hardships of the desert, and accept the law of Sinai because of the expectation of a land of their own, a land flowing with milk and honey. The pleasure of sexual love, in many quarters looked at askance as a block to virtue, is extoled in the Canticle and used as a metaphor for divine-human relationships. More than one of Jesus' parables uses feasting in the heavenly banquet as an image of the reign of God. Perhaps most tellingly, Jesus' own behavior and teaching were criticized as "dissolute" by Pharisees who prided themselves on their asceticism.

importance of involvement in profane participation

While not an ascetic, Jesus of Nazareth was profoundly disciplined by the Spirit of his Abba, the Spirit he embraced as his own spirit. All his choices and behavior were governed by an overriding eros, the fundamental option of working to establish the reign of God; in implementing that option, he celebrated the pleasures of a world created for humans' enjoyment, but always in accord with the goal to which he was passionately committed. He enjoyed that freedom of the Spirit that Paul would later advocate for his Christian converts.

But eros is not the whole story or even the most important chapter in the story of human affectivity. At the same time that one recognizes its intrinsic and inescapable role in human loving, there is an aspect of love that is more ultimate. Beyond the lover desiring the beloved for his or her own fulfillment, there is the altruistic self-giving outreach toward the beloved for the beloved's own sake. This is the realm of friendship and agapic love that we will explore in the following chapter.

14

The Power of Love (Agape?)

To call a person a "powerbroker" would not point to that individual's capacity to form deep and lasting friendships. Indeed, in some circles of power, being a loving person would probably be somewhat suspect; the question would be raised whether that individual might be swayed by friendship from following through on the kind of ruthless decision sometimes required to move up on the ladder of public power. At the same time, there seems to be a grassroots perception that love is a powerful force—as the popular song goes, "Love makes the world go round."

Actually, the experience of love and friendship, even apart from its link with sexuality, has always intrigued and attracted humans. Over the centuries, there have been innumerable treatises on friendship and/or love, some of them quite philosophical, like Cicero's *De amicitia*, some of them quite descriptive and "scandalous," like the treatise on honorable and dishonorable love by Andreas Capellanus. The Hebrew Bible itself bears witness to "heroic" friendships like that of David and Jonathan and to the erotic love reflected in the Canticle of Canticles. Ancient literature is filled with tales of love between men and women, gods and human beings, and companions in arms.

While history records a wide range of friendships that exerted lasting influence on events—Pericles and Aspasia; Abelard and Heloise; Francis and Clare; John Dewey, Oliver W. Holmes, Charles Peirce, and William James; Augustine and Monica; Dante and Beatrice—it also reflects the variety of relationships that fit under the canopy of "love and friendship." While the relationship between Pericles and Aspasia, publicly acknowledged as Pericles' mistress, certainly focused to a considerable extent on the sexual bond, Aspasia was considered to be not a prostitute, but a shrewd political adviser, personal support, and loyal friend. With Augustine and Monica, it was, obviously, quite different. Bonded as mother and son, they enjoyed an even deeper spiritual link, to the point where they apparently shared a common mystical experience. Quite different, again, was the love that bonded Francis and Clare. Without question a warm and affectionate human relationship, it was grounded in and gave expression to the love for God that both enjoyed and that they nurtured in one another. So also the deep affection that bonded the disciples of Bernard of Clairvaux to him and to one another. Different, very different, was the circle that included Olive Wendell Holmes, John Dewey, Charles Peirce, and William James, a group of friends that is credited with immense influence on the emergence of distinctive culture in the United States.[1] Perhaps most unusual of all was the one-sided love of Dante for Beatrice; without any reciprocation or even the hope of expressing directly his love, Dante cherished Beatrice as the "lode-star" of his personal maturation and his poetic genius.

Love has clearly been a major influence on human activity over the centuries. Perhaps one of the most revealing recognitions of its deserving characterization as "power" has been the frequent attempt of other forms of power to negate or at least restrict its influence—to take but one example, an example germane to our present discussion, the proscription of marriage to ordained ministers in Latin Christianity. Certainly, the demand for celibacy by the Church, like the same demand in ancient Rome for the Vestal Virgins, was tied in with a notion that sexual activity was incompatible with dedication to "the sacred." But beyond that was the view that love for a spouse and children could come into conflict with and overrule an ordained minister's total commitment to Church structures. It represented a power that threatened the absoluteness of ecclesiastical power. So, in the eleventh and twelfth centuries, during the papal campaign to solidify Church power, the full strength of law and social recognition was brought to bear by declaring clerical marriages invalid.

Unquestionably the power of love is intertwined with the power of sexual attraction and passion, and often a superficial view of love tends to identify them. In reality, love and friendship are a more profound and far-reaching reality in human life. In fact, genuine mature love has irreplaceable power to give meaning, balance, and experiential depth to sexuality. Though most cultures, including our own, still display less than accurate understanding and balance in their view and practice of sexuality, there are enough instances of persons in whom love has refined and humanized sexuality that the potential of love in this regard is undeniable.

Precisely because love is such a "many-colored thing," it is necessary to distinguish the diverse phenomena to which the term "love" is attached. We have already studied erotic attraction, the desire for a good that a person wishes to possess. In human relations, it can be a completely self-interested posses-siveness, but it can also be an element in genuine affection for another. Such amorous desire flows from perception of the beloved as almost irresistibly attractive and is rooted in human creatureliness and the incompleteness of isolated existing. Again, there is healthy self-love, authentic appreciation for one's worth and gratitude, at least implicitly directed to God, for one's being. But there is also the sick self-centeredness of narcissism. There is altruistic love, agapic love, sometimes one-sided as in a mother's love for her infant, at other times a central force in an adult's self-gift to another, the relation of an "I" to a "Thou." When such love is reciprocated, it is friendship—the Greek philia.

eros
agape
philia

desire

reciprocity

Traditionally, agapic love has been viewed as distinctively characteristic of God's relation to humans because it has been assumed that there can be no desire on the part of God. It has also been viewed as the best way for humans to love since it was looked on as "unselfish," the paradigm being mother love. Part of the perceived superiority of agape was its difference from eros; a certain negativity surrounded erotic loving because it involved passion, pleasure, and the lover's "selfishness." Friendship was evaluated more positively, for appar-ently, like agape, it was affection for another for that other's self and thus avoided selfish interest. However, in the normal experience of friendship, there is always a mixture of eros—one does desire that the other person become or remain one's friend. Actually, the loving involved in agape and philia seems to be distinguished only by the reciprocity involved in the latter.[2]

As we saw, attempts to separate eros and agape in human loving have proved futile. While there is a distinction to be made, the concrete experience of human loving—at least of mature loving—involves both. No doubt, on the one hand, there does exist infatuation that involves no lasting relationship, no true self-gift. On the other hand, there has also been the notion of love without feeling, "Christian charity," a dutiful concern for others that involves little, if any, warm human affection. At times, this latter view has been manifested by preference for the word "charity" instead of "love," perhaps because reference to two persons as "lovers" is commonly understood in sexual terms.[3]

Perhaps one should not argue with such attitudes and language that often are reflections of cultural mores, but there is a theological and religious issue at stake. Because human friendship is a basic sacrament of divine saving presence in human life, to deny warm affection and intimacy to these friendships would lead to viewing divine loving as disinterested and impersonal. The very heart of Christian belief in salvation and human destiny would be brought into question.

Theological Reflection

It is precisely in theological examination of love as power that one touches on the basic question: what truly is ultimate power? Taking as a very general notion of power "the ability to achieve a particular goal," theology begins with the issue of the divine goal for humanity—what is the intent, the will, of God for humans? In one form or another, theological responses are variations on Irenaeus's famous remark: "The glory of God is the human person fully alive." Today we would probably rephrase that in psychological terms: the fully alive person is the truly mature person; and we would extend that to human societies as well. The will of God, the goal of the divine creative/redemptive activity, that is, of divine providence, is that humans, individually and in communities, should realize as fully as possible their potential as persons.

Current reflection on human maturity leaves little doubt that the measure of maturity is a person's capacity to love and that one acquires this capacity most importantly through loving and being loved. Professional psychology would examine maturity in terms of a person's ability to deal with relationships—which is saying basically the same thing. Here we may be in the midst of a "revolution" in psychology: whereas the basic thrust of Freudian thought is that one attains to autonomy (and presumably to maturity) by freeing oneself from dependence on relationships, some current reflection (e.g., Jean Baker Miller and study at the Stone Center) insists rather on preserving, cherishing, and deepening key relationships.[4]

Love in the Bible

The biblical sources of theologizing about love are manifold and compeling. While the original stratum of Israelite thinking about their god Yahweh probably saw that god only as a fear-inspiring though protective divinity, this view shifted with the prophetic movement. The contrast of Elijah's encounter with Yahweh at Horeb and Moses' at Sinai is striking and intended: whereas at Sinai Moses met with Yahweh amid earthquake, thunder, and lighting, Elijah experiences this same god "in a gentle breeze." What begins with Elijah continues in Hosea's use of marital imagery to describe Yahweh, and this prophetic stream influences the very notion of the Torah that was so basic to Israelite belief. The book of Deuteronomy, though retaining much of the detailed legislation of Exodus 20-34, shifts the whole notion of law—instead of the apodictic "you shall not . . ." of the Mosaic formulation, Deuteronomy begins with "you shall *love* the Lord your God."

The Hebrew Bible bears constant witness to the power of love and reflects a positive view of love, both human and divine. Unquestionably, one must avoid attributing to their understanding all the overtones of romantic affection attached to "love" today, but one cannot avoid the tender familiarity expressed in Hosea 2. And one cannot avoid the constant implication that the love of Yahweh is the power that ultimately "wins the heart" of Israel.

That raises the question: to what extent, if at all, is the link between God's love and God's Spirit present in the Bible prior to Christianity? That the power associated with God's Spirit accompanies the prophetic word is clear and explicit, but that this power is the power of love is certainly not prominent, if present at all. However, with Wisdom developments comes the intriguing linkage of Word, Wisdom, Spirit, and Law. Love is not added to this list. It is not mentioned, as an abstract force or as a divine personification. At the same time, the "attitude" of the divine teacher, Wisdom, is one of loving concern and desire to benefit her disciples. She spreads her table and invites them to her banquet. She promises peace and rest and fulfillment to those who cherish her. In Sirach, the last of the wisdom writings, Yahweh's loving of his chosen people is epitomized in the gift of the Law's wisdom.

Christian Reflection on Love

Stress on the primacy of love in the Christian Scriptures is undeniable. Beginning with the teaching and ministry of Jesus himself, the law of loving concern for others dominates the perspective of Christianity on humans' relation with God and, derivative from this, humans' relationship to one another and to themselves. The Johannine tradition, in particular, places authentic human love at the very center of faith and discipleship. "This is my command, that you love one another as I have loved you."

While such statements may be the distillation of two generations of Christian reflection on Jesus' person, activity, and teaching, they clearly are grounded in the manner in which Jesus himself related to others, both to his close friends and to the wider group of humans who entered his life. In addition, they reflect the extent to which the earliest Christians placed love and friendship at the heart of desirable human behavior, beyond strict ethical demands.

But did Jesus regard love as power? Perhaps this question as such never occurred to him. However, it seems undeniable that in his public ministry, he felt himself empowered by God's Spirit, empowered to act lovingly as he did. His parables reflect his awareness that the healing/saving power, God's Spirit, to which he bore witness in word and deed was that of love, unconditional divine love. Furthermore, his own compassion and concern for those he encountered, especially for the marginalized, were the sacrament in which he experienced his Abba's love for those people. And he experienced the power of that love, the power of his Abba's Spirit, to heal.

Even more directly, as the scene of the desert temptations indicates, Jesus realized the conflict between his own empowerment and the empowerment that would have come with earthly wealth or political influence. In his "kingdom" the power to be exercised was not that of the rulers of this world but the mysterious power of self-sacrificing servanthood. Greater love than this no one has, to lay down one's life. So, it does seem rather clear that Jesus in his ministry lived with the constant awareness of the battle taking place between two "powers," the power of God's Spirit that was the power of love, and the powers of "this world."

The Battle between the Power of Love and the Power of Evil

If one follows through on the biblical worldview of a battle between God and evil, it is possible to see the "love dimension" of the Spirit as fundamental power. Sin, the most basic of evils, is essentially the denial of the love that is appropriate to any given situation; it need not be only hatred, for apathy and irresponsibility also qualify. It is precisely because of this absence of love as creative of life that evil can only be healed by the "insertion" of love into the situation. This was graphically illustrated in the ministry of Jesus: at one level, his response to the various forms of evil he encountered—hunger, disease, ignorance—was to counter them and work for a betterment of the human situation in question. But as his public ministry progressed, he apparently became increasingly aware that there was a deeper level to evil that could be overcome by only one power, a self-giving love that was willing to sacrifice physical life itself. What this implies is that the divine love, the Spirit, working in and through Jesus' self-giving love, is the very heart of salvation.

The earliest memories that fed into the gospel narratives retain the disciples' awareness of Jesus' friendship. Though it is a composite of many memories about Jesus, the "last discourse" in John's Gospel conveys in almost palpable form the love Jesus felt for his friends, even though he was aware of their weakness and inability to support him openly in his final ordeal. And like a parent with his or her children, as he faced death, he longed for them to love one another. "A new commandment I give you, that you love one another, even as I have loved you" (John 13:34). Though the last discourse does not explicitly link power and love, it does link loving friendship with God's/Christ's Spirit, a linkage that continues into the Johannine stories of Jesus' Easter appearances and giving of the Spirit.

What seems clear is that Jesus' immediate disciples and the first generations that produced the Christian Scriptures possessed a developed theology of love as power, a theology that focused on God's Spirit and that was expressed in servanthood. Matthew 20:26, the third temptation in the desert, Acts 2, and Philippians 2—related to one another, these passages attest to the power exercised by Jesus as the Suffering Servant. But this Jesus, raised to glory because of his servant "obedience" even unto death (Phil. 2), was God's embodied Word, spoke in his own human freedom the "mind," the Spirit, of his Abba.

While there is no explicit linking of "Spirit" and "love" in the remembered teaching of Jesus, his own attitudes and behavior, grounded as they were in the Spirit, spoke undeniably about the divine love. The Spirit that Jesus shared with his Abba was sacramentalized in his dealings with people—the power that moved Jesus was his Abba's love, for this was the deepest level of his relationship to God.[5]

Although the earliest generations of Christians were focused on love, divine and human (e.g., Paul's constant refrain "have concern for one another," 1 John's "Little children, love one another"), the influence of Platonic thought in the Mediterranean basin gradually turned the discussion of God's power at work in salvation from the affective to the intellectual. From the third century onward, God's activity was described in terms of "illumination."[6] In trinitarian reflection, it was not until the latter half of the fourth century, that is, after Nicaea, that attention was paid in the conciliar creed to the character and influence of the Spirit. Not that awareness of the Spirit was totally lacking—the notions of the "sphragis" imprinted on a Christian by the Spirit, of the sanctifying power of the Spirit in the baptismal water, of the Spirit's endowment of an ordinand were already present in second-century theology—but the dominance of Logos was already well established.

As Christianity moved out of its Semitic origins and into the Greco-Roman-Platonic-Stoic thought world, the cultural dominance of patriarchy overwhelmed it. The conflict of love and patriarchy was not immediately recognized or felt, nor did patriarchy totally triumph, but a combination of developments—clergy divided from laity, monastic asceticism, suspicion of sex and passion leading to celibacy as an ideal—made love "second-rate" as an influence on "educated" Christian faith and theological reflection. On the contrary, intellectualism/rationalism as characteristic of the male *imago Dei* fitted into patriarchal cultural domination. This stress on the intellect is strikingly apparent in the influential writings of Pseudo-Dionysius, where the symbolic theurgy central to the system functions primarily in the realm of hierarchically ordered intellectual activity—illumination, ecstatic insight, and so on. Dionysius does preserve the Platonic notion of the overarching impact of the Good, but human personal relations do not enter at all into the process of human striving for "perfection." Symptomatic of this is the total lack of reference to women in the Dionysian corpus.

Still, the belief persisted that love of God is the supreme expression of Christian faith and life. The Spirit was recognized as the power that would lead the Christian to this "perfection," the Spirit of life that animates the baptized with a share of divine life. There was overwhelming stress on the development of the *individual* Christian and on the influence of the Spirit in leading the person to that which is the acme of "perfection," that is, agape. The influence of Paul's writings was key to much of this development. While Paul is explicitly concerned about the well-being of communities, there does not seem to be much theological reflection on the role of the Spirit as divine Love forming Christian communities. For centuries, even up to today, spiritual theology and most of the reflection on "grace" are focused on the faith life of the individual. An obvious exception to this remark is, of course, the prominent but unappreciated role of the epiclesis in eucharistic celebration.

Christian writing in the patristic period and the Middle Ages provides ample evidence that love remained a focus in Christian teaching about virtue, salvation, perfection, imitation of Christ, and grace. There is considerable dispute, however, about the exact understanding of love that prevailed in those centuries. This disagreement came to a head in the mid–twentieth century with a flurry of debate triggered by Anders Nygren's *Eros and Agape*, Pierre Rousselot's *Problème de l'Amour au Moyen Age*, and C. S. Lewis's *The Analogy of Love*. [7] What emerged from the discussion was a greater appreciation of the diversity of Christian views about love prior to modern times. Though all admitted the necessary contribution of both thought and affectivity, leading theologians and theological traditions placed relatively greater stress on one or the other. However, as a result of studies like those just named, there emerged a question that is still open to debate: was, as some allege, the warmth and intimacy associated with romantic love lacking prior to the troubadours? Was God's love for humans and human agapic love for one another as well as for

God to be understood in terms of responsible concern, altruism, and unselfishness but without the feelings associated with eros?

What stands as a challenge to this entire discussion is the experience of mystics throughout Church history. Certainly, the experience of a given mystic was deeply influenced by the prevailing cultural understanding of love, influenced also by the particular spiritual tradition that she or he had inherited. However, there was a prevailing experience of intimate relationship to Christ and God that lay at the heart of mystical contemplation throughout the centuries, a feeling that at times found expression in explicitly erotic language. There was a knowledge of the heart that was admitted to be superior to purely rational understanding.

An intriguing tribute to the continuing tradition of love as central to Christian spirituality is the way in which it "infiltrated" the Dionysian influence. That the writing of Dionysius and in particular his *Mystical Theology* exerted a major influence on medieval spiritual theology and theology thereafter is beyond dispute. Moreover, that influence is most evident in the currents of mysticism that are notable for their stress on affectivity—the Cistercians, Bonaventure and other Franciscans, the Victorines, Mechtilde, Julian, and so on. The Dionysian image of the overflowing abundance of the divine goodness is pervasive in medieval spiritual literature and is consistently interpreted as the overflow of divine love. Yet, in Dionysius himself, there is a striking absence of reference to love. Instead, there is what Paul Rorem refers to as the "relentlessly intellectual approach to union with God and his [Dionysius's] omission of any reference to love in the *Mystical Theology*."[8]

Where, then, does the entrance of love into the Dionysian tradition come from? Obviously, the biblical texts are an immediate candidate; but no doubt the influence of Augustine, specifically the affective side of the Augustinian heritage, was also responsible. Probably the most powerful influence was the actual spiritual experience of the mystics and theologians concerned, their experience of intimate relationship to God, the experience of loving and being loved.

Postmedieval centuries saw such classic Christian reflection as Francis de Sales' *The Love of God*, John of the Cross's *Living Flame of Love*, Teresa of Avila's *Interior Castle*, and the final "Contemplation for Obtaining Divine Love" in Loyola's *Spiritual Exercises*. With all their distinctiveness, these writings maintain a fundamental alikeness that is characteristically Christian. They all see human destiny achieved in love of God; they all see the possibility of attaining such love as dependent upon God's prior loving of humans; they all see love for God necessarily finding expression in humans' love for one another. Along with many other expressions of Christian spirituality, they manifest a certain pre-Freudian innocence in their healthy positive regard for warm human friendships.

At the same time, in certain circles, often in seminaries and religious communities, there developed a suspicion of human friendships, especially what were considered "particular friendships." Some of this may have been connected to concern about homosexual relationships, but the more common worry was that such friendships could detract from a person's total love for God or could threaten the overall concern of members of a community for one another. It was also linked at times with a false understanding of celibacy, as if commitment to celibacy demanded renunciation of deep human friendship. Theologically, this has been offset more recently by increased appreciation of the sacramentality of friendship, the insight that genuine love between humans is the most basic symbol of the presence of a loving God in human life.

Love and the Spirit of God

Throughout the history of Christian understanding of love, there is a constant linkage of love with God's Spirit, therefore with the divine exercise of power. At times, the Spirit is simply equated with divine love. At other times, the name "Gift," that is, the expression of love, is seen as proper to the Spirit. Indeed, the reference to the Spirit as divine love is so constant and pervasive that it is, for all practical purposes, taken for granted in Christian doctrine and theology. However, as we will see in the next chapter, the manner in which this is modeled in people's understanding is manifold.

During the patristic and medieval periods, the Spirit was seen as the gift of divine love, and theological detailing of this Gift was in terms of the various charisms granted by the Spirit. The medieval summas, such as that of Thomas Aquinas,[9] based their treatment of the Spirit's "mission" on an explanation of the gifts given to humans by the Spirit, the gifts listed in Isaiah 11 and by Paul in I Corinthians 12. However, what was always viewed as the fundamental gift was, to quote Paul in Romans 5, "the divine love poured into our hearts through the Holy Spirit which is given to us." What is specially relevant to the topic of this book is that all these "gifts," including the Spirit as Gift, were regarded as empowerment of the human subject.

Speaking of divine gift giving inevitably raises the question of God's creative activity as self-giving and the link of *creator* Spirit with the Spirit as *gift*. Perhaps it is in viewing God's action of creating in terms of the creative power of love that one can make some sense of the kenosis that occurs in creation.[10] Seemingly in contradiction to God's infinite power, creating involves a divine relinquishing of absolute power; for the reality of creatures that exist with their own distinct being implies randomness in the universe. This "independence" is much more evident if human creatures possess genuine power of free self-determination. But it is characteristic of the power exerted in love, in this case the creative loving of God, that it influences the beloved with respect for the otherness of the beloved. God's creative loving is not dominating.

Long before the Middle Ages, the Spirit was linked with divine love. In the East, Didymus taught that the Spirit is within the Trinity the Gift of Father and Son and is the great Gift to humans in the process of sanctification because the Spirit is Love.[11] Basil of Caesarea in his treatise on the Spirit, though reflecting almost totally the intellectualism characteristic of the Platonic tradition, saw Gift as a name proper to the Spirit.[12] In the West, Augustine in particular referred repeatedly to this link. Yves Congar mentions the frequency of Augustine's reference to Paul's citation of Romans 5.[13] So, while, in the patristic and medieval periods, the principal focus in theological speculation about the divine Spirit had to do with the trinitarian relationship of the Spirit to Father and Son, there was a constant accompanying reflection about the Spirit's effect on human life in the mystery of "grace." So strong was this linkage that the Middle Ages witnessed an ongoing debate as to whether the Spirit caused grace or whether the Spirit *was* the grace.[14]

With the classic Reformers, the role of the Spirit as transforming love was overshadowed by the Spirit's work of supporting the power of the Word, particularly the biblical word in its witness to the saving activity of Christ. Justification came through imputation of the justifying act of Christ, and sanctification was achieved in attachment to Christ. Even in nineteenth-century liberal Protestantism, despite its emphasis on religious experience, no role in human transformation was assigned to God's Spirit as Love.[15] An important qualification to this negative judgment needs to be added: namely, the widespread influence of the various forms of Pietism. Embracing such diverse phenomena as the Moravian Brethren, American and English Methodism, and French Jansenism, the Pietist impulse brought to the fore the religious sentiment believed to flow from the animating presence of the Spirit. Though its influence waned in Europe, Pietism produced a lasting effect in pentecostal developments in the United States.[16]

In Catholic circles, the postmedieval traditions of mysticism, which included Teresa, Francis de Sales, Ignatius Loyola, and John of the Cross, reflected the same stress on Christ's redeeming role but maintained also the teaching of the Spirit's mission as divine Love. Relatively little attention, however, was paid to the role of the Spirit in the dogmatic theology that was taught in post-Reformation Catholic seminaries.

Recent developments in pneumatology have been deeply influenced by research and reflection on the life, death, and resurrection of Jesus and the resultant "Christology from below." Intrinsic to this christological development has been examination of the role in Jesus' career of the empowering presence to him of God's Spirit, God's love.[17] In some circles this has led to suggestive proposals of Spirit Christology.[18] Some theologians, like, Heribert Muehlen, Piet Schoonenberg, and Walter Kasper have more explicitly directed their reflection to the role of the Spirit. Karl Rahner, by contrast, apparently gives little direct attention to the Spirit, but this is deceiving. Actually, the Spirit's operation underlies the entire Rahnerian vision of the divine "gracing" of humanity that is central to Rahner's theological anthropology.[19]

At the same time, pneumatology has been enriched by the shifts in thinking about the Church, not just in theology but in the practical religious experience of the "ordinary" faithful that followed, for one thing, on Vatican II's description of the Church as "the people of God." Much of this has found expression in a widespread interest in "spirituality," in various forms of "the charismatic movement," and in a renewed sense of personal relatedness to God in response to the divine gift of love.

Summary. In a sense, if one thinks of "love" as the affective movement toward "the good," love deals with the ultimate exercise of power, that is, the motivations that lead humans to action. These motivations flow from the perception of something or some person or some activity as good; so, influence on people's values and perceptions is an exercise of power beyond any other.[20] Other forms of power—threats of violence, physical control, bribery, and so on—are exercised precisely to motivate people toward one or another course of action. Whether admitted by everyone or respected in a person's actual judgments, there is no good beyond a beloved friend. Consequently, friendship possesses a certain ultimate power to motivate, a power that at least theoretically overshadows the attracting power of anything else in human experience. There are striking instances of this, instances in which a person will give up wealth, political power, and public esteem because he or she has fallen in love and values the beloved above all else. It is because friendship has this basic power that it is the most fundamental sacrament of God's Spirit of love. It is true that some men and women judge wealth or earthly power as supreme goods and sacrifice personal relations to obtain material goals. Yet, there is a common sense judgment of most people that to forego human friendship is a tragic loss.

Seen from a theological point of view, love, ultimately the out-reaching "expression" of divine love that is God's Spirit, is the most powerful of powers. It is the power that breaks the cycle of violence in Jesus' dying and rising; it is

the creative source of the power of nature, life-power overcoming death; it is
the power bonding humans together in the eschatological community that is
the final destiny of human life; it is the prophetic power already working in
history to achieve that relating of humans to one another in justice and peace
that is the "reign of God." It is the bond of friendship, the pearl of great price
for which humans are willing to confront the criticism and disdain of "the wise
of this world" who place greater weight on the achievement of wealth and
political power.

Conclusion

The Divine Embrace

After a long period of relative neglect, pneumatology flourishes to-day as never before in Christian history. One need only read and then pray about the proceedings from the 1996 gathering of the Catholic Theological Society of America to realize the inexhaustible richness of theological reflection about God as Spirit that is taking place at the present moment. [1] At the center of this theological reflection is the awareness that it is in *faith experience* that this pneumatological explosion is rooted, and it is this experience, shared within the community of faithful (whether formal adherents of a Christian church or not), that needs to be mined for its riches. This present volume tries to tap only one aspect of human experience, the experience of power, as a vein of insight into the mystery of God's Spirit.

If one is to attempt some understanding of the reality referred to as "the Holy Spirit," there are certain presuppositions that establish the parameters within which the attempt can legitimately and profitably occur. Obviously, search for deepened knowledge of God's Spirit can occur only within the context of faith; it is *fides quaerens intellectum,* and the *intellectum* (understanding), when it occurs, is not the conclusion of careful reasoning but an insight that extends beyond justifying explanation.

Reason can, however, dictate the path one must walk in striving for an understanding of God. The truly transcendent reality we name "God" is by definition beyond human words or human thoughts, and consequently, only analogy and metaphor can provide a spring-board for the intellectual leap into mystery. This has been acknowledged for millennia and is currently reflected in the widespread interest in and use of "models" in theological discourse. This is not the place to undertake an analysis of the way in which metaphorical understanding works; but it should be clear that grasping the nature, contribution, and limitations of metaphor is intrinsic to understanding and evaluating the process of theologizing.

Before proposing a metaphorical approach to "understanding" the Spirit of God as power, which is the avowed and limited goal of this book, it is necessary to purify as far as possible our understanding of "God." This requires criticizing the understanding of God already acquired and rejecting those elements that are unjustified anthropomorphic projections. Clearly, this cannot mean that all transfer of understanding from our experience of being human persons is ruled out; if that were the case, we would be left completely thoughtless. What it does mean is that we realize that basically the way we imagine and think about God is not the way God is. To put it in classical terms, we need to employ both the *via positiva* and the *via negativa* and then make our "leap."

We are dealing with the Transcendent and must let God be God, and we must beware of thinking that our analogous projections are the way God actually is—such is the root of idolatry. However, it would seem that in some analogous way this Transcendent can be thought of as "spiritual," the analog being our human experience of spiritual existing as persons: thinking, loving, imagining, being free and so on. So, as we probe our knowledge/belief in the created character of ourselves and of the universe we know, we envisage this God thinking and loving the universe into existing. Divine creative thinking and loving, we believe, reach a new dimension with the evolutionary emergence of human persons capable of response to the divine initiative. Such reflection inevitably raises certain questions: how does this creator God work in human lives? What is providence? How is the divine power that is the Spirit of God operative in the ongoing process of creation?

Not only will the understanding of God have to be appraised; it will be necessary also to take a brief but probing look at the reality referred to by the word "*spirit*." Basically this demands insight into what we humans are as persons, demands that we go beyond the inadequate characterization of the human person as body and soul and define humans as incarnate (or embodied) spirits. This is far more than substituting the word "spirit" for "soul." It is grasping the fact that our dominant and controling way of being is as spirits, that our bodiliness flows from and exists in service of our spirit-being, but conversely that our human spirit-being cannot be what it is as spirit except in terms of its relation to bodiliness.

Reflecting on human experiences that we take for granted helps us grasp this fusion of spiritual and bodily existing that we are. While our ideas exist without weight or size or spatial location, they are drawn from and remain grounded in bodily exposure to sensations. Because we are spirits, self-aware even as we are aware of the world around us and engaged in self-giving friendships, we are capable of presence that is quite other than spatial proximity. Our thinking and loving are modes of being distinctively other than the complicated physical activity of the brain that provides the infrastructure for thought, self-awareness, and free choice. Like all created beings, we exist relationally, but beyond that we exist as self-consciously relational and to some extent freely choose our relations.

It is not the purpose here to probe further the nature of "spirit." Rather, it is to insist that in any discussion of pneumatology, indeed in any discussion of God, it is imperative that we constantly remind ourselves that God is spirit. So, in applying one or another metaphor to gain a glimpse into the reality of "the Spirit of God," we must highlight the spirit dimension of the metaphor and prescind as far as possible from the limiting elements of the embodiment that is always intrinsic to the analog we use.

In previous chapters that related the Spirit of God to various forms of power, we have inevitably utilized a number of models without drawing attention to their metaphorical functioning. However, before going on to suggest a metaphor that can enable an insight into God's Spirit as power, it may be helpful to review very briefly a number of metaphors currently used in pneumatology. This sampling may suggest some of the faith awareness of God's Spirit possessed by the Christian community, and this may help set in context my own metaphorical attempt to understand the Spirit of God as power.

Yves Congar in his magisterial *I Believe in the Holy Spirit* reviews a number of classic explanations of the Spirit, but his own view is perhaps best revealed subtly in his agreement with C. Buchsel, who describes the Spirit as divine *What is* communication by way of love. Clearly the metaphor being used (as it was a *Spirit?* number of times in history) is the human experience of <u>loving communication.</u>

Jurgen Moltmann devotes a chapter ("The Personhood of the Spirit") of *The Spirit of Life* to summary discussion of metaphors for the Spirit. These he classifies under four headings: personal (Lord, mother, judge), formative (energy, space, Gestalt), movement (tempest, fire, love), mystical (source of light, water, fertility). However, the basic metaphor used in the book is that of <u>vitality overflowing into life-giving.</u>[2]

In his 1986 encyclical letter on the Holy Spirit ("Dominum et vivificantem"), *Pope John Paul II* reviews a number of traditional metaphors. With his strong interest in ethical issues, the Pope stresses the Spirit's "judgment" on sin (John 16:8) and impact on conscience; the underlying metaphor appears to be that of *counselor/teacher*.[3]

Like the Pope, *John Haughey* treats the influence of the Spirit on a person's internal awareness but focuses on relation to Christ rather than on consciousness of sin; he uses the metaphor of a *witness* and the knowledge provided by a witness, leading to inner personal understanding of Christ.[4]

Donald Gelpi uses two metaphors—because he stresses the cognitive role of the Spirit, he uses *gracious enlightenment* and speaks of the Spirit as "the mind of God," but he also uses the metaphor of *mother*.[5]

Leonardo Boff in his *Trinity and Society* also draws attention to the feminine dimensions of the Spirit by using the metaphor of *mother*. However, in *Church, Charism and Power*, where his focus is on the charisms of the Spirit, his basic metaphor is that of internal *organizing power*.[6]

In the context of a doxological approach to understanding the Trinity, *Catherine LaCugna* speaks of the Spirit as the dynamic relating of humans to God. The metaphor in question is that of *personal relationship* but in the dynamic sense of actively relating. She links it with the Spirit as divine *freedom* in love-creating koinonia.[7]

As the title of his recent volume indicates, *Gary Badcock* focuses on the two classic metaphors of *light* (of truth) and *fire* (of love), examining the way they continue to function in current pneumatology.[8]

An intriguing study of metaphor applied to the Spirit is *Michael Lodahl's* linkage of Christian understanding of "divine *presence*" with the Jewish notion of *Shekhinah*.[9]

One of the most provocative metaphors and one that focuses on *power* is the one to which *Sally McFague* draws attention. It sees the Spirit of God as "the *breath of life* that gives all bodies, all forms of matter, the energy or power to become themselves." It is in the context of panentheism that she then speaks of the world as God's body. There is a certain congruence of this model with theistic stress on the divine transcendence, for breath is not a constitutive element of a body; it comes and goes, flows through, imparts life, and empowers but retains its autonomous reality—a transcendence along with immanence.[10]

Finally, one can add the summation of medieval metaphors provided by *Elizabeth Dreyer* in her 1996 CTSA address:

> agent of reconciliation and unity, as the one who offers comfort and
> confidence to those who suffer; as messenger of God the gift-giver;
> as the one who empowers the believer to act, especially in the
> realms of virtue and love of neighbor; and as the one who renews

the face of the earth. The Spirit is seen as the wind or breath that blows where it will, bringing freedom; as an aid to contemplation; as the fire of Love that transforms the affections; as the gift of insight leading to an intelligent grasp of the faith, and the ability to live it maturely; as courage to witness to the gospel and to prophesy.[11]

With no intent of comparing with these the metaphor I will use, but because the aim of this book is to develop a pneumatology out of the diverse human experiences of *power*, I hope to explore the _experience of a personal embrace_ as a unifying metaphor to aid an understanding of the Spirit of God. And I would wish to keep this in an active context: it is the divine "outreaching" in loving self-gift. While this metaphor can be used with regard to the inner life of the Trinity (as such it is akin to Bernard of Clairvaux's characterization of the Spirit as "the kiss" between Father and Son), I will treat its applicability to the divine "reaching out" with creative power to embrace the universe. While somewhat distinctive, this metaphor is consonant with the traditional metaphors through which Christian faith experiences of God's Spirit have been expressed. The objective will be to advance our understanding by seeing how this model relates to, unites, and throws light on the various connections of Spirit and power we have studied.

Throughout I hope to keep in mind that the experience and "reality" of God as revealed in Jesus exerts power in a *personal* way. This means that we are dealing with a spiritual embracing and therefore that our analog is foremost the spirit dimension in our experience of a personal embrace. After all, as we will see, without this spirit aspect, that is, without feeling, an embrace is inauthentic custom/routine and even at times hypocritical.

Reflection on Embrace

Presuming that we are dealing with a genuine embrace used as an expression of friendship, it involves a _knowing_ of self and "the other" as loving and loved. Nothing is more basic in the establishment and grateful acceptance of a person's self-identity than the experience of love. As the gesture in which this reciprocal love is expressed, a warm embrace is life-giving and personhood-creating.

To have another embrace me warmly is an _invitation_ to friendship, either new or continuing. To respond to this invitation and thereby gain a friend is attractive, but it may also involve an unknown and risky future.

Any genuine embrace must be two sided, precisely because it is a *com-*

mitment to friendship. It is a promise of fidelity in the relationship, a promise that each will be there for the other when needed. So, it provides _hope_ for the future, an assurance of support, assurance that one will not be alone to face life.

A genuine embrace of friends offers the _comfort_ of friendship: the peace of being unconditionally accepted, a sense of self-worth and being appreciated, a quiet recognition that one holds something of "supreme _value_," starting as early as a mother's embrace of her infant, an awareness of being at home. Embracing a friend symbolizes in profound fashion the reciprocity of friendship: it is one's _self-gift_ to a significant other (not necessarily "the" significant other), but at the same time it is _possessing_ the other as friend. It is I-Thou knowing that is I-Thou in both directions. It is truly a personal _union_, with no other goal than the union itself so that at that moment the new reality "we" comes into being. The union in no way diminishes the _otherness_ of the other; instead, it celebrates that otherness in respect and love. In the embrace, one experiences the excitement of _joy_, but it is a joy mixed with the calm of _peace_.

On many occasions, an embrace can be completely in silence; it speaks for itself. Indeed, in many situations, as on the occasion of consoling a bereaved friend at a death, it substitutes for one's inability to find any suitable words. But on other occasions, it is enriched by words whose sincerity and deeper meaning are conveyed by the embrace itself. There seems to exist a natural link between deeply personal conversation and reaching out to touch another.

If one looks carefully and reflectively at the experience of embracing another, it becomes evident that the very heart of the action is the "spiritual embracing" that is taking place. One is reaching out as a person, truly giving oneself as the subject he or she is. This is what one attempts to express in the physical gesture, but in the last analysis this bodily action is incapable of saying all that one wishes to say. Somehow, though, if this inner embracing is present, it gives to the physical embrace as symbol a genuineness that is inescapable. If the inner embrace is not there, if the embrace is a purely routine or formal gesture, that is immediately felt. On the other hand, there can be occasions when, without the outward embrace, a person's spiritual embrace can be conveyed by other body language, perhaps by nothing more than a look. Finally, it is in the realm of the spiritual embrace that a person can with full mature love reach out intentionally to embrace all creation and especially the poor, neglected, and oppressed. It is this spiritual embrace, with all the resonances of a bodily embrace that I have described, that is the heart of the metaphor I wish to apply to the Spirit of God. I believe, too, that in so doing, I am dealing with more than an analog; I am dealing with a sacrament. Because it is sacrament, it is a revelation of God's Spirit as divine love/power "outreaching" to embrace creation and especially humans, even as God's Word is "outreaching" in Incarnation. It is "panentheism" in terms of *presence*.

In experiencing and accepting this divine embrace, there are two distinct responses. From what we might call the "receptive" side, there is the awe and openness that accompanies being loved. This is not automatic; it engages a person's freedom because the believer must overcome the reluctance of apparent dependence and be willing to live with the implications of such a relationship. On the "active" side, the experience is one of being empowered to share ministerially in the divine outreaching by loving service to others.

Divine Power Exerted by Embrace

Exerting the kind of power suggested by our metaphor, God's Spirit-power encounters and interacts with the various exercises of power we have described in earlier chapters. Contrary to the dominating power that uses force to accomplish its purposes, divine Spirit-power works through nonviolent service. Instead of coercion, God's Spirit is an invitation to greater levels of life and happiness. Since it operates as friendship, God's Spirit is not forced upon humans; rather, it accepts and respects human freedom but seeks to elicit the response of friendship. In so doing, it reaches a depth of influence that domination cannot, for it engages the inner assent and unfettered cooperation of persons without the fear of "rebellion" that patriarchal control always faces. That such "gentle" power can counteract and overcome the power of force and violence is, of course, a matter of faith, but as I suggested in chapter 1, some events of recent decades suggest that it can happen. While many of those still holding political and economic power continue to trust in their ability to retain control through use of force, it is interesting to observe the way in which the theme song of the civil rights movement, "We Shall Overcome," has been picked up worldwide by oppressed peoples.

Is a new wind blowing? One indication that it may be is the lessening of capitulation to fear of violence among many dominated groups. Clearly, the fear remains, for the threat of violent control remains. Yet, women and men are persisting in their quest for liberation and freedom, even as they face torture and death for doing so. When questioned about what seems to be folly, their response is that despots can kill their bodies, but they cannot kill their spirit. The courage comes to many of them with the conviction that God's power is with them and therefore the triumph of their cause is inevitable. We have often admired the courage of early Christian martyrs and attributed their fearlessness to the continuation of the Pentecostal event, but today is witnessing at least as widespread incidence of martyrdom and the fortifying presence of God's Spirit. Theologically, this has found expression in the emergence of liberation theology, which, though generally associated with developments in Latin America, has probably found its most prominent voice in Christian feminism. Our metaphor applies to this situation: in the embrace of a powerful friend, one can experience both assurance and hope. Aware that one will not be abandoned in any circumstances by this friend, one is strengthened to encounter the objects of one's fears and not give way to them. Contrary to the assault of dominators who employ violence to exact vengeance, the divine power reaches out in mercy to protect; it is "soft" power that is the basis of hope because it is already possessed.

The centuries-long creedal description of God's Spirit as "giver of life" can find metaphorical clarification through the metaphor of "embrace." Obviously, an embrace of friends does not communicate biological life. The fact that a new human being can result from the marital embrace does serve as a symbol of the Spirit's creative power. However, it is in the realm of creating personal life that the embrace operates symbolically. Growth and maturation of personal existing comes about through humans' relating to one another. In dealing with another person, I either help to create or diminish that individual's self-identity and personal potential. A warm embrace conveys an evaluation of that person's importance to me; it signifies my unconditioned acceptance of him or her as friend; it adds my friendship as an element in that person's self-identity.

If "embracing" is used in the transferred sense of accepting the life circumstances that surround me, that is, I embrace life and the universe in which I live, this points to humans' role in advancing the processes of evolution. We are at that stage in that evolution when humans are assuming a new role in the development of the universe, but a role that must be acknowledged and honored. It is painfully evident that humans can despoil the world in which they live and thereby stunt or reverse that world's development, both the development of human life and the development of the environment. Embracing stewardship of the world is essential to the creative continuation of life. If it is accepted, it can and will then act sacramentally, signifying and "inserting" the presence of God's creative Spirit.

To the extent to which humans share in the creation of life, they participate in the eros of the universe, the universal drive of creatures toward fulfillment. An embrace of friends provides a clue to understanding the divine embrace and the way it brings about the world's eros. True human embracing is always erotic, not necessarily with sexual implications, but with expression of the desire to relate to the other as a friend. As such, it is a symbol of the mysterious fact that the Transcendent, which by definition seems to eliminate any erotic longings, desires humans and through them all creation to "return" to its creator. It is in so returning that humans become "fully alive" and the "glory of God."[12] Were it not for the divine revelation contained in the religious experience from which the Hebrew Bible and the Christian scriptures are derived, even faith could not imagine such an erotic aspect to the loving "reaching out to embrace" that is God's Spirit. The divine embrace is not itself the eros of creation, but it elicits that erotic response by its eschatological invitation to ultimate fulfillment.

In the context of the Spirit empowering Jesus' ministry, during his earthly career and continuing in the mystery of his risen breathing forth the Spirit, the invitation of the divine embrace includes the vocation to discipleship. To respond to another's embrace in friendship means that one accepts implicitly that friend's goals as one's own, shares that friend's "projects" if invited to do so. In human affairs, it is a common gesture when two persons have agreed to sharing a common task for the "inviter" to put an arm around the shoulder of the "disciple" in a modified embrace that is more side-by-side than face-to-face. Such a Spirit-embrace finds expression in the charisms' empowering a person for ministry. It finds expression also in the classic "spiritualities" that characterize the origin and history of the great religious communities—for example, the invitation to serving with Christ that is the meditation on "The Kingdom" in the Ignatian *Exercises*, to which the response is the exercitant's prayer: "Take, Lord, and receive *all*."

In previous chapters, we studied several forms of authority that come, not from the occupation of office, but from other sources such as knowledge. Perhaps the most basic of these is the authority one has as "good" and "important" because he or she is the object of divine love, embraced by God's Spirit. A true human embrace says to another person that she or he is most basically valued for who they are rather than for what they are or possess. If the human embrace grants this kind of dignity to a person, the divine embrace is an ultimate grounding for this fundamental human importance. Embraced by the Spirit, one has the authority of a friend of God.

Moreover, a person responding in openness to the divine embrace has a unique kind of authority in the area of knowledge. The authority to teach comes with possession of knowledge; one can teach with authority in proportion as one knows that about which one speaks and not just what has been said about the reality. Many languages use two different verbs to distinguish between knowing someone and knowing about someone—for example, the French *connaître* and *savoir*—though English does not. At the heart of the mystery of divine loving of humans is that a person enjoying this religious experience does not simply know about God, one knows God. Mystics over the centuries have referred to this as "the knowledge of the heart," a knowing that is not confined to those with extraordinary mystical gifts but to some extent belongs to all with faith.[13] Though this religious experience needs the normative guidance of a believing community if for no other reason than that it is open to self-deception, it does possess its own kind of authority.

In the case of Jesus of Nazareth, the Christian scriptures base his unique teaching authority precisely on this kind of intimate insight into the reality of God. At the end of the Johannine prologue that describes Jesus as embodied divine Wisdom, his empowerment to speak more authoritatively than even Moses flows from his intimate knowing of God—he is in the bosom of the Father. The same insight is contained in the synoptic scene of the Transfiguration in the divine words spoken about Jesus, "This is my beloved Son, listen to him." The authority to teach about God extends beyond Jesus himself; the basis for the distinctive religious teaching of Christianity is Jesus' awareness of God as his Abba.[14] Jesus was uniquely aware and empowered by the divine embrace, the Spirit he shared with his Abba.

Despite the tendency of humans to reduce religion to morality, they are not the same. Still, authentic faith-knowing that comes with the divine embrace does grant a capacity to judge the morality of human attitudes and actions that goes beyond ethical reflection. The truth and goodness of the God whose Spirit reaches out in love inescapably evaluates all else that a person encounters, including him-or herself. This empowers the loved person or community with the discernment that is central in the power over sin, the *potestas judiciaria*. Because such judgment on sin takes place in the "soft" though inescapable truth of an embrace, it immediately implies also the reconciliation of the sinner. It is the experience that in actuality divine justice and mercy are not distinguishable; God's Spirit passes judgment creatively by making one just. The Spirit-embrace is at the very heart of Jesus and Christianity's healing ministry.

An often forgotten aspect of this God-given discernment is the deepened awareness and appreciation for beauty. One can grasp some of this enhanced aesthetic sense and the creative impulse it triggers in the words of Gerard Manley Hopkins as he speaks about "the beauty of things deep down" or in the theological vision of Hugh of St. Victor that all things are sacramental. Again, our human experience of being embraced by a beloved gives us a window on the deepened awareness of creation's beauty that comes with being embraced by the creator. One of the most apt metaphors of this was provided by a friend of mine in describing his relation to his wife: "Before I met her everything was in black and white; after I came to know and love her it was in Technicolor." With this new awakening to beauty comes a transformation of the pleasure accompanying the use of the "good things" of life; no longer a temptation to substitute material enjoyments for greater goods, the pleasurable elements of life are freely and appreciatively used, with discipline against excess being provided by the experience of divine embrace. Truly, in gratefully using creatures in the presence of the Gift-giver, one is living the text of the Wisdom of Solomon, "Wisdom has spread her table. . . ."

Finally, it is essential to draw attention to the communal dimension of the Spirit's powerful embrace. Though it does touch each individual with creative regard for his or her distinctiveness, the outreaching of God that is the Spirit embraces humans in their relationships to one another, that is, as a community. Like a parent whose spiritual embrace of children reaches out to unite them as family, so the divine Parent reaches out to gather humans together into the reign of justice and peace. This is reflected in Jesus' parables that speak of God gathering in the harvest and in the ancient prayer of the *Didache* and early liturgy—"Like stalks of wheat gathered from the hillside. . . ." Ultimately, this is the story of humanity's advancing history: embraced by the Spirit-power of God, women and men will be able to conquer those powers that would diminish them and instead use beneficent powers to become united with God and one another in the power of the Spirit.

Notes

INTRODUCTION

1. H. Kung and D. Tracy, eds., *Paradigm Change in Theology* (New York, 1989).

2. T. Kuhn, *The Structure of Scientific Revolution*, 2nd ed. (Chicago, 1970).

3. Cf. D. Tracy, "Hermeneutical Reflections in the New Paradigm," in Kung and Tracy, *Paradigm Change*, pp. 34–62.

4. See F. Fiorenza, pp. 1–88 in *Systematic Theology*, vol. 1, ed. F. Fiorenza and J. Galvin (Minneapolis, 1991).

5. An instance of this is F. Fiorenza's *Foundational Theology: Jesus and the Church* (New York, 1984). Another is "The Christian Classic," pp. 249–338 in D. Tracy, *The Analogical Imagination* (New York, 1981).

6. W. Eichrodt, *Theology of the Old Testament* (Philadelphia, 1961); see also A. Gelin, *Key Concepts of the Old Testament* (New York, 1955).

7. G. von Rad, *Old Testament Theology* (New York, 1960).

8. J.D.G. Dunn, *Unity and Diversity in the New Testament* (Philadelphia, 1977).

9. On the role of experience in theology, see my article "The Experiential Word of God," in *Consensus in Theology*, ed. L. Swidler (Philadelphia, 1980), pp. 69–74. In Roman Catholic circles, the breakthrough in acceptance of religious experience as a springboard for theology came with the writings of Jean Mouroux, especially his *The Christian Experience* (New York, 1954).

10. On nominalism, cf. Paul Vignaux's classic article "Nominalisme" in the *Dictionnaire de théologie catholique*, vol. 11-1 (Paris, 1931), cols. 717–784. A somewhat different view is held by Heiko Obermann, *The Harvest of Medieval Theology*, 3rd ed. (Durham, 1983).

11. This shift is generally associated with the twentieth-century movement of "existentialism" or with the metaphysics of Heidegger. However, there was an important parallel development based on a reassessment of the philosophy of Thomas Aquinas and commonly referred to as "dynamic Thomism" (in distinction from "traditional" Thomistic philosophy), which exploited the existentialism involved in Aquinas's own thought. The seminal thinker in this dynamic Thomism was Joseph Marechal whose *Point de départ de la métaphysique* was a major influence on the philosophy and theology of Bernard Lonergan and Karl Rahner among others.

12. J. Steinbeck, *East of Eden* (New York, 1952).

13. Recently, there has been renewed attention to the work of Talcott Parsons and his emphasis on function, criticized by A. Giddens, who stresses the dominant role of structures in influencing people's behavior, and more positively viewed by Jurgen Habermas. For an analytic review of these positions, see S. Glegg, *Frameworks of Power* (London, 1989). Clegg's comparison of the position of S. Lukes and A. Giddens on agency and structure is particularly helpful; cf. pp. 138–148. On Parsons, cf. F. Bourricaud, *The Sociology of Talcott Parsons* (Chicago, 1981).

14. Overlapping the study of political structures and processes is consideration of the public power that has increasingly attached to economic activity. See J. Galbraith, *The Anatomy of Power*, (Boston, 1983). See also the writings of R. Heilbroner. The title of his book on leading economic theorists, *The Worldly Philosophers* (5th ed. [New York, 1980]) reflects the interrelatedness of social-scientific thinking about power. Power of wealth will be studied in chap. 6.

15. It would be an interesting study to compare this empowerment by situation within an organization with the ancient view of *potestas ordinis*, where an individual's power derived from his or her "location" in society.

16. J. Nye, *The Paradox of American Power* (New York, 2002).

17. M. French, *Beyond Power* (New York, 1985).

18. Especially in France, during the complicated philosophical discourse that followed on the existentialist phase of philosophy, there was increasing insistence that reality is complicated, that there are dialectical interactions of continuity and discontinuity, that there are many "hidden" influences that have been overlooked in the writing of history, that there are many kinds of influence (read "power"). Much of this led to and finds expression in Foucault's studies on various kinds of power. This is reminiscent of the 1950s, when in evening discussions of history at the Center for French Catholic Intellectuals, panelists like Paul Riceour, Jean Danielou, and Raymond Aron were wrestling with the interplay of diachrony and synchrony in analyzing history. While societal structures certainly affect historical developments, their influence is intertwined with such things as free decisions and the indeterminacy of events—such as the assassination of President Kennedy.

19. Cf. Jane Chance, *The Mythology of Power: Lord of the Rings* (Lexington, Ky., 2001). The power of language will be studied in chap. 10.

20. It would be the subject of another needed study to relate this to the gradual "secularization" of Christianity that has taken place in the past three centuries.

21. See, for example, Karl Rahner's discussion of using "person" in trinitarian

theology (*Foundations* [New York, 1986], pp. 134–137). For extensive review of present pneumatolotical reflection, cf. papers of the important Marquette University symposium referred to earlier: B. Hinze and L. Dabney, *Advents of the Spirit* (Milwaukee, 2001).

22. This was strikingly illustrated by the meeting of women in 1996 in Beijing at the United Nations Conference on Women. In addition to the official conference, which drew representatives from across the globe, the unofficial gathering associated with it was comprised of several thousand, a cross section of women, rich and poor, of diverse ethnic origins, from all parts of the world. For a systemic analysis of patriarchy and the shift away from it, cf. A. Johnson, *The Gender Knot* (Philadelphia, 1997).

23. Perhaps in the light of recent events in the former Yugoslavia or in Rwanda, it would be more accurate to speak of "tribalism" rather than nationalism.

24. In a recent survey of the members of the Catholic Theological Society of America, the issue mentioned as most important in theology today is the relation of Christianity to other world religions.

25. This is reflected in Rahner's turn to theological anthropology. For an insightful relating of Rahner's theological anthropology with that being developed within the U.S. Latino/a theological community, cf. M. Diaz, *On Being Human* (Maryknoll, 2001).

26. Reaction against this irrelevance of liturgy was a main thrust of Vatican II's *Constitution on the Liturgy* (*Sacrosanctum concilium*). See especially #48.

27. Cf. L. Snook, *What in the World Is God Doing?* (Minneapolis, 1999).

28. For an explanation of social construction of reality that distinguishes the various constructions flowing from differing ideological bases and social locations, cf. Susan Parsons, *Feminism and Christian Ethics* (New York, 1996), pp. 66–120.

CHAPTER I

1. Cf. Joseph Campbell, *The Hero with a Thousand Faces*, 2nd ed. (Princeton, 1972). In interesting deviation from individual glorification of the "strong" hero is the emergence in present-day literature of the "anti-hero," e.g., the "heroes" Sam and Frodo in Tolkien's *Lord of the Rings*. What this points to is the overarching and ultimately triumphant power of loving service and the importance of "little people" who overcome the violence of "big people."

2. For a social analysis of patriarchy as a system of control, cf. Johnson, *The Gender Knot.*

3. See Nye's recent *Paradox of American Power*. Though detailing the increasing role of U.S. economic power and the importance of "soft power," Nye indicates the continuing primacy of military strength.

4. Given this fact, today's revolutionary questioning of violence may find expression in Tolkien's *Lord of the Rings*: the hero is the basically nonviolent Frodo.

5. Plato, *Republic*, pp. 377–396.

6. For example, Psalms 25–28, 55–59 recalling God's help to David in his conflicts.

7. Cf. G. Von Rad, *The Message of the Prophets* (San Francisco, 1976), pp. 60–76.

8. On Israelite notions of Spirit, cf. G. Badcock, *Light of Truth and Fire of Love* (Cambridge, 1997), pp. 8–18.

9. Cf. E. Johnson, *She Who Is* (New York, 1992). Johnson focuses on divine Sophia in her important reorientation of trinitarian theology. A distinct but related element of late Jewish thought that touches on Spirit is that of divine presence; cf. Michael Lodahl's provocative book, *Shekhinah/Spirit* (Mahwah, N.J., 1992).

10. See R. Horsley, *Jesus and the Cycle of Violence* (San Francisco, 1989); *Bandits, Prophets and Messiahs* (Harrisburg, 1999).

11. Cf. E. Schussler Fiorenza, *Jesus: Miriam's Child, Sophia's Prophet* (New York, 1994); E. Johnson, *She Who Is*, pp. 150–169.

12. A distinctive aspect of this "power of weakness" has been highlighted by René Girard in his study of the saving role of "the victim," its celebration in sacrificial ritual as fundamental to religious practice, and the reversal of meanings of victimhood that occurred in the death of Jesus of Nazareth. See especially *The Scapegoat* (Baltimore, 1986).

13. Cf. A. Gelin, *The Poor of Yahweh* (Collegeville, 1964).

14. See my essay, "The 'War Myth' in 2nd Century Christian Teaching," pp. 235–250 in *No Famine in the Land*, ed. J. Flanagan (Missoula, 1975).

15. The account of Lactantius, reporting that Constantine in a dream was instructed to paint the Chi-Rho symbol on the shields of his warriors, is probably more trustworthy than Eusebius's story of the *In hoc signo vinces* vision.

16. Cf. pp. 105–150 in R. Bridenthal, Susan Stuart, and Merry Wieser, eds., *Becoming Visible: Women in European History*, 3rd ed. (Boston, 1998).

CHAPTER 2

1. On the nature of fear and its relation to anxiety, cf. pp. 287–306 in the essay by D. Barlow, B. Chorpita, and J. Tirovsky, in *Perspectives on Anxiety, Panic, and Fear*, ed. D. Hope, vol. 43 in Univ. of Nebraska Symposium on Motivation (Lincoln, 1996).

2. On the idea that a person's being subject to another's power is correlative to the subject's perception of the Other's power in relation to one's own power to resist and to the value each places on whatever is being contested, cf. S. Bacharach and E. Lawler, "The Perception of Power," *Social Forces* 55, no. 1 (1976): 123–134.

3. Johnson, *The Gender Knot*.

4. See G. Lerner, *The Creation of Patriarchy* (New York, 1986), pp. 15–100.

5. Cf. S. Brownmiller, *Against Our Will* (New York, 1975), pp. 14–15, and E. Janeway, *Man's World, Women's Place* (New York, 1971), pp. 92–93. See also Janeway, *Between Myth and Morning* (New York, 1975), especially chap. 13.

6. L. Schottroff, *Lydia's Impatient Sisters* (Louisville, 1995), pp. 104–112.

7. Recognizing the complex reality of patriarchy and the variety of its manifestations, some feminist scholars have turned to the term "kyriarchy" to pinpoint the op-

pressive elements in patriarchal cultures. Cf. Elizabeth Schussler Fiorenza, *But She Said* (Boston, 1992), pp. 117–123.

8. In his commentary on *Joshua* in the Anchor Bible series, 1982, R. Boling, without adopting Alt's thesis, refers to "the great revolutionary gathering at Shechem," pp. 545–546.

9. Elizabeth Johnson in *Friends of God and Prophets* (New York, 1998) lays open the stark reality of death; cf. pp. 181–201. It is instructive to compare her view regarding an afterlife, a view that is hopeful though anything but naïve, with Ernest Becker's hesitant and reluctant admission of humans' need for a transcendent "solution" to death. See his Pulitzer Prize–winning *The Denial of Death* (New York, 1973).

10. There is a mysterious kenotic dimension to divine creative love, a forfeiture of absolute control, that will be discussed in a later chapter on the power of love.

11. One of the most recent and most satisfactory studies of the theory of atonement is Michael Winter, *The Atonement* (Collegeville, 1995). His key insight deals with the sacramentality of Jesus' dying, sacramental of his internal "petitioning" for humanity's forgiveness. I believe that the sacramentality can be extended to the divine participation in Jesus' dying.

12. R. Girard, *Violence and the Sacred* (Baltimore, 1977) and *The Scapegoat.*

CHAPTER 3

1. Since this will be my approach, this chapter will not have a distinct section on "theological reflection."

2. For a philosophical approach to authority seen in the context of the common good, cf. Y. Simon, *The Nature and Function of Authority*, 1940 Aquinas Lecture, Marquette University, Milwaukee. See also Letty Russell, *Household of Freedom* (Philadelphia, 1987); E. Janeway *The Powers of the Weak* (New York, 1980); and the writings of Walter Wink. A detailed study of the varieties of authority is that of R. De George, *The Nature and Limits of Authority* (Lawrence, 1985); pp. 116–187 are particularly relevant to the topic of "office." On the basic distinction between "power over" and "empowerment," see T. Wartenberg, *The Forms of Power* (Philadelphia, 1908), pp. 9–31.

On the current discussion of public power from a somewhat different perspective, see the remarks in the chapter on "force" above. Governing authority attached to office necessarily involves the use of coercion when needed, whereas other types of authority, such as the authority connected with knowledge, use persuasion rather than domination. Such persuasive power will be studied in subsequent chapters.

For a general discussion of persuasion as different from coercion, see K. Reardon, *Persuasion in Practice* (Newbury Park, 1991), especially pp. 2–3.

3. In recent sociological debate about "power," the position of Talcott Parsons (functionalism) was attacked by others, especially Giddens, because it too closely linked social power and authority. However, for the purposes of my study, which employs a phenomenological approach to theological method and focuses on the power exercised in religious contexts, it is important to distinguish various kinds of power that are connected with public authority—the power of office as such being central.

Part of the problem comes because "authority" itself has various specifications and grounding—such as knowledge, experience, personal charism, etc. The "grid" I will be using is for that reason different from that employed by sociologists, though there is obvious overlap. Basically, discussion in mainline sociological circles seems to revolve around the interdependence and interaction of agency and structure. Connected with this is current study of organizational structure, processes, and power. Recently, however, such attempts to locate "power" have been challenged (as we will see) by Foucault and his "postmodern" followers who stress the influence of public discourse on the understandings and attitudes that shape the complex and ever changing exercise of power.

4. As we will see in another chapter, the power attached to public rituals intersects with and enhances the power attached to the office.

5. A lengthier discussion of leadership than is possible here would have to include an examination of group leadership and specifically the authority exercised by official commissions of one sort or another. For a study of the dynamics that operate in such groups, cf. E. Schein, *Organizational Psychology*, 3rd ed. (Englewood Cliffs, N.J., 1980).

6. For the linguistic and cultural differentiation of these two terms, cf. A. Gunneweg and W. Schmithals, *Authority* (Nashville, 1982).

7. In the history of Christianity, this became a very divisive issue that to some extent has never been satisfactorily settled: e.g., at the time of the Donatist heresy, in the fourth and fifth centuries, it was argued by the dissidents that a bishop's actions were incapable of producing their intended result if that official was not in the state of grace, not possessing the Holy Spirit and therefore unable to give that Spirit. The lurking question: is the office endowed with the power "to give grace" and does one upon occupying that office now become an effective grace-giver even if he or she is without grace or faith? On Donatism cf. G. Bareille, "Donatisme," Dictionnaire de Théologie Catholique, vol. 4–2 (Paris, 1939), cols. 1701–1728.

8. A distinctive case was that of the College of Cardinals claiming authority because they are *pars corporis papae*; cf. S. Chodorow, *Christian Political Theory and Church Politics* (Berkeley, 1972), p. 219, fn. 45.

9. One must add to this list the power, if not the authority, that comes from organization. This power attaches to those in positions of control in an organization, but it attaches as well to the organization itself. Enterprises that are efficiently structured are capable of achieving their goals precisely because of the power of their coordinated activity and their ability to draw upon a range of effectively interacting talents.

10. Cf. H. Frankfort, *The Intellectual Adventure of Ancient Man* (Chicago, 1977).

11. On the process by which official authority quickly displaced other sources of authority, such as the liturgy, cf. D. Power, "Power and Authority in Early Christian Centuries," in M. Downey, *That They Might Live* (New York, 1991), pp. 25–38. "The rather startling thing that the Church has ever to face, and to face more pragmatically today than ever before, is the early date at which a division is forged between the clergy and the laity" (p. 31).

12. On the nature and roots of continuity within the Church, cf. K. Rahner, *Foundations*, pp. 352–369.

13. In this regard, there is the interesting feature of the ancient rituals for ordination of an *episkopos*. Upon the head of the individual being ordained, the book of the Bible is laid. There is disagreement among liturgical scholars as to the exact meaning of this gesture; but it could well be that this is meant to sacramentalize the power of the revealed word empowering the ordinand to bear witness to the Spirit's truth contained in the sacred text. Cf. pp. 13–14 in Dom B. Botte, "Holy Orders in the Ordination Prayers," *The Sacrament of Holy Orders* (Collegeville, 1962), pp. 5–29.

14. Rather quickly, the notion of "priest" (*hiereus, sacerdos*) became prominent as the primary office that the bishop held. See T. O'Meara, *Theology of Ministry*, 2nd ed. (New York, 1999), pp. 57–98.

15. Cf. Y. Congar, *L'Ecclesiologie du haut Moyen Age* (Paris, 1968), p. 147.

16. On the centrality of teaching in the early Christian succession of bishops, see the recent study of F. Sullivan, *From Apostles to Bishops* (Mahwah, N.J., 1999).

17. On Gregory's social location as a wealthy and politically prominent Roman, then a monk, and finally pope, cf. J. Richards, *Consul of God* (London, 1980).

18. Gregory the Great, *Pastoral Care*, Ancient Christian Writers, no. 11, trans. H. Davis (New York, 1978).

19. On the use of the allegory of "the two swords," cf. W. Ullmann, *A Short History of the Papacy in the Middle Ages* (London, 1974), pp. 281–282. Ullmann attributes the full formulation of a doctrine of "the two swords" to Bernard of Clairvaux. See also Congar, *Ecclesiologie*, pp. 277–297.

20. On the distinction between *auctoritas sacra pontificum* and *regalis potestas*, cf. Congar, *Ecclesiologie*, p. 255.

21. The classic detailing of the bureaucratizing of the Church in the thirteenth century is that of G. LeBras, *Les Institutions de la Chrétienté médiévale* (vol. 12 in Fliche-Martin, *Histoire de l'Eglise*) (Paris, 1959).

22. For an interesting description of the shift from medieval views on economic activity to modern focus on profit as goal in economic life and the religious element in this shift, cf. R. Heilbroner, *The Making of Economic Society* (Englewood Cliffs, N.J., 1962).

23. On Vatican I, cf. J. Bury, *History of the Papacy in the nineteenth Century* (New York, 1964). A more recent appraisal of Vatican I's statement on infallibility is provided by M. O'Gara, *Triumph in Defeat* (Washington, 1988).

24. On the modernist controversy and its aftermath, cf. D. Jodock, ed., *Catholicism Contending with Modernity* (Cambridge, 2000).

25. Cf. F. Sullivan, *Magisterium: Teaching Authority in the Catholic Church* (Mahwah, N.J., 1983) for a discussion of the issues in official teaching authority being debated during the pontificate of John Paul II. See also R. Gaillaretz, *Teaching with Authority* (Collegeville, 1997).

26. See *The Catechism of the Catholic Church*, 2nd ed. (Washington, 1997), nos. 861–862, 874–875.

27. On current discussion of tradition, cf. T. Tilley, *Inventing Catholic Tradition* (Maryknoll, 2000); also J. Thiel, *Senses of Tradition* (New York, 2000).

CHAPTER 4

1. Cf. my essay "Fullness of Orders: Theological Reflections," *Jurist* 41 (1981): 405–421.

2. Cf. C. Toussaint, "Gloire de Dieu," *Dictionnaire de théologie catholique*, vol. 6–2, (Paris. 1920) cols. 1386–1393.

CHAPTER 5

1. For a basic study of law and its function in society, cf. T. Davitt, *The Basic Values in Law* (Milwaukee, 1978).

2. Cf. H. Frankfort, et al., *The Intellectual Adventure of Ancient Man* (Chicago, 1946).

3. Cf. "Conscience and the Holy Spirit," *Proceedings of CTSA*, 51 (1996): 227–246.

4. W. Conn, *Christian Conversion* (New York, 1986).

5. See, for example, the convergence of biblical study and reflection on spirituality in the work of Sandra Schneiders.

6. Cf. B. Tierney, *Foundation of the Conciliar Theory* (Leiden, 1998). See also his *Religion, Law and the Growth of Constitutional Thought, 1150–1650* (Cambridge, 1982).

7. As mentioned earlier, the basis for public authority is treated by Gunneweg and Schmithals, *Authority*.

Certainly, the power of a law is contested by its nonobservance and necessarily reinforced by the accompaniment of appropriate sanction. Cf. pp. 192–198 in *The Principles of Social Order, Selected Essays of Ron Fuller*, ed. K. Winston, where the distinction is made between *formal* power and *real* power, i.e., laws powerful enough to withstand physical force.

8. At present, there is considerable discussion about the validity of the "liberal" Enlightenment notion of the autonomous person with inalienable rights, etc. See the various "models" of human rights and responsibilities discussed in S. Parsons, *Feminism and Christian Ethics*.

9. Schottroff, *Lydia's Impatient Sisters*, especially pages 301–303.

10. Cf. E. Johnson, *She Who Is*, pp. 133–146.

11. On the relation of Jesus to Wisdom, cf. Johnson, *She Who Is*, pp. 94–100; E. Schussler Fiorenza, *Jesus: Miriam's Child, Sophia's Prophet*.

12. T. West, *Jesus and the Quest for Meaning* (Minneapolis, 2001), pp. 159–161.

13. While pervasive in Paul's letters, this theme is most clearly stated in Galatians.

14. For Rabbinic Judaism's understanding of Torah, cf. M. Kadushin, *The Rabbinic Mind* (New York, 1972).

15. For a study of the medieval debate about "obedience" in relationship to various exercises of official power, cf. Chodorow, *Christian Political Theory*, pp. 112–132.

16. For historical instances, cf. R. McClory, *Faithful Dissenters* (Maryknoll, 2000).

17. E. Schillebeeckx, *Ministry* (New York, 1981), pp. 76–80.

18. Rahner, *Foundations*, pp. 26–39; see also his important essay on nature and grace in vol. 4 of *Theological Investigations* (Baltimore 1967), pp. 165–188.

CHAPTER 6

1. Cf. the essay of John Sweeney, CIO-AFL President, "Making globalization work for all," published in the July 1999 *Call to Action, Spirituality and Justice Reprint.*

2. S. Huntington, *The Clash of Civilizations and the Remaking of World Order* (New York, 1996).

3. As early as 1962, attention was drawn to this as an international problem by Barbara Ward's *Rich Nations, Poor Nations*, and it has been highlighted in recent meetings of the World Bank.

4. Cf. Galbraith, *The Anatomy of Power*, which traces the way in which capitalism has emerged to central power in the world.

5. Already in 1974, R. Barnet and R. Mueller, in *Global Reach*, detailed the worldwide control exerted by transnational corporations and the banks to which they are allied.

6. For example, the pastoral letter "Economic Justice for All" (Washington, 1986) of the U.S. bishops.

7. Cf. *Gustavo Gutierrez, Essential Writings*, ed. J. Nickoloff (Maryknoll, 1996). Throughout his writings, Gutierrez stresses the power of the poor and the basic hermeneutic for assessing present-day developments as being "the preferential option for the poor."

8. While his perspective and concern are neither theological nor ethical, Robert Heilbroner makes an important and relevant observation in *The Making of Economic Society*. In tracing the historical shift from the Middle Ages to modern times, he points out that profit was not the goal of economic activity prior to the emergence of a market economy.

9. W. Wink, *Naming the Powers* (Philadelphia, 1984), *Unmasking the Powers* (Philadelphia, 1986), and *Engaging the Powers* (Philadelphia, 1992).

10. R. May, *Love and Will* (New York, 1969).

11. G. Mueller-Fahrenholz, *God's Spirit* (Geneva, 1995).

12. D. Soelle, *The Strength of the Weak* (Philadelphia, 1984), pp. 11–23.

13. I am indebted for reference to this quotation to Corita Kent, who used it in one of her most striking serigraphs.

14. Cf. G. Gutierrez, *The Power of the Poor in History* (Maryknoll, 1983).

CHAPTER 7

1. However, in recent years, there has been a considerable amount of irenic and substantive discussion between scientists and theologians. See, for example, I. Bar-

bour, *Religion and Science* (San Francisco, 1997); S. Jaki, *God and the Cosmologists* (Washington, 1989); J. Polkinghorne, *Faith, Science and the Understanding* (New Haven, 2000); J. Templeton, *The Humble Approach: Scientists Discover God* (Philadelphia, 1998).

2. On the wide-ranging historical and cultural reflection on "spirit," see *Spirit and Nature*, ed. J. Campbell (Princeton, 1954), selections drawn from vol. 45 and 46 of *Eranos Jahrbuch*.

3. For a more positive acceptance of teleology, cf. J. Templeton, *Evidence of Purpose* (New York, 1994).

4. Cf. Teilhard de Chardin, *The Human Phenomenon*, trans. S. Appleton-Weber (Portland, 1999), pp. 28–32.

5. On the ascendancy of mechanics, cf. H. Kearney, *Science and Change, 1500–1700* (New York, 1971), pp. 17–76.

6. A recent reflection on the panentheistic view of the creator-creature relation, admittedly influenced by Teilhard, is that of Sallie McFague in *The Body of God* (Minneapolis, 1993).

7. Cf. Lerner's *The Creation of Patriarchy*, a study of the rape and sexual enslavement of women as basic to the establishment of patriarchal cultures.

8. See E. Becker's contention, in *The Denial of Death* (New York, 1973), pp. 94–96, that Freud's focus on sexuality was an avoidance of facing death.

9. On chosen celibacy as a mature expression of sexuality, see D. Goergen, *The Sexual Celibate* (New York, 1974).

CHAPTER 8

1. On biblical inspiration, cf. R. Smith, pp. 499–501 in *Jerome Biblical Commentary*.

2. Cf. J. Guillet, *Themes of the Bible* (Notre Dame, 1960).

3. On the difference between reaction and revolution, cf. Hannah Arendt, *On Revolution* (New York, 1963).

4. Cf. Kung, Tracy, *Paradigm Change in Theology*.

CHAPTER 9

1. On creative imagination and theology, cf. *The Incarnate Imagination*, ed. I. Shafer (Bowling Green, Ohio, 1988), pp. 235–296.

2. Cf. T. McFarland, *Originality and Imagination* (Baltimore, 1985).

3. On Iconoclasm, cf. *Church History*, ed. J. Jedin and J. Dolan, vol. 2 (New York, 1980), pp. 26–53. For an explanation of icons' function in the Byzantine world, see J. Pelikan, *Imago Dei* (Princeton, 1990).

4. R. Haight, *Jesus, Symbol of God* (Maryknoll, 1999), pp. 188–202.

5. Cf. B. Cooke, *The Distancing of God*, (Minneapolis, 1990), pp. 97–109.

6. What is undoubtedly important in this connection, but is much too vast an

area to be treated here, is the character and reality of "the unconscious" and its influence in human thought and activity. What this would entail would be a description and validation—if that were appropriate—of the various psychoanalytic schools, the conflicting Freudian and Jungian views of "hidden" symbolisms in the human psyche and their impact on individuals and society, especially on the view people have of "God." To the extent that some clarity could be reached in this realm, it would raise intriguing questions about the operation of God's Spirit. Some of the most suggestive reflection has been provided by the Eranos group and in particular by Eric Neumann. See, for example, "Creative Man and Transformation," pp. 149–205 in Neumann's *Art and Creative Imagination* (Princeton, 1959); or *Spirit and Nature*, ed. Joseph Campbell, with essays drawn from the Eranos Jahrbuch of 1937, 1945, and 1946 (Princeton, 1954).

7. I. Kant, *Critique of Pure Reason*, trans. P. Geiger and A. Wood (Cambridge, 1998), A22–49.

8. On the symbolic power of music, cf. S. Langer, *Philosophy in a New Key*, 3rd ed. (Cambridge, Mass., 1957), pp. 204–245.

9. Longinus, *On the Sublime*, trans. Arieti and J. Crossett (New York, 1985); Aristotle, *Poetics*, ed. Stephen Halliwell (Chicago, 1998); J. Ruskin, *Modern Painters* (Boston, 1872); A. Malraux, *Les voix du silence* (Paris, 1951).

10. Cf. Guillet, *Themes of the Bible.*

11. Some feeling for the role of medieval symbolism can be gained by reading Abbot Suger's account of the consecration of the great abbey church of St. Denis.

12. M.-D. Chenu, *Nature, Man and Society* (Chicago, 1968), pp. 99–145.

13. Cf. Johnson's *Friends of God and Prophets* (New York, 1998), pp. 209–218.

CHAPTER 10

1. Chenu, *Nature, Man, and Society in the Twelfth Century.*

2. On the emergence and development of postmodernism, cf. H. Bertens, *The Idea of the Postmodern* (London, 1995). An advantage of Berten's treatment is his attention to elements, like architecture, beyond the literary.

3. Cf. Langer, *Philosophy in a New Key*; E. Cassirer, *Language and Myth* (New York, 1946).

4. On the iconoclastic controversy, see my *Distancing of God*, pp. 97–10.

5. Cf. J. Piaget, *The Language and Thought of the Child*, trans. M. Gabain (New York, 1955).

6. Cf. "Man as false generic," pp. 246–248 in C. Kramarae and P. Treichler, *A Feminist Dictionary* (Boston, 1985).

7. Cf. P. Berger and T. Luckmann, *The Social Construction of Reality* (New York, 1967).

8. Cf. *On Narrative*, ed. W. Mitchell (Chicago, 1981). As will be indicated later, study of narrative is part of the broader movements of structuralism, poststructuralism, and deconstruction.

9. On the intertwined development of "word, "spirit," and "wisdom" in late Jewish theology prior to Christianity and then its continuation into early Christian Christology, see the important discussion in West, *Jesus and the Quest for Meaning*, pp. 214–15.

10. On the relation of logos Christology to spirit Christology, see, besides R. Haight, pp. 445–466, P. Schoonenberg, "Spirit Christology and Logos Christology," *Bidragen* 38 (1977): 350–375, and P. Rosato, "Spirit Christology: Ambiguity and Promise," *Theological Studies* 38 (1977): 423–449.

11. Cf. the classic exposition of nominalism by Paul Vignaux in DTC; this was challenged and modified by Obermann's *Harvest of Medieval Theology*.

12. See for example Thomas Aquinas, *Summa Theologiae* III, q. 60, as. 7 and 8.

13. Rahner, *Theological Investigations*, vol. 4, pp. 253–286.

14. Ibid., pp. 77–102.

15. For example, his treatment of "the divine self-communication" and "grace" in pp. 116–132 of *Foundations*.

16. West, *Jesus and the Quest for Meaning*, p. 246, n. 16.

CHAPTER II

1. For example, Luis Schottroff (among others) has pointed to the way in which the power of Scripture has been "diverted" to support of patriarchy because of the fact that almost all exegesis of the Bible has until recently been done by men.

2. For a wide-ranging discussion of thought and power, cf. R. Fardon, ed., *Power and Knowledge: Anthropological and Sociological Approaches* (Edinburgh, 1985).

3. Cf. the *Dictionary of the History of Ideas*, 4 vols. (New York, 1970).

4. As early as the 1920s, Durkheim stressed the power of "moral regulation" that comes with education. Cf. his *Moral Education* (London, 1925). See also G. Walford and W. Pickering, eds., *Durkheim and Moral Education* (London, 1998). This anticipated the current stress on "disciplinary power" exerted by social structures. An "unfriendly" tribute to the power of thinking was the opposition to and exile of Paulo Freire by the Brazilian government because of the effectiveness of his educational theories.

5. Paulo Freire in his writings has advocated both a dialectic between instruction and the student's social location and an interactive relation of teacher and student. His most famous and influential book is *Pedagogy of the Oppressed* (Brazil, 1968; English ed., New York, 1972).

6. For an influential delineation of such a process, cf. B. Lonergan, *Insight* (London, 1958).

7. For a treatment of "revelation" in the broad context of human life, especially in its relation to imagination, memory, and open-ended human development, cf. R. Hart, *Unfinished Man and the Imagination* (New York, 1968). Incidentally, he has an interesting discussion of *potentia obedientialis*, Rahner's "supernatural existential," etc., pp. 170–179.

8. Beginning with the writings of J. Geiselmann in the 1950s and Jedin's history of the Council of Trent, there has been an increasing body of research reassessing the notion of "tradition"; see for example the 1998 proceedings of the College Theology Society, *Theology and the New Histories*," ed. G. Macy (Maryknoll, 1999), or Tilley, *Inventing Catholic Tradition*, or Thiel, *Senses of Tradition*.

9. G. Van Ackeren has made a convincing case that Thomas Aquinas in the first question of the *Summa Theologiae* understands the term "sacred doctrine" (*sacra doctrina*) not as a collection of articles of belief but as the process of divine to human revelatory communication in which the theologian/teacher participates.

10. In his essay "Towards the Construction of an Intercultural Theology of Tradition", ACHTUS 9(2002), p. 22, Orlando Espin provides an extended bibliography of current writing on tradition.

11. Cf. Tracy's treatment of "a classic" in *Analogical Imagination*, pp. 99–230.

12. Mueller-Fahrenholz, *God's Spirit*.

13. It is this power of truth to which, in the chapter above on the power of office, I referred as the heart of Christianity's power of judgment over evil.

CHAPTER 12

1. Among the many books that deal with ritual, I have found Catherine Bell's *Ritual Theory, Ritual Practice* (New York, 1992) especially helpful, both for its account of research in the field and for the clarity and depth of her own analysis.

2. *Communitas* is a main theme in Victor Turner, *Drama, Fields, and Metaphors* (Ithaca, 1974).

3. Bell, *Ritual Theory, Ritual Practice*, pp. 199–204, following Foucault, stresses the flexible interplay of power relationships that function in human groupings.

4. For example, in the eucharistic prayer of Hippolytus in *The Apostolic Tradition* and the *Anaphora of Addai and Mari*.

5. On folk religion, cf. O. Espin, *The Faith of the People* (Maryknoll, 1992).

CHAPTER 13

1. Rollo May in his *Love and Will* points to apathy as the basic ill affecting society today.

2. For an enlightening discussion of the link between hope, desire, and eschatology, cf. West, *Jesus and the Quest for Meaning*, pp. 264–266.

3. One interesting response to this question is Rosemary Haughton's *The Passionate God* (New York, 1981).

CHAPTER 14

1. Cf. L. Menand's recent book, *The Metaphysical Club* (New York, 2001).

2. On the distinctiveness of friendship as love, cf. C. S. Lewis, "Friendship—The

Least Necessary Love," pp. 39–47, and L. Thomas, "Friendship and Other Loves," pp. 48–64 in N. Kapur Badhwar, *Friendship* (Cornell, 1993).

3. For a recent discussion of friendship, cf. L. Rouner, ed., *The Changing Face of Friendship* (Notre Dame, 1994). The introduction mentions that the purpose of the essays is to rehabilitate "love" as more than sexual relationship.

4. J. B. Miller, *Toward a New Psychology of Women* (Boston, 1986). Also her essay "Women and Power," *Women's Growth in Connection*, ed. J. Jordan, et al. (New York, 1991).

5. On the Spirit's action in and through Jesus, especially after the resurrection, cf. West, *Jesus and the Quest for Meaning*, p. 225, n. 25.

6. However, it is good to remember that in Platonic and especially Neo-Platonic circles, "illumination" involves more than just rational thought. This is particularly true of Augustine and the Augustinian tradition. Gilson in *The Christian Philosophy of St. Augustine* (New York, 1960) remarks that "the Augustinian doctrine . . . refuses to separate illumination of the mind from purification of the heart" (p. 31). In that same volume, Gilson has a lengthy exposition (pp. 77–96) of "illumination" in Platonic and patristic thought.

7. See Martin D'Arcy, *The Mind and Heart of Love* (New York, 1947) for a review and commentary on this debate.

8. P. Rorem, *Pseudo-Dionysius* (New York, 1993), p. 223.

9. Cf. Aquinas *ST*, I–II, q. 68.

10. On the kenotic aspect of creation, cf. J. Haught, *God After Darwin* (Boston, 2000), pp. 53–54.

11. *On the Holy Spirit*, 28. Probably to be dated around 370–80.

12. See *On the Holy Spirit*, written about 375.

13. Y. Congar, *I Believe in the Holy Spirit*, vol. 3 (New York, 1983) p. 90.

14. See the article of M. Schmaus, pp. 647–648 in *Encyclopedia of Theology*, ed. K. Rahner (New York, 1975).

15. On Protestant approaches to pneumatology, cf. Badcock, *Light of Truth*, pp. 86–123.

16. Cf. F. Stoeffler, *Continental Pietism and Early American Christianity* (Grand Rapids, 1976); R. Knox, *Enthusiasm* (New York, 1950). The latter focuses on seventeenth and eighteenth-century European developments.

17. Cf. B. Cooke, *God's Beloved* (Philadelphia, 1992).

18. Cf. W. Kasper, *Jesus the Christ* (New York, 1976), pp. 245–268, and Haight, *Jesus, Symbol of God*, pp. 445–466.

19. A brief but helpful account of the pneumatological contribution of these and other contemporary theologians is provided by Badcock, *Light of Truth*, pp. 124–211. On the fundamental theme of "grace" in Rahner's theology, cf. L. O'Donovan, ed., *A World of Grace* (New York, 1980).

20. On the power of feeling and its relation to meaning and value, cf. West, *Jesus and the Quest for Meaning*, pp. 25–28.

CONCLUSION

1. For an indication of the extensive recent study of the Spirit, see the lengthy footnotes in E. Dreyer's essay in the 1996 *Proceedings of the Catholic Theology Society of America*, pp. 45–90.

2. J. Moltmann, *The Spirit of Life* (Philadelphia, 1982).

3. Pope John Paul II, *Lord and Giver of Life* (Washington, 1986).

4. J. Haughey, *The Conspiracy of God* (New York, 1973).

5. D. Gelpi, *The Divine Mother* (Lanham, Md., 1984).

6. L. Boff, *Trinity and Society* (Maryknoll, 1988), and *Church, Charism and Power* (New York, 1985).

7. C. LaCugna, *God for Us* (San Francisco, 1991), pp. 298–299, 362–363.

8. Badcock, *Light of Truth*.

9. M. Lodahl, *Shekhinah/Spirit*.

10. Pp. 142–150 in S. McFague, *The Body of God*.

11. E. Dreyer, "Narratives of the Spirit," *Proceedings of the Catholic Theological Society of America* 51 (1996), p. 53.

12. There seems to be a common awareness of this because of the frequent and affirming citation of Augustine's phrase, "Our hearts were made for you, O God, and they are restless until they rest in you." Interesting that some of the radical "postmoderns" want to eliminate all such teleological reference and "centering" relationship to Origin—thereby they eliminate the integrating role of eros in psychological health.

13. The mid–twentieth century debate about the distinctive character of mysticism vis-à-vis faith, represented for example by Garrigou-Lagrange's *The Three Ways of the Spiritual Life* (1938) and *The Three Ages of the Interior Life* (1947) was answered by Vatican II in its *Constitution on the Church*, especially the chapter on "The Universal Call to Holiness."

14. On Jesus' distinctive awareness of God, cf. B. Cooke, *God's Beloved*.

Index

LaVergne, TN USA
13 January 2010
169961LV00002B/266/P